THE MIND OF CHRIST

YOUTH EDITION

T.W. Hunt & Claude V. King

Youth Learning Activities Written by
James Jackson

LIFEWAY PRESS
Nashville, Tennessee

ISBN 0-7673-0000-9

Dewey Decimal Classification: 248.83
Subject Heading: CHRISTIAN LIFE/YOUTH-RELIGIOUS LIFE

This book is the text for course CG-0253 in the subject area
"Personal Life-Youth" of the Christian Growth Study Plan.
An application for course credit is located in the back of this book.

Printed in the United States of America
To order additional copies of this resource: WRITE LifeWay Church Resources
Customer Service, One LifeWay Plaza, Nashville, TN 37234-0113; FAX order to (615) 251-5933; PHONE 1-800-458-2772; EMAIL to CustomerService@lifeway.com; ONLINE at www.lifeway.com; or visit the LifeWay Christian Store serving you.

We believe that the Bible has God for its author; salvation for its end; and truth, without any mixture of error, for its matter and that all Scripture is totally true and trustworthy. The 2000 statement of *The Baptist Faith and Message* is our doctrinal guideline.

Student Ministry Publishing
LifeWay Church Resources
One LifeWay Plaza
Nashville, Tennessee 37234-0174

Contents

About the Writers

T. W. Hunt was the Prayer Specialist in the Adult Discipleship and Family Development Department of the Baptist Sunday School Board before he retired in September, 1994. He was Professor of Church Music at Southwestern Baptist Theological Seminary in Fort Worth, Texas, for 24 years. Dr. Hunt authored *Disciple's Prayer Life: Walking in Fellowship with God* (with Catherine Walker), *The Doctrine of Prayer, Music in Missions: Discipling Through Music*, and has written numerous articles for a variety of periodicals. A native of Arkansas, Dr. Hunt graduated from Ouachita Baptist College; and received the Master of Music and Doctor of Philosophy degrees from North Texas State University. He lives in Spring, Texas, with his wife Laverne. They have one daughter, Melana, and six grandchildren.

Claude V. King is Prayer Team Leader for New Hope New York. He is a former design editor in the Adult Discipleship and Family Development Department, Baptist Sunday School Board. He wrote the learning activities for *Experiencing God* and *Fresh Encounter*. A native of Tennessee, King is a graduate of Belmont College and New Orleans Baptist Theological Seminary. He lives in Murfreesboro, Tennessee, with his wife Reta and daughters Julie and Jenny.

James Jackson works with the Centrifuge Program in the Student Events Department of LifeWay Church Resources. He graduated from Georgia State University and The Southern Baptist Theological Seminary. James, his wife, Trish, and their sons, Caleb Benjamin and Joshua Allen, reside in Franklin, Tennessee with their beagle.

Preface

Let me ask you a question. What is your mind? You might be tapping your finger to your forehead right now in answer to that question. Your mind is that six or so inches between your ears, right? It's that complex system of billions of cells, neurons, dendrites, and synapses that control your body functions and muscle movements. It's where information is stored, and memories are retrieved. And, in some weird way that nobody really understands, it's also the place where emotions and feelings are generated. That's your mind, right?

Actually, that's your brain. The brain is the physical organ that fills up your skull. Your mind is something far more complex. If the brain is the organ that controls *how* the body will respond to different things, the mind controls *why* you respond to things the way you do. If the brain is *where* information is stored, the mind deals with *what* information gets up there in the first place. And if the brain is where emotions and feelings come from, the mind determines *what* those emotions are and *how* you feel about things.

Those are all crucial issues for you as a teenager. Wouldn't it be great if you had someone to help you "make up your mind?" Or imagine this: what if a scientist could somehow transplant the greatest mind that ever was into your head? You would still be you, of course; we're not talking some weird "Dr. Jekyll and Mr. Hyde" thing. Everything that makes you who you are would still be the same. Only now, you would have a mind that would always steer you in the right direction, always help you make right decisions, and give your life a sense of peace and joy that you never dreamed possible. Would you want to have a mind like that?

That mind is the mind of Christ. And for a Christian, having the mind of Christ is not just an option, it's an obligation! Paul said, *Let this mind be in you, which was also in Christ Jesus (Phil. 2:5,* KJV). That's a command!

Now, instead of just tapping your forehead, you might be scratching it. How is it possible for me to have the mind of Christ? I barely got through algebra, and you expect me to have the same mind as the Creator of the universe? You must be joking!

It sounds daring to talk about an ordinary, everyday teenager having the mind of Christ. But we have to realize that God wouldn't give us a command it was impossible for us to obey. The fact is, God created us to be like Jesus. The Bible says that *whom He foreknew,* (that's us!) *He also predestined to become conformed to the image of His Son, that He might be the first-born among many brethren (Rom. 8:29).* That means that God is constantly at work to make us more like Christ. Acting the way Jesus acts! Loving the way He loves! Thinking the way He thinks!

That's what this course is all about—learning to think the thoughts of Christ. In other words, this course will help you develop the mind of Christ.

If You're Not Sure You're a Christian

Have you ever heard the saying, "You have to learn to walk before you learn to fly?" That saying applies to this course. *The Mind of Christ* is designed to help you "take off" in your relationship with Christ. But, it assumes you already have a relationship with Christ. So, if you're not sure, **DO NOT SKIP THIS SECTION!**

The rest of this book will make no sense to you if you haven't taken this first step. So, spend some time reading the following Scriptures. Ask God to talk with you about your life.

- JOHN 3:16 — You matter to God, and He desires a relationship with you.
- ROMANS 3:23 — You, me, and everyone else in the world is guilty of sin.
- ROMANS 6:23 — The payment for that sin is death, but God has provided a way out through Jesus.
- ROMANS 5:8 — Jesus' death on the cross is the way God made for us to have a relationship with Him again.
- ROMANS 10:9-10 — Agree with God that Jesus is Lord, and believe God raised Him from the dead.
- ROMANS 10:13 — Ask God to save you and He will.

To place your faith in Jesus and receive His gift of eternal life, you must:

- Recognize that you are a sinner, and you need a saving relationship with Christ.
- Confess (agree with God about) your sins.
- Repent of your sins (Be sorry for them, turn away from them, and turn to God).
- Ask Jesus to save you by His grace.
- Turn over the rule of your life to Jesus. Let Him be your Lord (boss or manager).

If you need help, talk with your pastor, youth minister, parents, or a Christian friend. If you have taken these steps, and have just made this important decision, call somebody right now and tell them! Then, share the decision with your church.

The Purpose of This Course

The Mind of Christ is not a biography of Jesus. There are lots of those. Four of them, Matthew, Mark, Luke, and John are in the Bible. You may want to choose one of those to read on your own as we go through *The Mind of Christ* together. (Especially if you just became a Christian. I suggest you start with John.) *The Mind of Christ* focuses on the ideas found in *Philippians 2:5-11*. But I want this course to be more than just ideas in your everyday life. For that to happen, here's what you have to do:

- **Pray before every study time.** Ask the Holy Spirit to help you understand it and apply it to your everyday life.
- **Don't be afraid to go off on tangents.** That may be the Holy Spirit taking you on another learning adventure. Since it would be impossible for any one course to say everything there is to say about the mind of Christ, let this study be suggestive of other topics. Follow up on tangents. That's the Holy Spirit developing the mind of Christ in you!

My Prayer for You

I really hope this course will just be the beginning of a lifetime of developing the mind of Christ. Trust me—you're not going to have it all at the end of the next 12 weeks! But God will begin something in you in the next three months that will never stop. I'm praying for you as you work through this material.

> *God, I may never meet the brother or sister who is reading this book right now. But I pray that you would reveal your Son Jesus to him or her in the next several weeks. Jesus, be glorified as my friend reads and studies, and give my friend Your Holy Spirit to help make this apply to his or her everyday life at school, at church, at work, and at home. In Jesus' name I pray. Amen.*

T.W. Hunt
Spring, Texas
August, 1995

Overview of The Mind of Christ

Paul said, *Let this mind be in you, which was also in Christ Jesus (Phil. 2:5,* KJV). We want to help you keep that command. When Jesus said, *"the kingdom of God is within you" (Luke 17:21,* KJV), He was emphasizing an inner process of becoming more like Him. The place where that happens is the mind. That's where God wants to work. Each day of this course, God will be bringing changes into your life. Although they are inward changes, they will bear outward fruit as your attitudes, habits, and lifestyle become more pleasing to God.

With this in mind, we'll be looking at *Philippians 2:5-11,* a hymn that was probably used in early church worship. They hymn is divided into six parts for our study:

PHILIPPIANS 2:5-11

Part 1 The Freedom of Christ
Have this attitude in yourselves which was also in Christ Jesus (v. 5).

Part 2 The Lifestyle of Christ
Who, although He existed in the form of God, did not regard equality with God a thing to be grasped (v. 6).

Part 3 The Servanthood of Christ
But emptied Himself, taking the form of a bond-servant, and being made in the likeness of men (v. 7).

Part 4 The Humanity of Christ
And being found in appearance as a man (v. 8).

Part 5 The Holiness and Love of Christ
He humbled Himself and became obedient to the point of death, even death on a cross (v. 8).

Part 6 The Name of Christ
Therefore also God highly exalted Him, and bestowed on Him the name which is above every name, that at the name of Jesus every knee should bow, of those who are in heaven, and on earth, and under the earth, and that every tongue should confess that Jesus Christ is Lord, to the glory of God the Father (vv. 9-11).

We're going to look at the six parts of this hymn together, and see how God wants to work in you to make you more like His Son, Jesus.

- Unit 1 will help you understand the three-stage process through which God will guide you. You will see what having a Christlike mind is like.
- The work really begins in Units 2 and 3, as God sets you free from the bondage of sin.
- In Units 4 and 5, you will learn 17 virtues of the mind of Christ, and God will be working to develop these virtues in your life.
- Unit 6 will help you understand the importance of servanthood, following the example of Christ. God will be working on developing the characteristics of a servant in your life.

- Units 7-10 focus on the humanity of Christ. Sometimes we forget that Jesus was a real, flesh-and-blood person. But He was, and He is our perfect example of what God intends humanity to be. We will study the Beatitudes, emotions, relationships with things and people, and living in the Spirit.
- How do love and holiness work together? How do they enhance each other? That's what Unit 11 is all about. God will be working in you to make you holy and to teach you to love with a Christlike love.
- We will wrap up in Unit 12 with a high point of the hymn, as we examine how God has exalted Christ through His names. You will be challenged to allow Christ to be absolute Lord of your life.

Will you be finished developing the mind of Christ at the end of 12 weeks? I don't think so! This is just the beginning of a lifelong process for you as God continually renews your mind and life to reflect the image of His Son Jesus.

Getting the Most Out of This Course

The Mind of Christ is a course designed to provide quality Christian education to youth like you in the areas of discipleship, leadership, and ministry. These characteristics apply to *The Mind of Christ, Youth Edition.*

- You will spend between 30 and 60 minutes a day with this self-paced workbook, completing the learning activities as you go along.
- Once a week, you will meet in a small group session, which will last from one to two hours.
- You will have an adult course leader who will guide you and the other members of your group to reflect on and talk about what you have learned during the week, and how to apply it to your everyday life. Your small group will be a base of support for you as you help each other understand and apply the Scriptures to life.
- When you complete *The Mind of Christ, Youth Edition* you may receive a diploma from the Christian Growth Study Plan system. See page 224 for details.

Some Additional Tips

- Take the discipline of giving daily time to this study seriously. Don't just sign up for this course because everyone else in the youth group is. Pray about it first. If you're not going to have the time for it, then don't take it.
- Study only one lesson at a time. If you get behind, resist the temptation to "cram" a lot of lessons into a single day. This isn't like chemistry, where you memorize a lot of formulas for a test and then forget them as soon as the test is over. You've got to let these thoughts sink in to your understanding and practice. That takes time.
- Don't skip any of the learning activities. They will help you learn and apply these truths to your life, and will help you establish a personal daily walk with Christ. Many activities will lead you to interaction with God through prayer, meditation, and Bible Study. If you skip these, you may be skipping an encounter with God which could radically change your life. Your love relationship with God is the most important thing in your life. More important than school, more important than activities, even more important than family, friends, boyfriends, or girlfriends. Without an intimate relationship with God, you miss out on what He wants to do in and through your life.

✱ The activities will begin (like this paragraph) with a symbol next to bold, indented type. Follow the instructions given. After you have completed the activity, you will return to the content.

Answers may be given following the activity so you can check your work. Write your answer before reading ours. Sometimes the activity asks for your opinion, so there's no right or wrong answer. If you have difficulty with an activity, or don't understand a question, write a note out in the margin. Discuss your concern with your leader or small group.

Memorizing Scripture

Jesus knew Scripture. He quoted it all the time. If we are going to have the mind of Christ, we have to make the same commitment to knowing Scripture. Scripture memorization is an important discipline you will be called on to develop during this study. At the back of this book are cards containing all the key passages in *The Mind of Christ, Youth Edition* use the cards to help you memorize the Scriptures.

1. Read the verse and think about the meaning.
2. Put the card somewhere you'll see it every day, such as in your locker, on your bathroom mirror, or on the dashboard of your car. You may even want to make additional copies of the card, or write each phrase from the verse on a different card.
3. Glance at the first phrase and say it out loud. Glance at the next phrase and say both phrases out loud. Continue this process until you've said the whole verse.
4. Try to say the verse from memory later in the day. If you can't say the complete verse, glance at the card to refresh your memory.
5. Repeat the verse several times each day for a week or until you feel this verse is firmly implanted in your mind.

Lifelong Helps

Like we said before, you're not going to finish this course in three months. *The Mind of Christ* is simply an introduction to a lifelong process of allowing God to mold and shape your life into the image of Christ. God will work on you every day in a process that won't end on this side of heaven. You will always need God's renewal process in your mind and in your life.

We have provided some tools to help you in this process. The section at the back of this book called "Lifelong Helps" (pp. 189-220) will help you regularly examine your mind and your life. In that process God will be at work revealing the things that should be removed, and He will be transforming your thinking and your lifestyle to reflect Christ. You can turn to these Lifelong Helps long after our three months together are over.

Small Group

Your small-group time is crucial to your success in this course. Together you will discuss the content you studied the previous week, share insights and testimonies, encourage each other, and pray together. These groups should not be any larger than 10 people. The larger the group gets, the less closeness and intimacy they'll develop, the less they'll share, and the more people will be absent and eventually drop out. If more than 10 people want to study the course, enlist additional leaders for each group of 6 to 10.

If you've started studying *The Mind of Christ, Youth Edition* by yourself, get some friends to study the course with you. You will discover that your friends can help you more fully understand and know God's working in your life. The small group becomes a place where you can practice *Hebrews 10:23-25:*

> *Let us hold fast the confession of our hope without wavering, for He who promised is faithful; and let us consider how to stimulate one another to love and good deeds, not forsaking our own assembling together, as is the habit of some, but encouraging one another, and all the more, as you see the day drawing near.*
>
> *Hebrews 10:23-25*

God wants us to help each other, encourage each other towards love and good deeds, and be a support to one another. Don't try to do it all by yourself. God has already called us to be the body of Christ. Now, He is calling you to develop the mind of Christ as well.

Day 1
Characteristics of a Christlike Mind, Part 1

Day 2
Characteristics of a Christlike Mind, Part 2

Day 3
Philippians 2:5-11

Day 4
Developing the Mind of Christ

Day 5
Fix Your Thoughts on Jesus

Scripture Memory Verse
Do not be conformed to this world, but be transformed by the renewing of your mind, that you may prove what the will of God is, that which is good and acceptable and perfect.
Romans 12:2

Becoming Like Christ

Hymn Part 1—Christ's Freedom
Let this mind be in you, which was also in Christ Jesus (Phil. 2:5, KJV).

What Is in This Unit for Me?

This unit will help you understand what God wants to do with you during this course (and for the rest of your life). You will understand what God expects of you as you develop the mind of Christ. You will also begin to grow closer to God than you've ever been before as you practice prayer and Bible study.

Lifelong Objective

In Christ, you will set your mind, renew your mind, and prepare your mind. God will develop in you a spiritual mind that is characterized as alive, single-minded, lowly, pure, responsive, and peaceful.

How God Will be Working In You

God wants you to be like Christ. More than any other part of your personality, your mind is what He will measure most often for Christlikeness. God helps you grow by revealing His expectations for you in His Word. Through His Word, His work, His grace, and His Spirit, you can have the mind of Christ.

Unit Learning Goals

- You will understand the six characteristics of the Christlike mind.
- You will understand what God will be doing to develop these characteristics in your mind.
- You will understand the three stages in the process of developing the mind of Christ.
- You will show your willingness to set your mind on Christ and submit to His renewing of your mind.
- You will understand your role in developing the mind of Christ.
- You will understand the Apostle and the High Priest roles of Christ, and how to focus your thoughts in relation to them.
- You will demonstrate your commitment to developing the mind of Christ.
- You will study the characteristics of a Christlike mind.
- You will set your mind and attention on Christ.
- You will begin to allow Christ to renew your mind.
- You will strengthen your mind for action.

The Mind of Christ Cards Related to This Unit

1A. Scripture Memory—*Philippians 2:5-8*
1B. Scripture Memory—*Philippians 2:9-11*
2B. Three Stages in Developing the Mind of Christ
2A. Six Characteristics of a Christlike Mind
3A. Unit 1: Scripture Memory—*Romans 12:2*

Characteristics of a Christlike Mind, Part 1

DAY 1

Today's Bible Meditation
Do not be conformed to this world, but be transformed by the renewing of your mind, that you may prove what the will of God is, that which is good and acceptable and perfect.
Romans 12:2

Name of Christ for Today
The Bread of Life
(John 6:35)

Prayer to Begin the Lesson
Jesus, I am hungry and thirsty to be more like you. You are the Bread of Life itself. Fill me up with Your presence so that I can experience the abundant life You came to give.
Amen.

✳ Begin today's lesson by reading the Bible verse and the name of Christ for today. Work on your memory verse. Then use the suggested prayer to begin your study.

Here we go! Welcome to *The Mind of Christ.* Today is the start of a lifelong process of growth for you. You will develop the mind of Christ.

Let me say that again. You will develop the mind of Christ.

That statement is a little mind-blowing, isn't it? It seems a little too big to understand. But God has commanded us to *Let this mind be in you, which was also in Christ Jesus' (Phil. 2:5).* When you see that word *let* in there, that means it's not just a suggestion. It's a commandment! We're not supposed to just have a good mind, or a disciplined mind, or even a moral mind—we are to have Christ's mind! We're not supposed to just look like Jesus. We are to think His very thoughts! We are to have the mind of the only perfect human being who ever walked on the earth—the mind of Christ, who was completely human and completely God at the same time.

Do you think we can do this in twelve weeks? Not! Like we said, this is the beginning of a lifelong process! So, let's get started!

✳ If you haven't read the Introduction (pp. 8-11) you need to do that before you go any further. Please check the box when you've read it: ❑

✳ Did you read in the margin the Scripture for Meditation, the Name of Christ for Today, and the Prayer to Begin the Lesson? If not, do that now, every day begin with reading these items for the day. They will help prepare you for our time together.

✳ You will be learning many names of Christ in this study. What name did you learn today?

____

Those three activities were a breeze, weren't they? But future activities will become more challenging and more meaningful. We just wanted you to get off to a good start. Remember, for God to have maximum opportunity to work in your life, you will need to complete each instruction or activity as best you can.

There are six places in the New Testament where we get a description of what the Christian's mind is supposed to be like. In each place, the word *mind* is used. From these, we can come up with six characteristics of God's ideal for your mind.

We'll begin our study by looking at these six characteristics.

SIX CHARACTERISTICS OF A CHRISTLIKE MIND

1. **Alive**—*The mind set on the Spirit is life and peace (Rom. 8:6).*
2. **Single-Minded**—*I am afraid, lest... your minds should be led astray from the simplicity and purity of devotion to Christ (2 Cor. 11:3).*
3. **Lowly**—*In lowliness of mind let each esteem other better than themselves (Phil. 2:3,* KJV).
4. **Pure**—*To the pure, all things are pure, but to those who are corrupted and do not believe, nothing is pure (Titus 1:15,* NIV).
5. **Responsive**—*He opened their minds to understand the Scriptures (Luke 24:45).*
6. **Peaceful**—*The mind set on the Spirit is life and peace (Rom. 8:6).*

Throughout this course, you'll be looking in detail at the life of Jesus. Every one of these characteristics were obvious in the way He lived His life. Let's check out what each one means for your mind.

Alive

Paul tells us, *The mind set on the flesh is death, but the mind set on the Spirit is life and peace (Rom. 8:6,* NASB). Our first and last characteristics, alive and peaceful—come from this verse. A life without Christ is no life at all. In fact, Paul says without Christ we are dead *(Eph. 2:1)*. But in Christ, we have everlasting life *(John 3:36)*. Jesus isn't just talking about the fact of life either—you know, just breathing in and out. Jesus said that He came so that we could have abundant life *(John 10:10)*. There's a quality to life in Christ that those who don't know Him don't have. When you set your mind on the Spirit, you experience life.

✱ What is one characteristic of a Christlike mind?

____

Do you have any control over what you think about? Of course you do! That's why the will is so important. When Paul says, *The mind set on the flesh is death (Rom. 8:6),* he is talking about a decision of the will.

How can you tell if your mind is set on the Spirit? Life is distinguished by activity. The mind of Christ is never lazy. It enjoys being occupied. Sometimes it reflects on who God is. Sometimes it prays. It is evident when we talk to other people, Christian and non-Christians alike. The alive mind chooses the spiritual over the fleshly.

Single-Minded

A second description of the mind of Christ occurs in *2 Corinthians 11:3: I am afraid, lest as the serpent deceived Eve by his craftiness, your minds should be led astray from the simplicity and purity of devotion to Christ.* In other words, the Christlike mind is single-minded, or focused, in devotion to Christ.

We all struggle with being distracted. Especially these days. It's hard to concentrate when your mind is bombarded with so many distractions. Think about it. Even right now, as you're doing this study, there's a million other things for you to think about. Homework. Chores. Social activities this weekend. You're being pulled in a lot of different directions. But a single-minded Christian pays attention to Christ, His commands, His Person, and His ways.

Your mind needs to be preoccupied with sincere and pure devotion to Christ. Single-mindedness is the discipline of being focused. In future lessons, we will look at the importance of your will in depth. You can direct and control your attention with a focus on Christ and His kingdom.

✱ **What is a second characteristic of a Christlike mind?**

____

Lowly

Paul gives another description of the godly mind in *Philippians 2:3: Let nothing be done through strife or vainglory; but in lowliness of mind let each esteem other better than themselves.* The mind is to be lowly. Lowliness and humility are a lot alike, and we'll be looking at humility in unit 6. But humility deals with our relationships with others. Lowliness is a state of mind. Humility flows out of lowliness.

The opposite of lowliness is pride and arrogance, or thinking too much of ourselves. In our world today, it's not easy to be lowly. Lowliness is a trait which must be cultivated. Christians learn to submit to one another by lowliness. How do we work on our lowliness? By concentrating on genuine appreciation for God's holiness. When we start with how holy God is, it's hard to be full of ourselves. Lowliness helps keep things in perspective.

Think about the people who encountered God in the Bible. They almost always started off experiencing genuine fear or terror before Him. This is a godly fear. When they met God, they knew the need for lowliness. They immediately saw what a big difference there was between God and themselves. When you have a clear view of God's greatness, you will have a proper view of yourself. The lowly Christian has the security of understanding his or her position under the greatness of God.

✱ **What is a third characteristic of a Christlike mind?**

____

✱ **You have learned about the three characteristics of a Christlike mind. Write the appropriate characteristic in front of its definition.**

____________ A proper perspective of my position under the greatness of God.
____________ Focused attention on Christ and His kingdom.
____________ Activity of the mind which chooses the spiritual over the fleshly.

✱ **Wrap up today's lesson by focusing on Christ and His kingdom. Spend time in prayer.**

- **Talk to God about what He's doing or getting ready to do in your life, your church, and your school.**
- **Thank God for allowing you to become like His Son, Jesus Christ.**
- **Acknowledge your proper position of lowliness before His greatness.**

DAY 2

Today's Bible Meditation
The mind set on the flesh is death, but the mind set on the Spirit is life and peace.
Romans 8:6

Name of Christ for Today
Image of the Invisible God
(Col. 1:15)

Prayer to Begin the Lesson
Jesus, You are the Image of the Invisible God. Even though no one has ever seen God, thousands of people saw You, and praised You and worshiped You as God. I praise You also. Help me come to know the Father as I come to know You. And since I can't see God, help me to focus my eyes on You and the example of Your life. Amen.

Characteristics of a Christlike Mind, Part 2

✳ Begin today's lesson by reading the Bible verse and the name of Christ for today. Work on your memory verse. Then use the suggested prayer to begin your study.

✳ Think back to yesterday's lesson with me. What are three characteristics of a Christlike mind? Write them on the lines below. Then, flip back a few pages and check your work.

1.____

2.____

3.____

Pure

There is a good chance that the soap you used when you took a shower this morning (you did take a shower this morning, didn't you?) said "99.9% pure" on the label. But God desires that our minds be 100% pure. A pure mind is the natural state of the Christian. When the mind and conscience get corrupted, the result is impurity. Paul talks about the pure mind in *Titus 1:15: To the pure, all things are pure; but to those who are defiled and unbelieving, nothing is pure, but both their mind and their conscience are defiled.*

✳ What is one characteristic of the Christlike mind?

____

A pure mind is one of the toughest things for a Christian to maintain—especially these days. After all, think of all the impure images we encounter every time we turn on the TV, walk up and down the aisles at the local movie rental place, or switch on the radio! And when viewed on the 30-foot movie screen, lust is so much bigger! Jealousy is so much more spiteful! Greed is the way to get ahead, and cheating is the norm and not the exception. Sin is everywhere.

So if it sounds like an impossible battle, don't panic. Just because it's uphill doesn't mean it can't be done. Purity begins with the desire to be pure. Like anything in life, you have to want it bad enough first. And until the desire for purity becomes your passion, the impressions bombarding your senses will continue to get the best of you. If your desire for purity is sincere, God will provide you with the way to overcome impurity. Your best bet for resisting temptation is to escape it entirely. This is what the psalmist was talking about when he said, *I will set no wicked thing before mine eyes (Ps. 101:3,* KJV). Here's a key truth: Strength to resist temptation comes before you are tempted, not during it! Overcoming is a prior act. It involves making a decision to remain pure before the temptation comes.

✱ **What is the best bet for resisting temptation and remaining pure?**

____

Key Truth
Strength to resist temptation comes before you are tempted, not during it!

Responsive

When Jesus appeared to His disciples on the evening of the resurrection, the Bible says that *He opened their minds to understand the Scriptures (Luke 24:45)*. But He couldn't have done that if the disciples weren't open to having their minds open. In other words, the disciples had to be responsive. You see, when Jesus chose them, He recognized in them something that made them good candidates for a three-and-a-half year intensive training course. He saw responsiveness in them. They may not have always learned a lesson the first time, but at least they were teachable. They wanted to learn from Him. Now, we could call this quality "open-mindedness," but in today's world, that phrase doesn't really reflect what Jesus was looking for. There are some things Jesus doesn't want you to be open to. But Jesus always wants us to be responsive to His teaching.

The opposite of responsiveness is what we might call "blind-mindedness." Check out *2 Corinthians 3:12-16*. Paul is talking about the Israelites in the desert, and he says, *their minds were blinded (v. 14,* KJV). He is talking about the spiritual dullness that results when people do not open themselves up to Jesus' teaching. This is where the Pharisees and the Sadducees messed up. Their spiritual dullness was the result of a choice they made. They were so smug in their own self-righteousness that they missed the coming of the Messiah. To be unresponsive to God is to be spiritually dull.

Responsiveness must be to God. We can't just be responsive to anything and everything. Think about the disciples again. Remember when they said, *"Lord, teach us to pray" (Luke 11:1)?* When they asked this they showed Jesus that they really desired to have the kind of relationship with God that Jesus had. They didn't just envy the enormous power of Jesus to perform miracles. Jesus had already given them that. Rather, they wanted to imitate Jesus' close relationship to the Father. Jesus was intensely spiritual, and they wanted that level of spirituality in their own lives.

If you are ever going to grow in your spiritual life, responsiveness is not an option. You must be sensitive to God's Holy Spirit. How do you develop this kind of sensitivity? There are at least two ways. One is to spend time in God's Word. Remember: Jesus *opened* [the disciple's] *minds to understand the Scriptures (Luke 24:45)*. God wants you to understand His Word, but you can't understand it if you don't spend time in it! Another way to become sensitive to God's Spirit is through prayer. When the disciples wanted to imitate Jesus, they asked Him to teach them to pray.

✱ **What are two disciplines that indicate a responsive mind?**

1.____

2.____

The Mind of Christ cards in the back of this book are one of the tools provided to help you. You can carry these cards with you, tape them to the inside of your locker, stick them on the corner of your bathroom mirror, or even tape them on the middle of your steering wheel in your car! Any time you have free time during your day, you can use these cards to help you memorize Scripture. Some of the cards will also help

Key Thought
As the Father is to the Son, so Christ is to you.

you review the material in *The Mind of Christ.* Use these cards. Saturate your mind with the things of God.

✳ **Turn to the back of the book and cut out the following cards that relate to this unit.**

1A. Scripture Memory— ***Philippians 2:5-8***
1B. Scripture Memory— ***Philippians 2:9-11***
2A. Six Characteristics of a Christlike Mind
2B. Three Stages in Developing the Mind of Christ
3A. Unit 1: Scripture Memory— ***Romans 12:2***

✳ **Now, while the idea is still fresh in your mind, use your card to begin memorizing** ***Romans 12:2*** **(Card 3A).**

Jesus was sensitive and responsive in the utmost degree to His Father. He said, *"I do nothing on My own initiative, but I speak these things as the Father taught Me" (John 8:28).* Jesus saw what the Father was doing, He heard what the Father was saying, and He did nothing independently of the Father. He was taught by the Father. You see, Jesus devoted Himself to reflecting the mind of the Father, and the reflection was exact. And here's the key thought: As the Father is to the Son, so Christ is to you.

- Jesus imitated the Father. You are to imitate Christ.
- Jesus saw the activity of the Father. You are to pay close attention to the known earthly activity of Jesus, and to His present activity today.
- Jesus heard from the Father. You must hear from Jesus.
- Jesus was taught by the Father. You are to be taught by Jesus.
- Jesus could do nothing apart from the Father. You can do nothing apart from Jesus.
- Jesus stayed close to the Father. You must stay close to Jesus.

Peaceful

Romans 8:6 has already given us the adjective *alive* to apply to the spiritual mind. But it also gives us another word. Let's look at it again: *The mind set on the Spirit is life and peace.* The Christlike mind is peaceful. Now, is that something that's up to you? Not really. *Galatians 5:22* lists peace as one of the fruits of the Spirit. When a farmer takes care of a fruit tree, the tree bears fruit. Similarly, if you work on setting your mind, like the first half of the verse says, God will do His work of providing the peace. Jesus had peace. His life was totally free from sin and the effects of the world's way of looking at things. He promised rest to the weary and the burdened (check out *Matt. 11:28).* You will find rest (peace) by working for Jesus.

✳ **Name the three remaining characteristics of a Christlike mind:**

1. Alive	**3. Lowly**	**5. R____________**
2. Single-Minded	**4. P____________**	**6. P____________**

To summarize this week's unit so far, let's go back over the three things you need to do in developing the mind of Christ. You are to

- Set your mind;
- Renew your mind;
- Strengthen your mind.

When you do these things, you are being like Christ. All the work you'll do in this course is based on one of these three mental operations. The New Testament mentions six things your mind is to become: alive, single-minded, lowly, pure, responsive, and peaceful. As you work on these mental operations, you are obeying the Scripture and becoming like Christ. Each of our units will relate to one of these key adjectives of a Christlike mind.

✱ Pray as you finish out today's lesson. Review the six characteristics of a Christlike mind on Card 2A, and ask God to work in you to produce all six of these characteristics.

Philippians 2:5-11

DAY 3

Today's Bible Meditation
"Behold, the kingdom of God is in your midst."
Luke 17:21

Name of Christ for Today
The Christ [Anointed One]
(Matt. 16:16)

Prayer to Begin the Lesson
Christ Jesus, You are the Messiah. You were anointed by God to be my Savior. I can't wait to see progress as You develop Your mind in

✱ Begin today's lesson by reading the Bible verse and the name of Christ for today. Work on your memory verse. Then use the suggested prayer to begin your study.

So far, we've looked at six characteristics of a Christlike mind. They describe God's ideal plan for your mind. Possibly, you might be feeling discouraged right now, thinking, *I'm nowhere near where I'm supposed to be!* Don't lose heart. As we go along in this course, remember that this is a lifelong process! Hang in there!

Now, our primary text for this course is *Philippians 2:5-11*. This was one of the great hymns of the early Christian church. As I've studied this hymn, I've come to see six parts to it. Each one describes an aspect of Christ's life and mind. As we study these parts, God is going to be working in you to develop these same characteristics in your life. Today, we're going to look at how each part of the hymn relates to God's work in your life. Look again at today's Bible meditation, *Luke 17:21*. As you become more like Christ, God's kingdom is happening inside you! What God is doing on the inside will begin to be expressed in how you live your life on the outside.

✱ Get out your Mind of Christ Cards for this unit, and complete the following steps.
- **Read *Philippians 2:5-11* on Cards 1A and 1B.**
- **Start memorizing the hymn. Work on this at your own pace. This assignment is in addition to your weekly verse memorization work. Today, start memorizing *verse 5*. Make it a personal goal to have the entire hymn memorized by Week 12 of the course.**
- **Review the Six Characteristics of a Christlike Mind (Card 2A).**

Now, let's look at this passage in more detail. We're going to pay close attention to what God will be doing to develop a Christlike mind in you. Each section heading will *me, but at the same time, I know that it's a long process. Thank You that I don't have to do it alone. Thank You for my Mind of Christ small group and my leader. But most of all, thank You that You dwell in me to help me with the process. I love You, and I look forward to the closer relationship I'll have with You as we go along in this course.*

Amen.

have a part of the hymn, and a title related to the mind of Christ. Then, in parenthesis, you will see the unit or units in *The Mind of Christ* that are related to that part of the passage. Next, you will read that part of the passage. Finally, you will see the Christlike characteristic God will be developing in you.

Part 1—Christ's Freedom (Units 2-3)

Hymn: *Let this mind be in you, which was also in Christ Jesus (Phil. 2:5,* KJV).

Christlike Characteristic: Alive. If we are alive in Christ, then we are free from sin's control over our lives. As Christians, we can experience conflict when the desires of the flesh clash with the desires of the Spirit. But where spiritual life exists, real freedom occurs. Likewise, when life is fully free, it is fully spiritual. So, God will be working to give you life and freedom in Christ.

✷ Write in the characteristic below, and fill in the word to indicate what God will be doing in your life.

Characteristic— ________________________________: God will be working to give me _________________ and _________________ in Christ.

Part 2—Christ's Lifestyle (Units 4-5)

Hymn: *Although He existed in the form of God, did not regard equality with God a thing to be grasped (Phil. 2:6).*

Christlike Characteristic: Single-Minded. It is hard to be a single-minded teenager. Our minds wander like puppies playing in a yard. There are so many distractions around us, as the world and society tries to force us into its mold. But to be single-minded means to focus on seeking God's will first. As you make up your mind to put God's kingdom first, God will begin to give you the virtues of godly wisdom and the fruit of the Spirit.

✷ Write in the characteristic below, and fill in the word to indicate what God will be doing in your life.

Characteristic— ________________________________: God will be working to give me the virtues of godly ________________________________ and the _____________________ of the Spirit.

Part 3—Christ's Servanthood (Unit 6)

Hymn: *Made himself* [Jesus] *of no reputation, and took upon him the form of a servant, and was made in the likeness of men (Phil. 2:7,* KJV).

Christlike Characteristic: Lowly. Here's another one the world doesn't emphasize a whole lot. Pride has been the enemy of righteousness ever since the Garden of Eden, when Satan told Adam and Eve they could be like God. God can't stand pride, but He dwells with the lowly. Now, there is a big difference between lowliness and low self-esteem. Lowliness doesn't mean putting yourself down. Rather, it means building other people up. God will be working in you to help you see His greatness. With a lowly spirit, you will take on the characteristics of servanthood.

✱ **Write in the characteristic below, and fill in the word to indicate what God will be doing in your life.**

Characteristic— ______________________________: God will be working

to help me see His ____________________________________, and with a

______________________________ spirit I will take on the Characteristics

of ____________________________.

Part 4—Christ's Humanity (Units 7-10)

Hymn: [Jesus] *made in the likeness of men. And being found in appearance as a man (Phil. 2:7-8).*

Christlike Characteristic: Pure. When God became a human being, He showed His purpose for human beings—that they have great authority and nobility. In order to have these characteristics in your life, you must be pure. Purity shows in the way you live your life. How do you express your emotions? How do you treat people? What things are important to you? As you walk daily in the Spirit, God will be working in you to cleanse the impurities of your life and establish right patterns for living.

✱ **Write in the characteristic below, and fill in the word to indicate what God will be doing in your life.**

Characteristic— ______________________________: God will be working

to cleanse the ____, of my life and

establish ________________________ patterns for living.

Part 5—Christ's Holiness and Love (Unit 11)

Hymn: [Jesus] *humbled Himself by becoming obedient to the point of death, even death on a cross (Phil. 2:8).*

Christlike Characteristic: Responsive. Jesus became *obedient to the point of death.* His obedience bought our holiness. When Jesus died on the cross, it was the ultimate expression of God's love. When someone was willing to do that for you, doesn't that make you want to gratefully obey Him? Now, responsiveness is not "doing your duty." *Responsiveness* means "choosing to take on Christ's nature of holiness and love." God will be working to make you holy and to teach you to love with a Christlike love.

✱ **Write in the characteristic below, and fill in the word to indicate what God will be doing in your life.**

Characteristic— ______________________________: God will be working to make me ____________________ and to teach me to ________________ with a Christlike love.

Part 6—Christ's Name (Unit 12)

Hymn: *Therefore also God highly exalted Him, and bestowed on Him the name which is above every name, that at the name of Jesus every knee should bow, of those who are in heaven, and on earth, and under the earth, and that every tongue should confess that Jesus Christ is Lord, to the glory of God the Father (Phil. 2:9-11).*

Christlike Characteristic: Peaceful. Jesus' love is what makes peace possible for us. It was His love that took Him to Calvary, and through His death He brought us peace with God. Since Jesus conquered sin and death with His resurrection, peace can be a reality in our lives. When we exalt the risen Christ, we can experience genuine peace. Peace doesn't come when we fight God for control over our lives. Peace comes when we hit our knees, and allow Christ to be the absolute Lord of our lives. God will be working to exalt Christ before you so you will surrender completely to His lordship.

✳ Write in the characteristic below, and fill in the word to indicate what God will be doing in your life.

Characteristic— ______________________________: God will be working to exalt Christ before me so I will ______________________________ completely to His ________________________.

✳ Close your study today in prayer. Ask God to make you aware of the characteristic God wants most to work on in your life. Give God permission to mold you into the image of His Son. Thank God for the model He has given us in Jesus.

Developing the Mind of Christ

DAY 4

✱ **Begin today's lesson by reading the Bible verse and the name of Christ for today. Work on your memory verse. Then use the suggested prayer to begin your study.**

Okay. Time for an English lesson. Now, all along we've been talking about how developing the mind of Christ is a process. So, think of three verbs that describe a process. How about *beginning, middle,* and *end*? In the New Testament, three verbs are used concerning the mind. We can see these three verbs in terms of the beginning, middle and continuing stages of developing the Mind of Christ. (Notice I didn't say "ending" stage? That's because this is a lifelong process. You're catching on!)

Three Stages in Developing the Mind of Christ

Beginning Stage	The Will Principle	Set your mind on things above.
Growing Stage	The River Principle	Allow God to renew your mind.
Qualified Stage	The Readiness Principle	Gird up your mind for action.

The Will Principle

Look at *Colossians 3:2—Set your mind on the things above, not on the things that are on earth.* Paul emphasizes this theme again in *Philippians 4:8: Finally, brethren, whatever is true, whatever is honorable, whatever is right, whatever is pure, whatever is lovely, whatever is of good repute, if there is any excellence and if anything worthy of praise, let your mind dwell on these things.* Do you see the theme here? The goal is to make a conscious decision to think about certain things. We call this the Will Principle, and it is the first stage toward developing the mind of Christ. Imagine that on the first day of a new semester at school, you make a conscious decision to get good grades. If you are a runner or know someone who is, imagine focusing on the finish line when you start the race. In both these examples, a person sees the end from the beginning, and sets his or her mind on accomplishing a certain goal. This is the Will Principle.

One thing that separates people from animals is the ability to make decisions. Animals can't do it. They rely on instinct. But instinct is the opposite of will. The will is what enables us to make decisions in spite of feelings or intuitions. While we can't always control our emotions, we can always control our will. The goal, according to *2 Corinthians 10:5* is to take *Every thought captive to the obedience of Christ.* Giving God your will is the first step toward developing the mind of Christ.

✱ **What do you do during the first stage—the Beginning Stage?**

I ___________ my mind.

Today's Bible Meditation
Set your mind on the things above, not on the things that are on earth.
Colossians 3:2

Name of Christ for Today
The Lord Our Righteousness
(Jer. 23:6)

Prayer to Begin the Lesson
Dear Lord, You are my Righteousness. My own righteousness is like worthless, filthy rags next to You. Please help Your life become my life, and where Your righteousness becomes my righteousness. Guide me in that process. Help me to set my mind and heart on You.
Amen.

In your own words, define what it means to *set* your mind.

____

How did Jesus demonstrate the Will Principle? Think about the last week of His life. As He thought about the cross, His instinct might have said, "Run away!" His feelings and emotions probably said, "Don't do this! You don't want this pain!" But Jesus made a conscious decision to set His mind on God's will. He said, in *John 12:27-28, "Now My soul has become troubled; and what shall I say, 'Father, save Me from this hour'? But for this purpose I came to this hour. Father, glorify Thy name."* You see, while Jesus' emotions said one thing, His will did another. This decision to let His will rule over His emotions is also seen in the Garden of Gethsemane. Remember what Jesus prayed? *"Father . . . remove this cup from Me; yet not what I will, but what Thou wilt" (Mark 14:36).* Jesus came through with flying colors, because He set His will from the beginning. Jesus gave His mind to God. Therefore, His actions were in line with God's will. Jesus' mind was set on things above.

Have you ever had to make a decision between what you knew was the right thing to do and what your feelings said? Once, I was asked to take a certain ministry position. I knew that if I took it, it would involve a tremendous personal sacrifice, not to mention a huge salary cut! But on the other hand, it offered an opportunity to expand God's kingdom like nothing else I'd ever been offered. So, even though my feelings said "no," my will chose the will of God. Only the will can choose beyond feelings.

The River Principle

Heraclitus, an ancient Greek philosopher, once said, "You cannot step twice in the same river." What he meant was that a river is always flowing, always changing, and always being renewed. Nature is that way. Your body is that way, too. You are constantly reproducing new cells as old cells die away. As long as your body keeps producing new cells, you are alive. But what happens when your body is no longer renewing itself? Simple. You die.

This principle is at work in our spiritual life also. In *Romans 12:2,* Paul says, *Be transformed by the renewing of your mind.* If we are to continue to grow in our Christian lives, we must be continually renewed. Once you give your will to God (The Will Principle), you continue to allow your mind to be transformed, or renewed, by God. We can call this the River Principle. Jesus said, *"He who believes in Me, as the Scripture said, 'From his innermost being shall flow rivers of living water'" (John 7:38).* Living water! That's the kind that flows, and is always changing. Fresh water flows in and washes out what's old and dead. However, water becomes stagnant and foul when it stops flowing. You've all seen stagnant, scummy ponds. They are that way because there's nowhere for the old water to go, and there's no new water coming in.

Is your spiritual life more like a river or a pond? A pond eventually dries up and becomes a puddle. But a river keeps flowing, and eventually becomes an ocean! You are called to grow spiritually, and your growth in Christ ultimately will be enormous!

Spiritual newness comes in many shapes and forms. Sometimes, it hits you when you're reading a verse you've seen a million times before, but this time you see something you've never noticed before. Sometimes, it comes in the form of renewed energy to accomplish things for God. You may begin to make spiritual connections to your normal school day. You can experience newness as you develop deeper relationships with other Christians and within your youth group. Or as you make a new commitment. Sometimes, newness comes in the form of renewed strength to resist temptation. Newness helps you chart your progress in developing the mind of Christ (see *2 Cor. 3:18).*

✳ What do you do during the second stage—the Growing Stage?

I (a verb) ____________ my mind.

Which of the following indicate renewal? Check all that apply.

a. Newness of spiritual growth.
b. No signs of spiritual growth.
c. New insights into what the Scripture means, or how to apply it.
d. Failure to understand Scriptures or apply them to my life.
e. New energy to accomplish things for God.
f. Weakness, tiredness, and lack of spiritual energy to do anything for God.

Allow God to renew your mind in the Growing Stage. Keep in mind the difference between a river and a pond. Renewal beings newness, new insights, and fresh spiritual energy (a,c,e). Jesus demonstrated progress and growth in His life. In fact, while there is nothing written about Jesus as a teenager, we can assume from *Luke 2:52* that as a teenager, *Jesus kept increasing in wisdom and stature, and in favor with God and men.* If you are to have the mind of Christ, expect newness! That's how we grow. That's renewal!

The Readiness Principle

In ancient Greece, athletic competition was just as big as it is now. However, people dressed a lot differently then. Imagine our modern Olympic athletes trying to run track or jump hurdles wearing long, flowing togas! Those first-century athletes had the same problem. In order to compete, the athlete had to lift up the edge of his robe and tuck it under his belt. This was called "girding up the robe."

This is the image Peter uses in *1 Peter 1:13*. The third stage in developing the mind of Christ is to "gird up" our minds for action. In modern terms, you might think about "rolling up your sleeves." It's the same image. This is the Readiness Principle. Our minds are to be prepared for action.

✳ What do you do during the third stage—the Qualified Stage?

I (a verb) ________________ my mind.

What does that mean? Define it in your own words.

____

In the Qualified Stage, you prepare your mind for action. Remember how different groups would try to trap Jesus with questions (see *Luke 20:20-40)?* One group asked Him if Jews should pay taxes to the Roman government. Jesus was ready for them. He said they should give both God and Caesar what they are owed. Another group, the Sadducees, questioned Him about resurrection. Because Jesus knew the Scripture so well, He was prepared to correct their wrong ideas about the future life. Jesus was mentally ready at all times. Readiness means being qualified for service. If your will is set and your mind has grown through constant renewal, you will be qualified for any test God sends your way. Maybe you've seen the slogan, "24 / 7." That means that a Christian should be alert 24 hours a day, 7 days a week.

✱ Write each verb (prepare, renew, set) beside its description below.

_______________ focused attention

_______________ growth and newness

_______________ getting ready for action

✱ Match the verbs on the right to the proper stage and principle listed on the left. Write the letter of the verb on the line beside the stage.

_____ 1. Beginning: The Will Principle	**a. Prepare**
_____ 2. Growing: The River Principle	**b. Set**
_____ 3. Qualified: The Readiness Principle	**c. Renew**

✱ Close this session by setting your mind on God in prayer.

- **Ask God to give you focused attention to things above.**
- **Offer your will to God. Seek His will as you begin the three-stage process of developing the mind of Christ.**

Fix Your Thoughts on Jesus

DAY 5

Today's Bible Meditations
The steadfast of mind Thou wilt keep in perfect peace, because he trusts in Thee.
Isaiah 26:3

Therefore, holy brethren, partakers of a heavenly calling, consider Jesus, the Apostle and High Priest of our confession.
Hebrews 3:1

Name of Christ for Today
Apostle and High Priest of Our Profession
(Heb. 3:1)

Prayer to Begin the Lesson
Lord Jesus, You are the Apostle and the High Priest that I profess. I'm taking this course because I want to know You better. I want You to develop Your mind in me. Help me to begin today by fixing my mind and thoughts on You. No matter how many distractions there are at school or work, help me to keep my mind fixed on You in the coming weeks.

Amen.

✷ Begin today's lesson by reading the Bible verse and the name of Christ for today. Work on your memory verse. Then use the suggested prayer to begin your study.

Do you have a little brother or sister? Have you ever been around a baby for an extended stretch of time? Think about how their mind develops. At birth, they have all the right equipment. They have a brain. But as they grow, their mind develops. They learn habits and behaviors, and they also learn how to change habits and behaviors. Growth is a process of learning and developing. The spiritual world is the same way. Developing the mind of Christ involves many of the same elements. When you become a Christian, you have the mind of Christ (see *1 Cor. 2:16*). But it isn't developed yet. As we grow, the mind of Christ has to deal with habits we've developed that need to change, our culture, and the work of Satan that stunt its growth. There are also other factors which we'll deal with later. The mind of Christ matures in a process of growth.

✷ Based on yesterday's lesson, write in the three verbs that describe the three stages of the process. Try to do it without looking back at yesterday.

Beginning: S ____________________________

Growing: R ______________________________

Qualified: P _____________________________

First John 3:2 says, *We know that, when He appears, we shall be like Him, because we shall see Him just as He is.* As long as we're on earth, we can't match that final degree of perfection of being just like Jesus. But when Jesus comes back, we will be united with Him forever. And in His presence, we will become like Him, without spot or stain. Our ultimate destiny is to be like Christ. It's what God wants, it's what God commanded, and it's what the Bible says we are to work on until He comes back.

✷ As a child of God, what is your ultimate destiny?

____

Yes! You are going to be like Christ in eternity. Look at *Matthew 10:24* and *25*: *"A disciple is not above his teacher, nor a slave above his master. It is enough for the disciple that he become as his teacher, and the slave as his master."* Obviously, Jesus wants us to be like Him. Peter says, *You have been called for this purpose, since Christ also suffered for you, leaving you an example for you to follow in His steps (1 Pet. 2:21).* Not only are you to think like Christ, but you are to follow His lifestyle as well. Peter also gives us this command: *Therefore, since Christ has suffered in the flesh, arm yourselves also with the same purpose, because he who has suffered in the flesh has ceased from sin (1 Pet. 4:1).* Now, here's something serious for you to think about: God uses suffering in your life as a tool to put the flesh to death, so that you can become more like Christ. Developing the mind of Christ will cost you a great deal. But it is worth more than you could ever imagine.

✻ Be honest. What are you feeling right now about developing the mind of Christ?
- ❑ **I'm overwhelmed. This is too much. I can't do it.**
- ❑ **Whoa! I'm afraid! The idea of suffering sounds scary.**
- ❑ **I'm excited. I know this is going to be costly, but the results are worth it all.**
- ❑ **I'm confused. I still don't really understand what I'm getting into.**
- ❑ **Other: ______________________________**

God Is At Work

It's okay if you're feeling any or all of these emotions right now. Believe me, I've felt them all myself at one time or another. But God's goal for us is that we look like His Son. *For whom He foreknew, He also predestined to become conformed to the image of His Son, that He might be the first-born among many brethren (Rom. 8:29).* Paul also wrote, *But we all, with unveiled face beholding as in a mirror the glory of the Lord, are being transformed into the same image from glory to glory, just as from the Lord, the Spirit (2 Cor. 3:18).* What an awesome thing—to be like Christ! It's scary, it's overwhelming, it's a little confusing, but it's also incredibly exciting! Although it's overwhelming, there's good news!

If you look closely at New Testament passages, you'll see that becoming like Christ is not really your work, it's primarily God's work. Imagine yourself as a lump of clay, or as a blank canvas. God is the potter, or the artist. You are the subject of change; God is the agent of change. You see, it doesn't all depend on you. God promises that He will do two things for you. First, He will cause you to want the mind of Christ, then He will enable you to develop it.

Have you ever felt like a math teacher gave you an assignment without telling you how to do the problem? That's not how God works at all! *For it is God who is at work in you, both to will and to work for His good pleasure (Phil. 2:13).* Paul also told the Philippians, *For I am confident of this very thing, that He who began a good work in you will perfect it until the day of Christ Jesus (Phil. 1:6).* We are simply commanded to [fix] *our eyes on Jesus, the author and perfecter of our faith (Heb. 12:2).* Since God started the work in you, He will finish it. Although you will face discouragement in developing the mind of Christ, you need not despair. You don't complete the work, Jesus does. Our eyes are fixed on Him specifically as the Perfecter of our faith.

God wants us to develop the mind of Christ. He causes you to want it, He enables you to do it, and He allows His son to perfect the work He Himself began. It's a rock-solid guarantee for an incredible deal.

✻ Check the statement that most closely describes your role in developing the mind of Christ.
- ❑ **I'm in this alone. If anything is going to happen, it's up to me. If I don't do it, nothing will get done.**
- ❑ **I'm not alone. God is helping me. But still the main assignment is on my shoulders, and God just helps me out when I get stuck.**
- ❑ **God is at work in me, molding me into the image of His Son. As I submit to His work and cooperate with Him, God will bring it to pass.**

Apostle and High Priest

Hebrews tells us to *consider Jesus, the Apostle and High Priest of our confession (Heb. 3:1)*. An *apostle* is "one who has been sent." Jesus was sent from heaven to earth. Consider Jesus. That means to fix your mind, thoughts, and attention on Him— to set your mind on Christ. In order to do that, you must give total focus to what you can learn about Him from the Gospels. Then, you are to follow in His steps *(1 Pet. 2:21)*.

That same passage in Hebrews calls Jesus the High Priest. When Jesus made His own life the perfect sacrifice for our sins, He was acting as our High Priest. Even now, Jesus still serves as our High Priest. The Bible says that Jesus intercedes to the Father on our behalf *(Heb. 7:25)*. That means that He is our spokesman in prayer. As we look at the letters in the New Testament, a lot of Jesus' role as High Priest is revealed.

Let's put all this together. If we are to consider Jesus as both Apostle and High Priest, we have to have a good understanding of the New Testament. You see, the Gospels give us information about how Jesus was sent to earth (as Apostle). When we fix our thoughts on His lifestyle, we can model our lives after His example. The Letters give us insight into His function as High Priest. They describe the meaning of Jesus' work on earth, and also His intercessory role as High Priest in Heaven. We are to fix our thoughts on His divine work on our behalf.

✻ **Match the roles of Christ in the left column with the intended focus of our thoughts in the middle column. Then, indicate where we learn about that focus by matching the names to an item in the third column. Write two letters in front of each name.**

__ __ Apostle	a. His divine work in Heaven	x. Gospels
__ __ High Priest	b. His earthly life	y. New Testament Letters

Summary

Our goal as Christians is to become like Christ. Our role in that process is to think like Christ. The main work, however, is God's. God intends us to be like Christ. He has predetermined it, and is currently at work transforming us *(2 Cor. 3:18)*. In working with God in the process, we carefully study what we know about the human life of Christ and seek to follow in His steps. By the way, the answers to the test you just took were: Apostle— b, x; High Priest— a, y.

✻ **As you finish this first unit, review your memory verse. Remember how Jesus was prepared for all the questions and traps people threw at Him? He knew Scripture. Work at hiding God's Word in your heart so you will be better prepared for temptation when it comes. Ask God to be at work in you during this course to open your mind and heart to the Scriptures. Commit to God your intention of responding to all that He may reveal to you during your study. Consider praying this prayer:**

God, the idea of being like Your Son both frightens me and thrills me. He is so perfect, and I am so flawed. Will I really be "without spot or blemish" the way He is? At this point, that seems incredible. But I truly want to be obedient. I want to be like Jesus.

Thank You for giving me a place to start. For Jesus' sake, and in His name, I give my mind to You. I've set my mind on things above, as best as I know how. I'm seeking continual renewal, and I thank You for it. I will prepare my mind and live in a state of readiness to witness to the glories of Jesus. It seems that my mind must be alive, or I wouldn't want to be like Him. Thanks that Jesus was single-minded, lowly, pure, responsive, and peaceful. Help me to be more like Him in these specific ways. Amen.

Experiencing Freedom in Christ

UNIT 2

Day 1
A Disordered Mind

Day 2
Making a List of Your Desires

Day 3
Christ Sets You Free!

Day 4
The Ordered Mind of Christ

Day 5
One Great Passion

Scripture Memory Verse
"Seek first His kingdom and His righteousness; and all these things shall be added to you."
Matthew 6:33

Hymn Part 1—Christ's Freedom
Let this mind be in you, which was also in Christ Jesus (Phil. 2:5, KJV).

What Is in This Unit for Me?

You will learn that the control of sin in your life causes mental conflicts as your flesh fights against the Spirit, as Christ's desires become your desires, you will experience genuine freedom in Christ.

Lifelong Objective

You will live in peace in Christ, and you will have freedom from the control of sin. As you seek first His kingdom, you will develop Christ's desires as your desires.

How God Will Be Working in You

Christ's desires within you help bring about the work of God in your life. God's goal is Christ's fullness in your life. Your growth toward holy desires is only possible by seeking God's kingdom above everything else. Christ helps you develop that desire by His example. Christ wants you to want the same things He wants.

Unit Learning Goals

- You will understand how your desires can cause conflict with Christ's desires.
- You will understand how a disordered mind leads to ungodly living.
- You will see how Christ sets you free from mental conflict and the control of sin.
- You will know 17 virtues that are true of Christ's mind.
- You will demonstrate a willingness to seek the kingdom of God above all other things.

What You Will Do to Begin Experiencing Freedom in Christ

- You will begin to make a private list of your wants and desires.
- You will evaluate your list of wants to see if they conflict with Christ's desires.
- You will begin to study 17 virtues of Christ's mind in order to understand what His mind is like.
- You will ask God to renew your mind and give you the desires of Christ in place of your own desires.

Lifelong Helps Related to This Unit

Bondage to Freedom Lists (pp. 189-191)

The Mind of Christ Cards Related to This Unit

3A. Unit 2: Scripture Memory—*Matthew 6:33*
7A. Eight Virtues of Godly Wisdom
7B. Fruit of the Spirit

DAY

1

Today's Bible Meditation
What is the source of quarrels and conflicts among you? Is not the source your pleasures that wage war in your members?
James 4:1

Name of Christ for Today
The Desire of All Nations
(Hag. 2:7, KJV)

Prayer to Begin the Lesson
Lord Jesus, just as You are the desire of all nations, be my ultimate desire today. Help me understand how my desires conflict with your desires. Give me the desire to have the mind of Christ.
Amen.

A Disordered Mind

✳ Begin today's lesson by reading the Bible verse and the name of Christ for today. Work on your memory verse. Then use the suggested prayer to begin your study.

I want to share with you one of the ways God worked in my life to begin developing the mind of Christ in me. Read my story, and then make a list like the one I describe.

A Time for Meditation

On a Saturday morning in August of 1972, I was alone in the house. My wife had gone to the beauty shop, and my daughter was at orchestra practice. I took advantage of the quiet to focus on my walk with the Lord. I had memorized the Book of James, so I spent that Saturday meditating on *James 3:13-4:3.* Beginning with *verse 18,* James says:

> [18]*And the seed whose fruit is righteousness is sown in peace by those who make peace.*
> [4:1]*What is the source of quarrels and conflicts among you? Is not the source your pleasures that wage war in your members?*
> [2]*You lust and do not have; so you commit murder. And you are envious and cannot obtain; so you fight and quarrel. You do not have because you do not ask.*
> [3]*You ask and do not receive, because you ask with wrong motives, so that you may spend it on your pleasures.*

✳ As you look at this passage, ask yourself this: Has there ever been a time when you asked God for something that primarily was for selfish reasons? Check one:

❑ Yes ❑ Not that I can recall
If you answered yes, name one thing you asked for.

____

As I was meditating on the words of James, I realized that the things I wanted, desired, or lusted after could cause conflict within me. Even the things that gave me pleasure and the things that I was passionate about were often in conflict with one another. I'll explain more in a minute. But look again at the passage from James. Circle the phrase *wage war in your members.* Your lusts and passions are like opposing soldiers inside you, lining up for battle.

✳ Have you ever had a mental battle within yourself when two different wants argued with each other? Check one:

❑ Yes ❑ Not that I can recall
If you answered yes, briefly describe one such battle. For example, maybe you saw an outfit at the mall that you really wanted to buy and knew you couldn't afford, but you were also trying to save money for the youth mission trip.

____

____

Testing the Scripture in My Life

I decided to put the Scripture to the test. I listed all my lusts, wants, desires, pleasures, and passions on a legal pad. I wrote down everything I could think of, both good and bad. No particular order, just anything that came to mind. Then, I would see if they really did war against each other. I made up my mind that I would be totally honest before God with this list (Of course, I also planned to burn the list before anyone came home!) My list started off like this:

I want:
1. A new suit
2. A washer and dryer
3. Jesus Christ to be honored on the seminary campus where I teach
4. ________________ (an itch)
5. A consistent faith
6. ________________ (another thing)

The first two desires had been on my mind for a long time because for four years, we had been without either, and I hated the Laundromat! Honoring Jesus, I'm ashamed to say, was not the first thing I thought of. I'm not going to tell you what item number four was, but I will say that it was like an itch. That's how I describe tempting desires. You know how, once you start thinking about an itch, you can't stop thinking about it until you scratch it? That's how this desire was for me. I didn't want to honor it, but often it came to mind. Have you ever had an itch like that? Satan knows that if he can get our attention for five seconds, he's got our mind for five minutes! The itch was bad, but its persistence was worse.

The fifth desire I wrote was for a consistent faith. I had a friend who seemed to model that kind of faith. Even though he'd been through a lot of trials, his faith stayed steady. I looked at my own faith, and it seemed like a roller coaster. As circumstances went up and down, so did my faith. I wanted the same kind of consistent faith my friend had.

My sixth desire, like my first and second, was for a material thing. I had come to a point in my life where I figured I had the issue of materialism settled. But under the leadership of the Holy Spirit, I found that I still wanted things. God was showing me things I had not consciously been aware of.

And that's how it went. I filled up the page with desires, both good and bad, however they came to mind. As I looked at the list, it occurred to me that I was looking at a picture of how my mind normally worked. It was inconsistent and disordered.

✳ Let's practice (You're going to do this more in-depth tomorrow anyway). If you were to make a list like mine, what are four desires or wants that would be on your list? "I want… "

1. ____

2. ____

3. ____

4. ____

The Inner Conflict

So, did my desires "war" with one another? That is, were they in conflict? I looked at how my desires related to each other. Desire #4 was an unholy itch. I didn't want it, but it was often there. My third desire, on the other hand, was a desire to honor Christ. So there was one war right there! I truly wanted to honor the Lord, but I sometimes violated that desire by allowing an opposite, conflicting desire to surface. One desire fought the other!

I realized after this that the reason my faith was inconsistent (my fifth desire) was that I had not yet resolved the issue of materialism (my sixth desire). My concern for things increased my tendency to go up and down according to my circumstances. So once again, there was friction between two desires. Usually, when I made a choice over what to think about, the lower won out over the higher. And then I realized that my so-called "choices" over what to think about were really pretty thoughtless. Very little of my thinking was controlled by my will. The Bible was right! My passions produced conflicts within me!

✱ According to James, what is the reason a Christian has mental conflict or battles?

____

✱ Check each of the following items that describes a disordered mind.

- ❑ **a. only good desires**
- ❑ **b. good and bad desires mixed together**
- ❑ **c. clear choices are made about what to think about**
- ❑ **d. little thought is given to what to think about**
- ❑ **e. the will is in control of thinking**
- ❑ **f. the will is not in control of thinking**

According to James, the war that rages inside us is due to our desires that battle for control. The disordered mind has all sorts of desires, both good and bad, jumbled together in no particular order. The will isn't in control of your thinking. Therefore, little thought is given to what we think about. (Answers: b, d, f.) Our thoughts then often lead to actions—godly thoughts to godly actions, wrong thoughts to wrong actions.

The mind of Christ is not disordered but ordered. Jesus was able to control His thinking in such a way that only godly actions came through His life. This is one reason why you and I need the mind of Christ.

The next few lessons are going to require you to make some lists of different things. If you do not already have some kind of journal in which you record private thoughts, you may want to think about picking one up before tomorrow's lesson.

✱ Close this lesson in prayer, asking Jesus to begin doing the work He needs to do to set you free from the effects of a disordered mind.

Making a List of Your Desires

DAY 2

Today's Bible Meditation
Wretched man that I am! Who will set me free from the body of this death? Thanks be to God through Jesus Christ our Lord! So then, on the one hand I myself with my mind am serving the law of God, but on the other, with my flesh the law of sin.
Romans 7:24-25

Name of Christ for Today
Jesus Christ Our Lord
(Rom. 7:25)

Prayer to Begin the Lesson
Jesus Christ, my Lord! I thank my Heavenly Father for You. Because of You, I can be free from the bondage of sin and death. Lead me to get rid of my desires that conflict with Your desires. You are my Lord. I will do whatever You ask.
Amen.

✳ Begin today's lesson by reading the Bible verse and the name of Christ for today. Work on your memory verse. Then use the suggested prayer in the margin to begin your study.

Yesterday, you learned that desires can war against each other inside you, causing great mental conflict. This results in a disordered mind. A disordered mind can lead to ungodly or evil actions. Read Paul's description of the conflict he felt in *Romans 7:18-25,* and see if you can relate:

> 18*For I know that nothing good dwells in me, that is, in my flesh; for the*
> *wishing is present in me, but the doing of the good is not.* 19*For the good that*
> *I wish, I do not do; but I practice the very evil that I do not wish.* 20*But if I*
> *am doing the very thing I do not wish, I am no longer the one doing it, but*
> *sin which dwells in me.* 21*I find then the principle that evil is present in me,*
> *the one who wishes to do good.* 22*For I joyfully concur with the law of God*
> *in the inner man,* 23*but I see a different law in the members of my body, wag-*
> *ing war against the law of my mind, and making me a prisoner of the law of*
> *sin which is in my members.* 24*Wretched man that I am! Who will set me free*
> *from the body of this death?* 25*Thanks be to God through Jesus Christ our*
> *Lord! So then, on the one hand I myself with my mind am serving the law of*
> *God, but on the other, with my flesh the law of sin.*

✳ What kind of mind do you think Paul was describing?

- ❑ **A disordered mind, dominated by the flesh.**
- ❑ **An ordered mind, controlled by the Spirit.**

✳ Draw a line matching the mind on the left with the kind of living it produces on the right.

A disordered mind	**• godly living**
An ordered mind	**• ungodly living**

It's like this. Imagine your room when you haven't cleaned it for weeks (If that's a stretch for you, imagine a friend's room that hasn't been cleaned for weeks!) A mom would probably say that it's "disordered." Stuff in it is lost—even really important stuff that might be needed such as assignments, bills, keys—all buried beneath layers of junk.

Do you see the analogy? When your mind is disordered, really important priorities, such as godly living, can get buried beneath layers of less important, or even impure things. The result is ungodly living.

Now, look back up at the verses from *Romans 7*. In *verse 25,* Paul praised God that Jesus could set him free from this pattern of disorder. In other words, Jesus can be the Master Housekeeper, who can help you clean up the disorder in your own mind, and allow you to serve God more effectively.

How can He start doing that? First, you must let your mind be controlled by the will. You need to make mental decisions about what you're going to think about. You must come to the point where you choose to deny your desires that conflict with God's desires, and to choose to make Christ's desires your desires. The end result will be a freedom in Christ that will allow you to experience life to its fullest! Let me show you where we'll be going in the next few days.

Heading Toward Freedom

You can remember this process by remembering the acronym **L.I.G.H.T.**:

1. Make your own **List of desires.** This will be the start of an ongoing process for your life.
2. **Identify desires that may conflict** with other desires.
3. Pray that Christ will help you **Get rid of desires** that are in conflict with His.
4. Pray that Christ will help you **Have His desires.**
5. Begin to **Take Action** to follow Christ's desires rather than your own.

To get started, I'd like you to identify your desires—the good ones and the bad ones. Then, you'll evaluate which of those desires may be causing conflict with godly desires.

✷ **Follow these instructions to begin making a list of your lusts, wants, desires, and passions. If you bought a separate journal, now's the time to get it out.**

MAKING A LIST OF YOUR DESIRES

1. Write the title "My List of Desires" and today's date at the top of the page.
2. Pray that you can be totally honest with God as you make your list. No one else is going to see this list. Ask God to help you identify lusts, desires, wants, and passions in your life.
3. Make your list. Write down everything that comes to mind. Number the items, starting with the four desires you listed in yesterday's lesson.
4. If you're worried about someone else reading your list, you can label them as *Itch #1, Thing 2,* and so forth. Just make sure you give yourself enough information so you can remember what you're talking about. Ask yourself:
   - What do I really want in life?
   - What are my desires or passions?
5. Don't try to evaluate, judge, grade, or censor anything right now. Just write it down. The evaluation part comes later.
6. If you get stuck, turn to the Lifelong Helps on pages 189-191 and use the guide to help you make your list more complete.
7. Take whatever time you can today. You probably won't finish your list today, and that's okay. You may want to carry the journal with you today, or else a small note pad, so that you can jot down other desires that come to mind throughout the day. Once you start your list, sign and date below:

I've started making a list of my desires, being as honest with God as I can.

Signature: ______________________________ Date ____________________

You will continue to work with this list over a period of time. Add to it any time during the course when you become aware of additional desires.

✳ Close your study today by asking Jesus to give you unbiased spiritual eyes to begin seeing the desires you have that conflict with His desires.

Christ Sets You Free!

DAY 3

✳ Begin today's lesson by reading the Bible verse and the name of Christ for today. Work on your memory verse. Then use the suggested prayer to begin your study.

✳ Look over the list you made yesterday. Which desires conflict with each other? On your list, write down the number of conflicting desires (example: "4 vs. 2"). Try to identify several pairs, but remember that not every desire will have a specific conflict. You may not have time to cover the entire list today. That's okay. Always remember that this is the start of a lifelong process. You will continue to process this list over the coming months.

Here. Let me give you an example from my own list. Remember that my fourth desire was an unholy itch, one I didn't want but was often there. My third desire was that Christ be honored where I taught. There was a conflict there. I couldn't dwell on the unholy itch and honor Christ at the same time. So, on my list, I wrote down "#4 vs. #3."

✳ Describe one of the conflicts you identified.

____

____

____

Remember what *James 4:1* says about the source of mental conflicts? It says, *What is the source of quarrels and conflicts among you? Is not the source your pleasures that wage war in your members?* When your desires conflict with God's desires for you, you will experience mental conflict. Ungodly desires mixed with godly desires create a disordered mind which can lead to ungodly living.

The mind of Christ can help you resolve those conflicts. But don't think of this as some method or program to straighten out your thinking. Jesus Himself will set you free. As Paul says in *Romans 7,* which we studied yesterday, Christ is the One who sets you free.

Today's Bible Meditations

For the law of the Spirit of life in Christ Jesus has set you free from the law of sin and of death.

Romans 8:2

It was for freedom that Christ set us free.

Galatians 5:1

Name of Christ for Today

The Deliverer

(Rom. 11:26)

Prayer to Begin the Lesson

Lord Jesus,
You are my deliverer. Please begin to deliver me,
or set me free, from mental conflict and the control of sinful desires.

Amen.

A Process Toward Freedom (LIGHT)

List your desires.
Identify conflicting desires.
Get rid of wrong desires.
Have Christ's Desires.
Take action (Decide to follow His desires).

✱ Cover up the left margin and see if you can remember the steps in "A Process Toward Freedom." (Hint: L.I.G.H.T.) Uncover the margin and see how you did.

This process relates to what you do. But Jesus is the One at work in you throughout the process. Here is what He is doing.

- Christ creates in you the desire to be like Him.
- Christ begins to give you desires for the things He wants.
- Christ's desires within you enable the Father to work in your life.
- God's goal is for you to experience Christ's fullness so that He becomes your life.
- You grow in having godly desires by seeking the Kingdom (the will of Christ) above all other things.
- Christ helps you develop that desire by His example.
- Christ wants you to share His wants.

✱ Which of the following best describes what needs to happen for you to be set free from conflicting desires? Check one.

❑ a. I find an approved list of desires somewhere in the Bible, get rid of desires that are not on the list, and replace them with ones that are on the list.
❑ b. I sit back and wait until God changes me to be everything He wants me to be. I don't do anything until then.
❑ c. Christ encourages me to be like Him. I release my desires and allow Him to give me His desires.

God doesn't automatically change you, like "*b*" says. He won't violate your will. You make the choice whether you will be involved in the process. On the other hand, you can't do it all by yourself, rather, like "*a*" says. You can't be what God wants if you don't allow Him to work in your life. No, the right answer is "*c.*" Christ takes the initiative to cause you to want to be like Him. When you respond and submit your desires to Him, Christ gives you a new set of desires. Tomorrow, you'll see how His desires don't conflict with themselves.

Alive in Christ

In Unit 1, we studied how the word *mind* is used in six places in the New Testament. From these passages, we identified six characteristics of the Christlike mind. The first characteristic is *alive.* True life is in the Spirit. Those persons without the Spirit are spiritually dead. You need a mind that is alive in the Spirit.

✱ Read *Romans 8: 1-17* below and circle words related to life and death.

> 1 *There is therefore now no condemnation for those who are in Christ Jesus.*
> 2 *For the law of the Spirit of life in Christ Jesus has set you free from the law of sin and of death.*
> 3 *For what the Law was could not do, weak as it was through the flesh, God did: sending His own Son in the likeness of sinful flesh and as an offering for sin, He condemned sin in the flesh,*
> 4 *in order that the requirement of the Law might be fulfilled in us, who do not walk according to the flesh, but according to the Spirit.*
> 5 *For those who are according to the flesh set their minds on the things of the flesh, but those who are according to the Spirit, the things of the Spirit.*
> 6 *For the mind set on the flesh is death,*

but the mind set on the the Spirit is life and peace, 7 *because the mind set on*
the flesh is hostile toward God; for it does not subject itself to the law of God,
for it is not even able to do so; 8 *and those who are in the flesh cannot please*
God. 9 *However, you are not in the flesh but in the Spirit, if indeed the Spirit*
of God dwells in you. But if anyone does not have the Spirit of Christ, he does
not belong to Him. 10 *And if Christ is in you, though the body is dead because*
of sin, yet the spirit is alive because of righteousness. 11 *But if the Spirit of Him*
who raised Jesus from the dead dwells in you, He who raised Christ Jesus
from the dead will also give life to your mortal bodies through His Spirit who
indwells you. 12 *So then, brethren, we are under obligation, not to the flesh,*
to live according to the flesh— 13 *for if you are living according to the flesh,*
you must die; but if by the Spirit you are putting to death the deeds of the
body, you will live. 14 *For all who are being led by the Spirit of God, these are*
sons of God. 15 *For you have not received a spirit of slavery leading to fear*
again, but you have received a spirit of adoption as sons by which we cry
out, "Abba! Father!" 16 *The Spirit Himself bears witness with our spirit that*
we are children of God, 17 *and if children, heirs also, heirs of God and fellow*
heirs with Christ, if indeed we suffer with Him in order that we may also be
glorified with Him.

✳ **This passage describes spiritual life and death. Each of the following words or phrases relates to either life or death. On the line in front of each word or phrase, write *L* for Life and *D* for Death.**

___ a. bondage to fear
___ b. sinfully minded
___ c. hostile to God
___ d. put to death the misdeeds of the body
___ e. righteousness
___ f. sin
___ g. in the Spirit
___ h. led by the Sprit of God
___ i. live after the flesh
___ j. Spirit of adoption
___ k. spiritually minded
___ l. walk after the Spirit

Christ's Freedom

This first characteristic of the Christian mind—*alive*—corresponds to the first part of the hymn in *Philippians* 2. When we have freedom in Christ, we are spiritually alive. Genuine freedom only occurs where spiritual life exists.

When you are free in Christ, you are free to live in the fullest sense of the word! Spiritual life is not the absence of death, but the presence of Christ—Christ in you. When you allow Christ to make you like Himself, He sets you free to fully live. (Answers: *L*— d, e, g, h, j, k, l; *D*— a, b, c, f, i.)

✳ **Close today's lesson by asking Jesus to begin renewing your mind in such a way that you walk after the Spirit.**

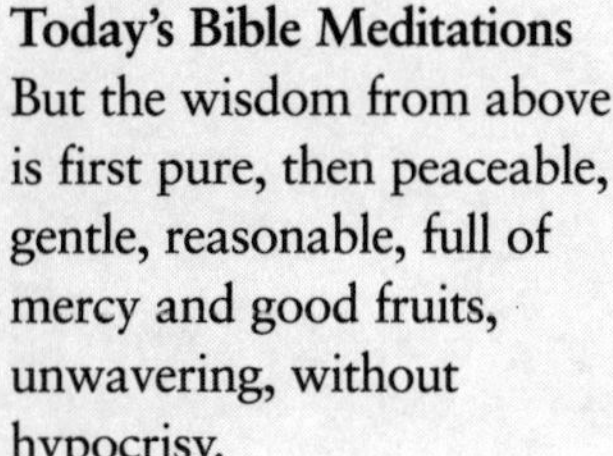

DAY 4

Today's Bible Meditations
But the wisdom from above is first pure, then peaceable, gentle, reasonable, full of mercy and good fruits, unwavering, without hypocrisy.

James 3:17

But the fruit of the Spirit is love, joy, peace, patience, kindness, goodness, faithfulness, gentleness, self-control; against such things there is no law.

Galatians 5:22-23

Name of Christ for Today
Our Hope

(1 Tim. 1:1)

Prayer to Begin the Lesson
My only hope is You, Jesus. If I'm ever going to be set free to live fully, You are the One who can do it. Please continue the process of setting me free.

Amen.

Eight Virtues—*James 3:17*

- pure
- peaceable
- gentle
- reasonable
- merciful
- fruitful
- unwavering
- honest

The Ordered Mind of Christ

✻ **Begin today's lesson by reading the Bible verse and the name of Christ for today. Work on your memory verse. Then use the suggested prayer to begin your study.**

Have you ever seen the cartoon where the lifeguard is doing CPR on a drowning victim? As he's pressing down on the guy's chest, he's saying, "Out with the bad air; in with the good." That's basically the same process God is going through with you as you develop the mind of Christ. "Out with the wrong desires; in with the good." Knowing what Jesus thought about, and the things He was concerned with can help you understand what He wants to work on in you. So today, we're going to look at 17 virtues that are true of Christ's mind. I know 17 sounds like a lot to handle for one day, but don't worry. We're just going to look at them briefly today. In later units, we'll look at each one in depth. These virtues describe some of the ideal qualities of the mind of Christ that God wants you to exhibit also.

I'd like you to meditate on *James 3:13-17* for a little while today. Notice how James describes a wise person. There are eight words that describe godly thinking in this passage. They are part of the mind of Christ.

✻ **Read *James 3:13-17* and circle the eight virtues of godly wisdom in *verse 17.***

> 13*Who among you is wise and understanding? Let him show by his good behavior his deeds in the gentleness of wisdom.* 14*But if you have bitter jealousy and selfish ambition in your heart, do not be arrogant and so lie against the truth.* 15*This wisdom is not that which comes down from above, but is earthly, natural, demonic.* 16*For where jealousy and selfish ambition exist, there is disorder and every evil thing.* 17*But the wisdom from above is first pure, then peaceable, gentle, reasonable, full of mercy and good fruits, unwavering, without hypocrisy.*

✻ ***Verse 14* also describes the conflict or battles that can rage in your mind and heart. When you have these feelings inside you, what should you do about it?**

____

✻ **Look at *verse 15*. Where does this kind of wisdom come from?**

____

✻ **What is present where jealousy and selfish ambition exist?**

____

Do not take pride in bitterness and selfish ambition. Maybe you've been told by friends at school that you have a right to your bitterness when a boyfriend or girlfriend breaks up with you. The world constantly gives us the message that selfish ambition is a virtue. But when this kind of wisdom is present, confusion and evil work (ungodly actions) are present. Don't you see how badly we need to be set free from this earthly, sensual, and demonic way of thinking? Only Christ can bring order to our minds and replace earthly wisdom with godly wisdom.

Eight Virtues in *James 3:17*

There are eight virtues of godly wisdom listed in *verse 17*. These virtues show us part of the mind of Christ. Since Christ is God, He had this godly wisdom. Jesus Christ was pure, peaceable, gentle, reasonable, merciful, fruitful, unwavering, and honest. He was perfect in every one of these virtues.

✱ Read the virtues in the left margin. They are so important I want you to begin memorizing them. Read through the list several more times, then see if you can write the eight virtues from memory.

1. P ____________________ **5. M** ____________________

2. P ____________________ **6. F** ____________________

3. G ____________________ **7. U** ____________________

4. R ____________________ **8. H** ____________________

When I experienced conflict between the items on my list, it was because of conflicting desires. But what if I had the characteristics of *James 3:17*? What if I was perfectly pure as Christ is, perfectly peaceable, perfectly gentle, and all the rest? If these were part of my mind, would I be experiencing the same conflict?

✱ Do any of these qualities conflict with any of the others? Does purity ever conflict with peace? Or peace with gentleness? Or being reasonable with being honest? Check one:
❏ Yes, they conflict all over the place.
❏ Nope. There's no conflict at all.

If you selected "Nope," give yourself a pat on the back. There is no conflict in the mind of Christ. These virtues don't clash with each other. They blend and harmonize. They work with each other, not against each other. The virtues of the Christlike mind enhance each other!

The Fruit of the Spirit in *Galatians 5:22-23*

There was a time in my life when I had been studying Galatians intensely. More than anything else in my life, I wanted God to work out the nine qualities found in *Galatians 5:22-23*. We call these values the Fruit of the Spirit.

✱ Read *Galatians 5:22-23* and circle the nine qualities or fruit of the Spirit.

> ***The fruit of the Spirit is love, joy, peace, patience, kindness, goodness, faithfulness, gentleness, self-control; against such things there is no law.***

Nine Virtues
Galatians 5:22-23

- love
- joy
- peace
- patience
- kindness
- goodness
- faithfulness
- gentleness
- self-control

The fruit of the Spirit shows what God is like. Therefore, these nine qualities are true of Christ, also. I wrote down the fruit of the Spirit in a vertical column, like the one in the margin. Then, I applied the same test to them as I did to the list out of James. Did they conflict? Judge for yourself!

✳ Does love: ❑ conflict with joy, or ❑ produce joy?
Do peace and gentleness: ❑ clash, like plaid and polka dots, or ❑ go together?

Love produces joy. Peace and gentleness go together. You can line up all of these virtues next to each other, and see that they all work together. Each one increases the power of the others. They are like the different instruments in an orchestra. When these virtues are present in your life, your life can be characterized by harmony and unity.

✳ Just as you did for the list of virtues in James, start working on memorizing the fruit of the Spirit. After reading through the list at the left a few times, try to write the virtues from memory on the lines below.

1. L ____________________	6. G ____________________
2. J ____________________	7. F ____________________
3. P ____________________	8. G ____________________
4. P ____________________	9. S ________- C __________
5. K ____________________	

An Integrated Mind

Okay. So now, we have two lists of virtues—one from *James 3:17,* and one from *Galatians 5:22-23.* Each one is complete by itself. Each one can stand on its own. But can they harmonize with each other? If you look at the two lists (and if you paid attention in English class!) you'll notice that all the words in James are adjectives, while all the ones in Galatians are nouns. And since adjectives are words that describe nouns, I decided to apply James' adjectives to Galatians' nouns to see if they made sense together.

✳ What do you think?

a lovely peace	a peaceful love	a gentle love
a pure joy	a gentle goodness	an honest joy
a patient mercy	a steadfast purity	a faithful love

Add some of your own combinations.

____

____

____

When you put these two lists together, you see how they fit with each other seamlessly. I learned from this little word game that the mind of Christ is an integrated mind. It has order, harmony, and unity. Each virtue works with all the others.

Compare that to your own list of desires. When I did that, I felt helpless against the conflicting itches, materialism, and desires God had revealed to me. But how could I change? The term *change your mind* is a cliche, but how do you do it? Tomorrow, I'll share with you how I responded to God.

✷ **Conclude your study today by asking God to produce these 17 virtues in your life more clearly each day.**

One Great Passion

DAY 5

Today's Bible Meditations
"But seek first His kingdom and His righteousness; and all these things shall be added to you."
Matthew 6:33

Name of Christ for Today
King of Saints
(Rev. 15:3, KJV*)*

Prayer to Begin the Lesson
Lord Jesus,
You are my King,
and I want to be a loyal subject. I want to see Your kingdom come.Give me a passion to seek Your kingdom above everything else.
Amen.

✷ **Begin today's lesson by reading the Bible verse and the name of Christ for today. Work on your memory verse. Then use the suggested prayer to begin your study.**

All week long we've been talking about "letting Jesus' desires become your desires." Well, what were Jesus' desires? From childhood on, Jesus expressed a consistent desire:
Age 12: *"I must be about my Father's business" (Luke 2:49,* KJV).
Age 30: *"My food is to do the will of Him who sent Me, and to accomplish His work" (John 4:34).*
Age 32: *"I have come down from heaven, not to do My own will, but the will of Him who sent Me"(John 6:38).*

✷ **What was Jesus' one great passion or desire? Check one.**
- ❏ **Jesus wanted to be popular—a people pleaser.**
- ❏ **Jesus wanted to do His Father's will and please God.**
- ❏ **Jesus wanted to do things to please Himself.**

Jesus' One Passion

Jesus' one passion was to do His Father's will. According to Scripture, this desire dominated His life at least from the time He was 12, through the beginning of His ministry at age 30, even up to His death. The night before He died, Jesus prayed, *"I glorified Thee on the earth, having accomplished the work which Thou hast given Me to do" (John 17:4).* All the way to the end of His life, Jesus was more concerned with what His Father wanted than with what He wanted. Minutes before He was arrested and led away, He was praying, *"Not My will, but Thine be done" (Luke 22:42).* Jesus was the ultimate example of an ordered mind focused on the will of the Father.

Since Jesus was dominated by this one great passion, all His characteristics and virtues had the kind of harmony and balance we talked about yesterday. And that is His personality now. There is nothing in Christ that contradicts with anything else.

Getting My Wanter Fixed

Which brings me back to my story. The more I learned about Jesus' unified desires, the more frustrated I was at my own conflicting ones. And worse, I felt trapped by my own weaknesses. Then I remembered *Romans 6:14—Sin shall not be master over you.* How could I get to the point where sin would not be master over me? The rest of the verse tells why sin can't have dominion: *You are not under law, but under grace.* Mastery over my mind cannot be done by willpower, but by the power of the Holy Spirit and by His grace.

✱ As you think about your own list of desires, what are you feeling about the conflicts you may have encountered?

- ❑ **Helpless. I feel trapped by my own weakness.**
- ❑ **Hopeful. God is already working in me to set me free by His grace.**
- ❑ **Ho-Hum. So I've got conflicting desires. That's just the way I am.**
- ❑ **Other: ____**

I guess you would say I felt both helpless and hopeful at the same time. I knew that God was bigger than my sins, and that His grace was greater. So, I took my list of desires, knelt down on the floor, held the list up toward heaven, and said, "Lord, what I need is to get my 'wanter' fixed. In my own strength, I am captive to my own lusts. But I don't have to depend on my own strength. I am under your grace. I want your grace to be active in my life. So in Jesus' name, I ask you to 'fix my wanter.' "

Had I stopped there, I would probably still be having the same struggle. You see, for God to accomplish real change in your life, there is an additional requirement: you have to give Him the freedom to do whatever it takes. So, I added this to my prayer: "And in Jesus' name, I free You to do anything You have to do to 'fix my wanter.' I won't argue with any procedure You consider necessary, and will accept the fact that You really do want me to be like Jesus, no matter what the cost."

Help!

My plan was to destroy my list. But in the face of one of the greatest challenges of my Christian growth, I felt I could not do it alone. When my wife came home that morning, I shared the list with her, the things God had shown me, and the prayer I had prayed. I asked her to pray with me that God would completely free me from the mastery of any sin in my mind. This was another step toward achieving an ordered mind like the mind of Christ.

✱ Asking for help is a scary thing. As you look at your list, you may feel ashamed about what's on it. But having someone you can trust to pray for you can help you experience the freedom from sin that God wants for you. Is there someone like that for you? It might be a Christian friend, teacher, coach, or youth minister. It might be someone in your Mind of Christ group. If you feel like you need a prayer partner, who is this person?

____

God Gets Busy

Right away, God began to answer my prayer. To accomplish His purpose, He reminded me of a single verse, *Matthew 6:33—"Seek first His* [God's] *kingdom and His right-*

eousness." That verse was like a steady drumbeat in my head. Night and day, the Holy Spirit kept reminding me of that verse. I would get into an argument with someone, and in the midst of trying to prove my point—*"Seek first His* [God's] *kingdom and His righteousness."* If an unholy lust popped into my head, right on the heels of it would be, *Seek first His kingdom and His righteousness."*

Romans 12:2 commands us to *Be transformed by the renewing of your mind.* This was precisely what was happening to me now. On my own, I could not change my mind, but God knew how to give me a greater passion. My self-seeking will was now being transformed into seeking God's kingdom and righteousness. By the end of the fall, God had completely renewed my mind in the area of my desires.

One of God's desires for you is that you seek His kingdom and His righteousness. I pray that by now you have that desire too. But the desire and the seeking are not the same thing. How can you live in a way that indicates you are seeking the Kingdom? Listed below are some ways you could demonstrate your willingness to seek God's kingdom first:

- choose to deny self and follow Christ *(Luke 9:23);*
- memorize *Matthew 6:33* and ask God to do what it takes to help you live that way;
- pray to seek God's guidance and follow it, rather than doing just what you think you ought to do without even checking it out with Him;
- give God control of your money by asking Him what to do with excess amounts of it (Ask yourself, is this something I want to buy but don't really need? Can it be used to build up God's kingdom instead?);
- choose to follow God's desires rather than your desires;
- rush away from temptations, impure thoughts and lusts, and focus on godly living, righteousness, and pure thoughts.

✱ **Ask God how He would have you begin seeking first His kingdom in your life. Agree to do whatever He wants you to do.**

And Now—The Rest of the Story

The first half of *Matthew 6:33* says, *"Seek first His* [God's] *kingdom and His righteousness."* Let me share with you how the second half, *"And all these things shall be added to you"* became true in my life. Remember the things that were on my original list (flip back a few pages if you don't)? Well, by the end of the fall, Laverne (that's my wife) and I discovered we had saved enough to buy me a new suit—Item #1 on my list. Then, I judged some music auditions, and was paid the exact amount we needed for a sale-priced washer—half of Item #2. Later that fall, I went to teach at a missionary orientation center. While there, I was having lunch with a missionary on his way to Africa. As we talked, I asked him where in Africa he was going. He told me that he and his family were going to Upper Volta, which is now Burkina Faso, Inland Africa, below the Sahara Desert.

"We've been told," said the missionary, "that it is so hot and dry we shouldn't bring our clothes dryer, so we need to get rid of it. You couldn't use a dryer, could you?"

Zing! I almost couldn't believe it, but I told him that we definitely could. Then he asked, "What kind of dryer connections do you have?" When I told him that they were electric, Norman told me that his dryer connections were gas.

I didn't think much more about it until the next morning. We were getting ready to leave when another missionary, this one on his way to Brazil, came in and pleaded,

"My wife and I are having an emergency! We've been packing our crates for shipping, and we just got a letter telling us that our dryer connections are gas. We've got an electric dryer! Is there anyone who would be willing to swap a gas dryer for an electric one?"

Zing!!! Item #2 had now been *added to us!*

After getting both washer and dryer installed, I said to Laverne, "You know, we used to pray for things, and often didn't get them. Now, we're praying for God's kingdom and aren't really concerned about things. Yet, God provided all the items from my original want list I made last August, and I didn't pray for a single one of them. Why didn't we get them when we prayed for them, but got them when we didn't pray for them?"

She asked me, "What is the verse that meant so much to you in the fall?"

I reminded her, *"Matthew 6:33—Seek first His kingdom and His righteousness."*

"But what does the rest of the verse say? *And all these things shall be added unto you."*

With a burst of insight, I told my wife, "All my life I have been going about it the wrong way. I thought my things were my business, and the kingdom of God was God's business. But now I realize that God's kingdom and righteousness are my business, and my things are God's business. When I gave up my things to God, and started being more concerned with His kingdom, I freed God to be concerned with His business—my things. As long as I insisted on taking care of my things, I was tying God's hands. But now, I've released the hand of God to work in what He loves to work in—our things. Our things are His business!"

✱ As you conclude this unit, consider praying this prayer:

Lord, what I need is to get my "wanter" fixed. In my own strength, I am captive to my own lusts. But I don't have to depend on my own strength. I am under Your grace. I want Your grace to be active in my life. So in Jesus' name, I ask you to "fix my wanter." And in Jesus' name, I free You to do anything You have to do to "fix my wanter." I won't argue with any procedure You consider necessary, and will accept the fact that You really do want me to be like Jesus, no matter what the cost.

Free Indeed

UNIT 3

Hymn Part 1—Christ's Freedom
Let this mind be in you, which was also in Christ Jesus (Phil. 2:5, KJV*).*

What Is in This Unit for Me?
You will continue the process you began last week of examining different areas in your life. This week we're going to look at eight areas in which we experience bondage to sin. In each area, you'll begin to experience the freedom of Christ as He renews your thinking, mind-set, and outlook on life.

Lifelong Objective
In Christ you will live in peace with freedom from the control of sin.

How God Will be Working In You
God's goal for you is complete freedom from any bondage to this world's system. As Christ works within you, you will begin to be more attentive to areas in your life that you need to surrender to Him. The standard we will use to measure our growth in freedom from sin is Christ's sinlessness. One of the names of Christ is Deliverer. Christ sets us free.

Unit Learning Goals
- You will show a willingness to be set free from areas of bondage.
- You will understand why God wants you to be free from bondage to sin.
- You will understand ways God wants to set you free in the areas of habits, loyalties, relationships, prejudices, ambitions, duties, debts, and possessions.
- You will show a continued willingness to seek the kingdom of God above all other things.

What You Will Do to Continue Growing in Christ's Freedom
- You will ask Christ to continue His work of producing freedom in you until you are free indeed.
- You will begin making lists of your habits, loyalties, relationships, prejudices, ambitions, duties, debts, and possessions.
- You will begin to evaluate your lists to identify items that lead to bondage.
- You will seek Christ's help to be set free in those areas.

Lifelong Helps Related to This Unit
Bondage to Freedom Lists (pp. 189-191)

The Mind of Christ Cards Related to This Unit
3B. Unit 3: Scripture Memory—*John 8:32, 36*

Day 1
God's Goal:
Your Freedom

Day 2
Habits and Loyalties

Day 3
Relationships and
Prejudices

Day 4
Ambitions and Duties

Day 5
Debts and Possessions

Scripture Memory Verse
"You shall know the truth, and the truth shall make you free."
"If therefore the Son shall make you free, you shall be free indeed."
John 8:32,36

Today's Bible Meditation
It was for freedom that Christ set us free; therefore keep standing firm and do not be subject again to a yoke of slavery.
Galatians 5:1

Name of Christ for Today
The Truth
(John 14:6)

Prayer to Begin the Lesson
Jesus, You are the Truth. You are the One who sets me free—free indeed. Please continue Your work in me, producing the freedom You desire. Amen.

God's Goal: Your Freedom

✳ Begin today's lesson by reading the Bible verse and the name of Christ for today. Work on your memory verse. Then use the suggested prayer to begin your study.

God's Purpose in Freedom

When you think about freedom, what comes to mind? Getting your license when you're 16? A longer curfew on the weekends? A life without restrictions or boundaries?

That's not really an accurate description of freedom in Christ. Our freedom in Christ serves the purpose of being able to serve Christ. You see, you're going to serve somebody. When you use your so-called freedom to do the things of the world, you are being a servant to the world's system. But when you use your freedom to glorify God, then you are a servant to Christ. Serving the world means freedom from Christ. On the other hand, serving Christ means freedom from the world!

God inspired Peter to say, *Act as free men, and do not use your freedom as a covering for evil, but use it as bondslaves of God (1 Pet. 2:16)*. Or, as another modern translation puts it, "Exercise your freedom by serving God, not by breaking the rules" *(The Message)*. We can easily misinterpret the purpose of our freedom. You could see the experience of God's grace and freedom from the law as an invitation to live any way you want to—sort of the "I know God's going to forgive me, so I can do whatever I want" attitude. That is not what God had in mind when He set you free in Christ! God's commandments are guidelines for right living, and they are meant to be taken seriously. When you live within those guidelines, you can experience the fullness of life God intends for you. but when you cross over those boundaries, you become a slave to sin. And as a slave to sin, you'll miss God's best for you. You can't be an effective servant to Christ.

Perhaps you're saying to yourself, *Boundaries? Living within God's commandments? That's not real freedom!* Think back to the example of getting your driver's license. Most teenagers see that as the ultimate example of freedom. But there are rules and restrictions to that license, aren't there? Speed limits. Traffic lights. Road signs. As long as you stay within those limits, you can experience the freedom of driving. Break those rules, and you may no longer be free to drive.

✳ Make the two statements below correct by crossing out the incorrect word in the parentheses ( ).

- **When I live like the world and do (right / evil), I am a slave to sin.**
- **When I live like a servant of God and do (right / evil), I am truly free.**

✳ Read *John 8:31-36* below, and underline statements that describe what a servant (a disciple) of God does and what a servant of sin does.

Jesus therefore was saying to those Jews who had believed Him, "If you abide in My word, then you are truly disciples of Mine; and you shall know the truth, and the truth shall make you free." They answered Him, "We are

Abraham's offspring, and have never yet been enslaved to anyone; how is it that You say, 'You shall become free?' " Jesus answered them, "Truly truly, I say to you, everyone who commits sin is the slave of sin. And the slave does not remain in the house forever; the son does remain forever. If therefore the Son shall make you free, you shall be free indeed."

✱ ***Verses 32*** **and *36* are your memory verses for this week. As a way to begin memorizing them, write the verses below or in the margin.**

Someone who commits sin is a slave of sin *(v. 34)*. When you commit sin, you put yourself in bondage to it. You are a slave to sin. But a disciple of Jesus, on the other hand, is one who continues in Christ's Word *(v. 31)*. He or she knows the truth *(v. 32)*. This is a person who lives according to Christ's commands. When you are Christ's disciple, He sets you free!

God's Process Toward Freedom

Last week I explained the process God has taken me through to move me toward freedom in Christ. For a long time, I figured that this was just something God was doing in my own personal life. I never intended to share them publicly. But through an unusual series of events, I was led to share these insights publicly. I am convinced that God wants His children free from all bondage to sin. God wants you to be free.

I asked you last week to make a list of your desires or lusts. You've already begun to evaluate your desires and remove those that are in conflict with Christ's desires. During this unit and the next unit, we're going to look at some other areas where bondage occurs. This week, we're looking at neutral areas of bondage. These items can be good or bad, depending on how they measure up against God's desires for you.

During this week, I'd like you to begin prayerfully making lists in the neutral and damaging areas in the left-hand margin.

Neutral Areas
- desires
- habits
- loyalties
- relationships
- prejudices
- ambitions
- duties
- debts
- possessions

Damaging Areas
- fears
- weaknesses
- hurts

✱ **Read through the list of 12 areas of bondage in the margin. Circle the one or two that you think may be toughest for you to deal with.**

Some Words of Warning

This unit is going to be intense. You'll be making lots of lists of areas in your life. It's crucial to remember not to rush God! Please keep in mind that it took me 14 months to make and process the lists you're going to be working on in the next two weeks. Bear in mind what I've said before—This course is an introduction to a lifetime of study towards developing the mind of Christ. For each list I had to pray for freedom and allow God time to guide me in working out the requirements for real freedom. As you make your lists, pray through each one. After you make the list, give God the liberty to do anything He needs to give you complete freedom. Don't be surprised if the Holy Spirit requires you to remake and add to the lists from time to time. He may direct you to areas and categories I didn't name here. He may work your transformation completely differently than He did mine. Let God direct this process, and let Him set the time schedule.

As you make these lists this week, make sure you budget your time. I know that making four lists a day is asking a lot. Notice that I only asked you to list five or six items in each area. Again, this is meant to be an introduction to a process. If you try to do too much in each session, you will get overwhelmed quickly.

A third word of warning: ACCEPT THE LIMITATIONS GOD GIVES YOU. God assigns us responsibilities that limit us. No child is ever completely free. They always have responsibilities to their parents. No mother or father can declare freedom from obligations to their children. The limitations which God assigns us are a training ground for Christlikeness.

✱ Are you willing to give God all the time He needs to work out your freedom?
❑ yes ❑ no
If you checked yes, tell God. Right now. If you checked no, ask Him to make you willing.

The Mind-Set of Christ

Anyone can be free from the 12 areas of bondage I've listed. God wants you to be free from the world's mind-set, and to accept the mind-set of Christ. In this way, you can experience true freedom.

There's never been a more free human being than Jesus Christ, and He desires your freedom. He promised, *"If therefore the Son shall make you free, you shall be free indeed" (John 8:36).* There is nothing in the world that can disturb the kind of freedom Christ gives, and it will endure forever. Paul gives us a warning about that, though. He says, *It was for freedom that Christ set us free; therefore keep standing firm and do not be subject again to a yoke of slavery (Gal. 5:1).* When we use our freedom as an excuse to sin, our very freedom can enslave us.

What's the big deal about freedom from bondage to sin? Why is that so crucial to the mind of Christ? It's because to have the mind of Christ is to have focused attention. When you're in bondage to sin, your focus is on your lusts, loyalties, ambitions, grudges, and other things that bind you to the world. Christ's freedom from these snares allows you to totally focus on the kingdom of God, His Word, and His voice.

✱ Why is freedom from the bondage of sin important?______________________

✱ What is God's desire for you? My f ______________________

This freedom that God desires for you is measured only by Jesus Christ. As you think about how free you are from sin, don't compare yourself to other people in your youth group, or even your youth minister. You will catch yourself trying to play some kind of holier-than-thou game if you try to measure your growth in Christ against other human beings. And don't try to make some sort of checklist, either. You can't mark off items on a list, saying, "Well, I didn't do that particular sin today, so I must be growing." When you start to do that, you may blind yourself to sin in other areas. No. Your standard needs to be Christ's sinlessness.

✱ What is the standard for measuring your growth in freedom?

We aren't talking about righteousness that God gives through faith in Christ. We are talking about the working out of your faith in practical terms. Fruitful faith is practical, and God wants you to be free, just as His Son, Jesus, is.

✳ *"If therefore the Son shall make you free, you shall be free indeed."* **Meditate on this statement as you close the lesson today. Ask Christ to set you free. Ask God to make you fruitful and faithful like His Son, Jesus.**

Habits and Loyalties

DAY 2

Today's Bible Meditation
Commit your works to the Lord, and your plans will be established.
Proverbs 16:3

Name of Christ for Today
The Way
(John 14:6)

Prayer to Begin the Lesson
Not only are You the Truth, Lord Jesus, You are the Way to truth about life. Apart from You, I'll lose my way. Keep me with You and keep me focused on the path You lay out for me. Amen.

✳ **Begin today's lesson by reading the Bible verse and the name of Christ for today. Work on your memory verse. Then use the suggested prayer to begin your study.**

Habits

I was supposed to pick up my wife Laverne one afternoon.

I forgot.

I did that pretty often. Usually, I made some kind of excuse like, "Well, I'm a professor; I had my mind on deeper things." So when I finally remembered the appointment, my wife had been waiting on me for an hour. I apologized profusely, and begged her forgiveness. Being the wonderful Christian woman my wife is, she forgave me immediately. But then she said something that really stuck with me. She looked at me and said, "If you were serious about sin not being master over you, don't you think you ought to pray about your absent-mindedness? After all, does a bad habit honor the indwelling Spirit?"

Wow! That really nailed me! A few days later, I came across this statement in *Mark 10:1: According to His custom, He once more began to teach them.* According to His custom! Jesus had habits, too. He was in the habit of going to the synagogue on the Sabbath (see *Luke 4:16)*. Another habit was going to the Mount of Olives, perhaps to the garden of Gethsemane *(Luke 22:39)*. Prayer was a very important habit to Jesus (see *Mark 1:35* and *Luke 6:12)*. Jesus had a lot of good habits and no bad ones. In contrast, I had some habits, but I knew that not all of them were good. The more I thought about Jesus' habits, the more I realized God was pointing out another area of bondage in my life—my habits.

If we are really going to be doers of the Word and not merely hearers (see *Jas. 1:22)*, then as soon as the Lord reveals something in our lives, we need to take action. So in my next quiet time, I prayed for the Lord to reveal to me all my habits, both good and bad. I wrote down the habits, and it was obvious to me which ones needed to go. Again, I prayed for the Lord to show me how to get rid of everything that was not pleasing to Him. A bad habit reveals an area of life which is not under the control of the Holy Spirit. Most of my bad habits, such as my absent-mindedness, were the result of carelessness. Now, there were some of my bad habits that I had to do certain things to get rid of. But most of the changes happened not because of my own personal discipline, but by being conscious of the rule of the Holy Spirit.

God's desire is to move your habits from being careless to being Spirit-controlled.

✳ In your journal, begin to make a list of your habits. At the top of a blank sheet, write "My Habits List" and today's date. If you get stuck, turn to pages 189-191 and use the guide there to make your list more complete. Keep in mind this is the first of four lists you'll be making today, so budget your time. List at least five or six habits as a start.

✳ Begin to evaluate your habits. Ask God to help you identify which ones are careless and which ones are Spirit-controlled. Write a *C* next to the ones that are careless and need to come under the Spirit's control.

Loyalties

Do you have more than one high school represented in your youth group? Have you ever been discussing something about your school with a friend from another school, and found yourself getting defensive? If so, you understand something about loyalties. Loyalty is simply the feeling of devotion to a certain institution or group.

Loyalty itself is a neutral trait. Jesus certainly had loyalties. He was loyal to His Father. He was loyal to His disciples, even protecting them at the time of His own arrest.

But loyalties can easily become misplaced. I have seen lifelong friendships jeopardized by football rivalries. And any loyalty which comes between yourself and God is certainly misplaced. To take the example about rival schools, when you feel yourself getting defensive, that may be the Holy Spirit giving you a signal. When that happened to me, I prayed through the matter. God pointed out to me that I sometimes defended false or misplaced loyalties.

So, once again, I made a list of all my loyalties, and then prayed through each one. My list was way too long! Loyalties, like wants, should be pure before the Lord. I discovered that my loyalties, even the legitimate ones, were not prioritized according to spiritual value. Some of them were totally valueless and needed to be eliminated. Others I prioritized according to spiritual weight. Basically, I gave myself this test. If I could pray for it, then I could be loyal to it. (In other words, if you feel silly praying for your favorite movie, you have a scattered loyalty!)

The final result was an almost complete restructuring of my value system. My loyalties were changed from being scattered to being prayerful.

God's desire is to move your loyalties from being scattered to being prayerful.

✳ In your journal, flip over one or two pages from your previous list, and write "My Loyalties" across the top of a new page, along with today's date. List a few of your loyalties to get yourself started. If you get stuck, turn to pages 189-191 to help you round out your list.

✳ Pray through your list, asking God to help you identify which ones are scattered and which ones are prayerful. Write an *S* beside the ones that seem to be scattered or unnecessary.

✳ Close today's lesson by looking through both lists one more time. Thank God for the ability to examine yourself. Humans are the only creatures God made that can do that!

Relationships and Prejudices

DAY 3

✻ **Begin today's lesson by reading the Bible verse and the name of Christ for today. Work on your memory verse. Then use the suggested prayer to begin your study.**

Relationships

There aren't too many bigger issues to a teenager than relationships. Changing relationships with parents, friendships, and relationships with the opposite sex are all extremely important. And like habits and loyalties, relationships are a neutral area—neither good nor bad by itself. But as I began to look at my relationships, I began to see another area in which the Holy Spirit needed to free me from the bondage of sin. Sin traps us in this area when we begin to feel ownership over our relationships. Sure, you talk about "your" girlfriend/boyfriend, "your" friends, and so on. But spiritually speaking, the relationships in your life need to be turned over to God. For me, I had to deliberately give my wife to the Lord. I prayed, "Lord, I ask You to make her love You more than she loves me." I asked God to make her priorities those of *Mark 12:30-31.*

Would it make you feel uncomfortable or jealous if your boyfriend or girlfriend showed love for God more than love for you? This may be an area of bondage in your life, also. Our love for God has got to be first, far above all earthly loves. Your prayer for every significant person in your life is that they are more concerned about God than they even are about you.

I found the Spirit leading me to make a list of my relationships—to my boss, my friends, my colleagues at the seminary, and others. Then I gave each one to the Lord to serve whatever purposes He had in mind for bringing them into my life. I began to realize that every relationship in my life was to be one of service to God. I really was being transformed. My relationships had changed from serving self to serving God.

God's desire is to move your relationships from serving yourself to serving God.

✻ **In your journal, begin to prepare a list of your relationships. Title and date the list. If you get stuck, turn to pages 189-191 and use the guide to make your list more complete. List three or four relationships for a start.**

✻ **Evaluate your relationships, ask God to help you identify which ones are serving self and which are serving God. Write an *S* by the ones that seem to be serving self.**

Prejudices

The next area that God began working on was prejudices. I didn't think I had any! But under the leadership of the Spirit, I found some deep, hidden prejudices.

The dictionary defines *prejudice* as "An adverse judgment or opinion formed beforehand or without knowledge or examination of the facts," or "A preconceived preference or idea."[1] We have listed prejudice as a neutral area, neither good nor bad.

Today's Bible Meditation
It is required of stewards that one be found trustworthy.
1 Corinthians 4:2

Name of Christ for Today
The Life
(John 14:6)

Prayer to Begin the Lesson
Lord Jesus, You are my life. Without You, I would be dead in my own sin. Please set me free from the things that keep me from living life to the fullest extent You have planned for me. Amen.

But are there any "good" prejudices? As Christians we ought to be prejudiced against anything that is not of God. There are some scriptural areas of prejudice, never against people, but against beliefs or practices which undermine the kingdom of God.

Many believers have dealt with the more common prejudices, concerning race or ethnic groups through the work of the Holy Spirit in their thinking. This may not be the case with you. Prayerfully examine your attitudes toward other races, other cultures, people with physical challenges, and people from different educational or economic backgrounds. Even believers can find prejudice lurking in unsuspecting places!

There are even more subtle prejudices, however. For example, some believers unconsciously think that if God works a certain way in their life, He is bound to work the same way in everybody else's life, also. Sometimes we think that the way God does things in our youth group is the only way for Him to do things.

If we are prejudiced about the way God works in anyone's life, we are limiting the kingdom rule of God. If God is sovereign, no prejudice of any kind on our part can exist if it will limit His working in our lives. Once again, I had to make a list. I had not suspected the presence of prejudice in my life, but prejudice limits God's control.

God's desire is to move your prejudices from being contrary to Scripture to being scriptural.

✷ In your journal, begin to prepare a list of your prejudices. Title and date the list. If you get stuck, turn to pages 189-191 and use the guide to make your list more complete. List three or four prejudices for a start.

✷ As you begin to evaluate your prejudices, ask God to help you identify which ones are contrary to Scripture and which ones are scriptural. Write a *C* beside the ones that seem to be contrary to Scripture.

In each of the areas named so far—habits, loyalties, relationships, and prejudices—I had to make a list and pray fervently about the bondage to sin each one involved. It was through prayer that the Spirit began to do His work.

✷ Pray about the areas God seems to emphasize that need changing the most. Allow Him to do whatever is necessary to renew your mind in these areas.

[1]The *American Heritage® Dictionary of the English Language, Third Edition* © 1992 by Houghton Mifflin Company. Electronic version licensed from InfoSoft International, Inc. All rights reserved.

Ambitions and Duties

DAY 4

✳ **Begin today's lesson by reading the Bible verse and the name of Christ for today. Work on your memory verse. Then use the suggested prayer to begin your study.**

Ambitions

The next area of bondage God dealt with in my life was the bondage that comes from my ambitions. Ambitions deal with all the "What do you want to be when you grow up?" issues. Your goals, purposes, objectives, hopes, and dreams are all wrapped up in your ambitions. These are what drives us to achievement. And in a balanced Christian life, ambitions are a healthy thing. You all know people at your school who are outstanding students. They know where they're going to college, they know what it takes to get there, and they are doing it. You would say that they are ambitious, goal-oriented people, and they have risen to the top of the class.

Ambitions reveal sin in the area of pride. Just as we talked about relationships yesterday, when ambitions become our ambitions and are not given over to God, they lead to bondage.

John the Baptist demonstrated the proper attitude toward ambition. One day, his disciples came to him and said, "John, that new prophet, Jesus, is baptizing more people these days than you are. What are you going to do about it?" John looked at them and told them that was how it was supposed to be. *"He must increase,"* he said. *"but I must decrease"* (see *John 3:30).*

It isn't easy to be honest with God about our ambitions, but it's necessary. As I made my list, I prayed that God would help me be open to His leadership. As I made the list, I became aware of ambitions I had never admitted openly, even to myself.

After I made the list, I tried sincerely to give these ambitions to the Lord. Again I freed God to do anything He needed to do to accomplish His aim. Many of my ambitions would have brought honor to me. But now the transformation began. The Spirit wanted me to put to death my personal ambitions and to develop ambitions that would honor the Lord and advance His kingdom.

God's desire is to move your ambitions from honoring self to honoring God.

✳ **In your journal, begin to prepare a list of your ambitions. Title and date the list. If you get stuck, turn to pages 189-191 and use the guide to make your list more complete. List five or six ambitions for a start. Remember to budget your time. You'll be making four lists today.**

✳ **As you begin to evaluate your ambitions, ask God to help you identify which ones are honoring self and which are honoring God. Write an *S* beside the ones that seem to be honoring self or have pride as a root cause.**

Duties

Think of the stuff that you have to do every day. Studying is probably in there somewhere, along with chores around the house (making your bed, feeding the dog, and so on). You might also have obligations to clubs and organizations at school. Then, of

Today's Bible Meditation
"He must increase, but I must decrease."
John 3:30

Name of Christ for Today
Spiritual Rock
(1 Cor. 10:4)

Prayer to Begin the Lesson
Lord Jesus,
You are My Rock. My only ambition is to become like You. My only duty is to serve You. Please let everything else in my life decrease, and let that desire increase.
Amen.

course, there are church activities. Not to mention doing things with your boyfriend or girlfriend. Then, you might have a part-time job every day after school.

When you think about all the obligations and duties you have, the list gets pretty long pretty fast, doesn't it? That's how I was when the Holy Spirit started work on this area of my life. He convicted me that there were a lot of things I was doing that I really wasn't gifted in or called to be doing. Now, before you start saying, "Well, I'm just not gifted or called to clean my room," let me make some distinctions. There are some duties that you have as a teenager that are not a matter of choice. Homework, for example, is a non-negotiable. Obedience to your parents, provided they are not telling you to do something contrary to Scripture, is also a non-negotiable (see *Eph. 6:2).* What I am talking about are the duties we have a choice about, such as extra-curricular activities, church activities, and even, in some cases part-time jobs.

Certainly, not all duties are wrong. There are some things about which we feel a sense of divine obligation. As the Holy Spirit began to deal with me on this, I started studying the times Jesus said, *"I must." "I must be about my Father's business…." "I must preach to other cities also: for therefore am I sent…" "I must journey on* [to Jerusalem]…." In all of Jesus' duties, there was a sense that Jesus had His mind on the eternal. Jesus knew from the very beginning the course and outcome of His life. Notice how many times He referred to His coming death (see *Matt. 16:21).* He had duties, and He never strayed from performing them.

While we do not have the same supernatural insight into the outcome of our lives that Jesus had, it is possible to know what God's will for our lives is. We know that all of our duties must be part of the eternal work of the kingdom. Paul tells us that *We are His workmanship, created in Christ Jesus for good works, which God prepared beforehand, that we should walk in them (Eph. 2:10).* We can figure out God's will for us through the patterns He establishes in our lives, the teaching of Scripture, the authorities He places over us, and the advice of wise Christians.

Part of having the mind of Christ is knowing what God wants us to do. But just as big a part is knowing what God doesn't want us to do. As you look at your own schedule, you may find, under God's leadership, that there are some things you are doing that really have no eternal significance. Remember how everything Jesus did pointed to eternity? What about you?

Don't quit the cheerleading team just because, on the surface, it doesn't seem to have any "eternal significance." God may have placed you on the cheerleading team to reach one of the other cheerleaders for Him. There are two ways to evaluate the duties in your life. Discard the things that don't contribute to the work of the kingdom and figure out how what you're doing can contribute to the kingdom. God wants purpose in everything you do, and He wants everything you do to have a purpose.

God's desire is to move your duties from insignificance to eternal significance.

✳ In your journal, begin to prepare a list of your duties. Title and date the list. If you get stuck, turn to pages 189-191 and use the guide to make your list more complete. List five or six duties for a start.

✳ As you begin to evaluate your duties, ask God to help you identify which ones seem insignificant and which ones seem eternally significant. Write an *I* beside the ones that seem to be insignificant.

Debts and Possessions

DAY 5

✷ **Begin today's lesson by reading the Bible verse and the name of Christ for today. Work on your memory verse. Then use the suggested prayer to begin your study.**

Debts

You may or may not be in monetary debt right now. If you are, then you have an appreciation for what it means to owe somebody else, whether it's your parents, your best friend, or a bank or credit card company.

Being in financial debt is a dangerous habit. There are few things that can get your eyes off the Lord faster than owing money. Financial debt can feel like bondage.

So when God began to speak to me about the bondage of debt, I at first thought I was off the hook because I had worked myself out of monetary debt. But then the Holy Spirit introduced a new way of looking at debt. There are things that I owe people that go beyond money. I am indebted to my parents for the way they raised me. I'm in debt to my teachers for the education they provided me. There are too many examples to count of things friends have done for me. In many cases, people have done things for me simply out of love. As an infant, there wasn't a thing I could do to repay my parents for the care they gave me. They took care of me because they loved me.

How do I respond to the people to whom I am indebted? Certainly I should express gratitude. But the grace shown to me should also be given to others. I should demonstrate grace (giving what has not been earned by the recipient) without expecting to be repaid.

As I listed these non-monetary debts, I discovered how much God was a part of each one. I am incredibly indebted to God for all He has done for me. Because of this, I am indebted to carry out His work—not begrudgingly, but out of gratitude.

God's desire is to move your debts from obligation to gratitude.

✷ **In your journal, begin to prepare a list of your debts—both financial and interpersonal. Title and date the list. If you get stuck, turn to pages 189-191 and use the guide to make your list more complete.**

✷ **As you begin to evaluate your debts, ask God to help you identify which ones are out of obligation and which are out of gratitude. Write an O beside the ones that seem to be out of obligation.**

Possessions

Jennifer had had her eye on an expensive leather jacket for months. So when she got $200.00 of Christmas money, she went straight to the mall and bought it. The first day of school after the Christmas break, she wore that jacket. All that day, she never let it out of her sight. She was scared to put it in her locker, because someone might break in and steal it. She refused to dress out for gym class because she just knew that someone would walk off with her new jacket if she left it on the bleachers. Although Jennifer didn't realize it, she did not really own that jacket. The jacket owned her.

More than we realize, we are bound by our possessions. We protect them, and we take measures to safeguard their security. What a contrast to the kind of life Christ lived. Jesus owned nothing except for the clothes on His back.

Today's Bible Meditation
For you have been bought with a price: therefore glorify God in your body.
1 Corinthians 6:20

Name of Christ for Today
Redeemer
(Job 19:25)

Prayer to Begin the Lesson
Jesus, You are my redeemer. You paid a debt for me that You did not owe. I owed a debt to You that I couldn't pay. I am so thankful that You paid the ultimate price for my sins. As I look today at the things I owe and the things I own, help me remember what You have done for me. I owe You everything. Amen.

What does God require of you in terms of the things you own? For Laverne and me, the first thing was our house. We agreed that God should dictate our use of our house. So, we dedicated it to God, and made up our minds that we were not really the owners of it. We were merely stewards. Almost as soon as we made that decision, God began sending us a series of guests—students, friends, homeless persons—as a test of the commitment we had made. The Lord also led me to disciple or teach each of these guests as well as I could, depending on the circumstances. Eventually, we were required to sell the house as a part of God's call to a new job assignment.

At that time, we had two cars. We had a young friend who was about to be married and had no car. The Lord led me to go to the filing cabinet, get the title to one of the cars, and give it (as a gift from God, not us) to the young man. The Lord seemed either to find unusual uses for our possessions, or to rid us of them altogether!

I am talking about the same principles regardless of what you own. Little by little, God was transforming mine and Laverne's thinking from a mind set of ownership to a mind set of stewardship. In order to have the mind of Christ, the same transformation is necessary in your life.

God's desire is to move your possessions from ownership to stewardship.

✳ **In your journal, begin to prepare a list of your possessions. You may want to place some in big categories, like clothes, stereo equipment, etc. Title and date the list. If you get stuck, turn to page 190 and use the guide to make your list more complete.**

✳ **As you begin to evaluate your possessions, ask God to help you identify which ones you relate to as owner and which you relate to as steward. Write an O beside the ones that you feel ownership over.**

You've made quite a few lists this week. In each of these transformations, God is working on freeing you from:

- the world as you have known it;
- inhibitions;
- the necessity to look a certain way at our friends and the world;
- false conceptions of happiness and well-being;
- bonds you didn't even realize were there.

At the same time, God is freeing you to

- let Him have first place;
- minister to others;
- and become more and more like His Son.

Sin will not be your master in any area (see *Rom. 6:14)*. It's dominion in your life is to be zero.

Fears

I wrote down all the fears I could think of and gave them to the Lord and asked Him to transform my mind in whatever direction He wished. Christ began to develop in me a unique sense of security. The only security I now am allowed to have is in Christ. In God's process, I realized that I was manipulative in ways I had not suspected. Some of my behavior was a false bravery that covered a fear of being perceived as simple or naive. Sometimes my innocent remarks were really self-protective or self-securing. The Lord became the only security on which I could count. In spite of my fears, I was being changed form one who is self-protective to one who is secure in Christ.

Most gladly therefore will I rather glory in my infirmities, that the power of Christ may rest upon me. Therefore I take pleasure in infirmities, in reproaches, in necessities, in persecutions, in distresses for Christ's sake: for when I am weak, then am I strong.
—2 Corinthians 12:9-10

✱ **Prepare your list of fears. As you begin to evaluate your fears, ask God to reveal ways you seek security through being self-protective. Ask Him to begin moving you toward finding your only security in Christ.**

Weaknesses

Three times Paul asked the Lord to remove his "thorn in the flesh" or a weakness. God's response was: "My grace is sufficient for thee: for my strength is made perfect in weakness *(2 Cor. 12:9).* Read Paul's response *(2 Cor. 12: 9-10)* in the margin.

I never had talked to the Lord about my weaknesses. I made my list. I prayed carefully about it and asked the Lord to strengthen me where necessary. I asked Him somehow to use my weak points for His glory. In this way, my weaknesses were transformed from being a tool of Satan to being a tool of God.

God's desire is to move your weaknesses from being tools of Satan to being tools of God.

✱ **Prepare a list of your weaknesses. Title and date the list. As you evaluate your weaknesses, ask God to help you identify the one which are being used against you as tools of Satan. Ask God to transform these weaknesses into tools that bring Him glory.**

If thy brother trespass against thee, rebuke him; and if he repent, forgive him. And if he trespass against thee seven times in a day, and seven times in a day turn again to thee, saying, I repent; thou shalt forgive him.
—Luke 17:3-4

Hurts or Grudges

Hurts are perhaps the most difficult of all areas of bondage to deal with. As with all the other areas of bondage, I made my list of hurts or grudges. My list was long. Over the years a friend thought I had become a religious fanatic. I bottled it up and resented him. Another man lied in order to worm his way into a position I was occupying. Others took advantage of me. I was dismayed at the depth of the resentments that were bottled up within me. I finished the list and prayed over each one. I asked the Lord to forgive me for the resentment I felt and to forgive them for the wrongs they had done in selfishness.

✱ **In your notebook, begin to prepare a list of your hurts, resentments, or grudges. Title and date the list. Ask God to heal your hurts.**

God's desire is to move your hurts from producing resentment to producing love.

✱ **As you conclude this lesson:**

- **Ask God to forgive you for any resentment or bitterness in your life.**
- **Ask God to enable you to forgive those who have hurt you.**
- **Ask God to forgive those who have hurt you.**
- **Ask God to begin changing your resentment to love.**

✱ **Close today's lesson and this unit by praying about the areas God seems to emphasize that need changing first or most. Give Him permission to do whatever is necessary to help renew your mind in these areas.**

Day 1
Washing Your Mind

Day 2
Pure

Day 3
Peaceable

Day 4
Gentle, Reasonable, and Merciful

Day 5
Fruitful, Steadfast, and Honest

Scripture Memory Verse
The wisdom from above is first pure, then peaceable, gentle, reasonable, full of mercy and good fruits, unwavering, without hypocrisy.
James 3:17

Virtues of Godly Wisdom

Hymn Part 2—Christ's Lifestyle
Who, although He existed in the form of God, did not regard equality with God a thing to be grasped (Phil. 2:6).

What Is in This Unit for Me?

God's goal for you is to become like Jesus. That's a high standard. Without Christ, it's impossible. The good news is, He's ready to help! You will study eight virtues of Christ as your Model. God will be working in you and with you to give you the mental quality of discernment. As you measure your thoughts and actions against the perfection of Christ, God will work to renew your mind to reflect Christ's virtues.

Lifelong Objective

In Christ you will become pure, peaceable, gentle, approachable, merciful, fruitful, steadfast, and honest.

How God Will be Working In You

Christ's lifestyle in you is based on the mental quality of discernment. God's goal is your virtue. Your growth in Christ's character can be measured only by Christ's perfection. Jesus' life is your model, and He makes your virtue possible.

Unit Learning Goals

- You will understand the importance of God's Word as a tool for cleaning up your mind and keeping you from sin.
- You will show a willingness to submit to God's cleansing through His Word.
- You will understand the difference between the eight virtues of godly wisdom in *James 3:17* and their opposites and perversions.
- You will know eight virtues of godly wisdom.
- You will show a willingness for Christ to establish these virtues in your mind.

What You Will Do to Begin Developing the Virtues of Godly Wisdom

- You will study the eight virtues, with their opposites and perversions.
- You will become familiar with the Lifelong Helps on pages 189-220.
- You will identify a virtue and use the Helps to mature in that virtue.
- You will seek Christ's help to be set free in those areas.

Lifelong Helps Related to This Unit

Christlike Virtues (pp. 192-202)

The Mind of Christ Cards Related to This Unit

3B. Unit 4: Scripture Memory—*James 3:17*
7A. Eight Virtues of Godly Wisdom
8A. Pure
8B. Peaceable
9A. Gentle
9B. Reasonable
10A. Merciful
10B. Fruitful
11A. Steadfast
11B. Honest

Washing Your Mind

DAY 1

✱ **Begin today's lesson by reading the Bible verses and the name of Christ for today. Work on your memory verse. Then use the suggested prayer to begin your study.**

Hymn Part 2—Christ's Lifestyle

There was a popular song on MTV recently that asked the question, "What if God was one of us?" The singer was wondering how God would behave if He came to earth and walked around with us. What would His actions be like?

I don't know if the singer realized that God did become one of us. Another popular song, one that was popular in the early church about two thousand years ago, answers all the questions she brings up. That song is found in *Philippians 2:5-11*. God came to earth as Jesus Christ. He came to show us in the flesh what God is like, and what His purpose is for us. Jesus, *Who, although He existed in the form of God, did not regard equality with God a thing to be grasped (Phil. 2:6)*.

Since we can see the actions of God in Christ's lifestyle, we can learn about His mind. *For as he* [man] *thinks within himself, so is he (Prov. 23:7)*. Outer actions are a reflection of inner thoughts. So, during the next two units, we'll look at the virtues of Christ that are reflected in His lifestyle.

✱ **Read the following account of Jesus' temptation in the wilderness from *Matthew 4:1-11*. Pay attention to how Jesus responded to Satan. As you read, underline the words of Jesus.**

> *Then Jesus was led up by the Spirit into the wilderness to be tempted by the devil. And after He had fasted forty days and forty nights, He then became hungry. And the tempter came and said to him, "If You are the Son of God, command that these stones become bread."*
>
> *But He* [Jesus] *answered and said, "It is written: 'Man shall not live on bread alone, but on every word that proceeds out of the mouth of God.' "*
>
> *Then the devil took Him into the holy city; and he had Him stand on the pinnacle of the temple, and said to Him, "If you are the Son of God throw Yourself down; for it is written,*
>
> *'He will give His angels charge concerning you';*
> *and 'On their hands they will bear You up,*
> *lest You strike Your foot against a stone.' "*
>
> *Jesus said to him, "On the other hand, it is written: 'You shall not put the Lord your God to the test.' "*
>
> *Again, the devil took Him to a very high mountain, and showed Him all the kingdoms of the world, and their glory; and he said to Him, "All these things will I give You, if You fall down and worship me."*
>
> *Then Jesus said to him, "Begone, Satan! For it is written: 'You shall worship the Lord your God, and serve Him only.' "*
>
> *Then the devil left Him; and behold, angels came and began to minister to Him (Matt. 4:1-11).*

Today's Bible Meditations
Who, although He existed in the form of God, did not regard equality with God a thing to be grasped.
Philippians 2:6

Christ also loved the church and gave Himself up for her; that He might sanctify her, having cleansed her by the washing of water with the word, that He might present to Himself the church in all her glory, having no spot or wrinkle or any such thing; but that she should be holy and blameless.
Ephesians 5:25-27

Name of Christ for Today
The Word
(John 1:1)

Prayer to Begin the Lesson
Jesus, You are the Word of God. You are God. I want to know You like I know the words to my favorite song. Please cleanse me and fill me with Yourself.
Amen.

✱ In all three responses, Jesus used a phrase to begin His response. What was it?

____

Jesus quoted Scripture when He was tempted to sin. He said, "It is written..." Now, Jesus didn't have a pocket King James Version with Him in the wilderness! He had committed large portions of Scripture to memory, and therefore was able to resist temptation. By knowing God's commands, Jesus knew the proper way to respond to each temptation. As the Psalmist said, *Thy word I have treasured in my heart, that I may not sin against Thee (Ps. 119:11).*

✱ Why should we become familiar with what God has said in the Bible?

____

One thing we learn about the mind of Christ is that Christ filled His mind with the Scriptures. Jesus knew the will of His father and was prepared to resist temptation when it came. By the way, you can resist temptation much more successfully if you prepare beforehand. The Scripture helped Jesus keep His mind clean and unpolluted.

The Cleansing Power of God's Word

The word of God has a cleansing effect on the mind. Jesus told the disciples, *"You are already clean because of the word which I have spoken to you" (John 15:3).* Later Jesus prayed, *"Sanctify* [His disciples] *in the truth; Thy word is truth" (John 17:17).* The Lord cleanses the church by *the washing of water with the word (Eph. 5:26).*

Today, our minds get mixed up with the world's way of thinking. That's why we constantly need to be reoriented to God's way of thinking. We need a thorough scrub-down with God's Word. God's Word washes away things that are wrong or impure. God's Word cleanses as it replaces wrong with right ways of thinking. One step in developing the mind of Christ is to let God cleanse your mind through His Word.

Hindered by Humanism

After I had been working on my areas of bondage to sin, I set out to study what the Bible says about the 17 virtues of *James 3:17* and *Galatians 5:22-23.* These virtues show a part of the ideal mind of Christ that I was trying to attain. I knew that once I was free from the bondage of sin, God would work on developing these virtues in my life. So, using my concordance (a Bible study tool that allows you to look up a key word and find all the Scripture passages containing that word), I compiled several passages about the virtues mentioned in these two Scriptures.

In the process, I began to discover aspects of my education and background that were keeping me from gaining these virtues. There is a philosophy called humanism, which teaches that human beings can achieve happiness and fulfillment through reason. Humanism glorifies what humans can do apart from God. Humanism had been a subtle part of much of my education. So I kept looking at these virtues as something that if I worked hard enough, I could achieve. I figured if I read the Bible more, or prayed more, or memorized more, I would become all the things that James and Galatians talk about. I had a hard time accepting that these virtues were a gift given to us at our spiritual birth. When we become Christians, these virtues are part of our standard equipment package. Look at *1 Corinthians 2:14-16:*

> *But a natural man does not accept the things of the Spirit of God; for they are foolishness to him, and he cannot understand them, because they are spiritually appraised. But he who is spiritual appraises all things, yet he himself is appraised by no man. For who has known the mind of the Lord, that he should instruct Him? But we have the mind of Christ.*

You see, *verse 16* doesn't say, "we can get the mind of Christ," or that you can work towards the mind of Christ. It says *we **have** the mind of Christ.*

Standard Equipment!

✱ Identify the two statements below by marking them God's perspective or Humanism's perspective.

____________ I can develop these godly virtues in my life by hard work.

____________ Godly virtues are a gift to me at spiritual birth and show when I allow Christ to live His life in me.

Sure, Bible study helps. They help define the virtues enough so that you can recognize them. My spiritual knowledge was growing. The problem was, humanism teaches you to be proud of the knowledge itself. When we achieve certain things in the world's system, the act of achieving becomes part of our unconscious mind. But these Christlike virtues can't be developed by hard work, as humanism teaches. I needed God to do a work that would allow Christ's presence and mind to show through my life.

A Special Vow

It was hard for me to let God have His way. I had been so influenced by the idea that I could work to achieve these virtues that I had to take drastic action. I made a vow to the Lord: from that time on, I would not read anything but the Bible until God signaled me that I had begun to think biblically. I was determined to saturate my mind with God's way of thinking.

That period lasted four years. During that time, I didn't read anything but the Bible. I didn't even read Bible commentaries. I memorized several books of the Bible and many passages of the Bible. I studied intensely, and prayed constantly. And I felt a real change taking place in my mind. I felt like I was actually understanding the deeper meaning and implications of the virtues in *James 3:17* and *Galatians 5:22-23.* The Word of God reached into the deepest parts of who I was and impacted every part of my mind. And God's Word will have the same effect on you, if you allow it to.

As a junior high or high school student, you are not in a position right now to read nothing but the Bible for the next four years. But I want you to consider these thoughts. Do you think that these virtues are something you can arrive at on your own, through any amount of hard work? If that's even a possibility to you, then you have been effected by humanism. This course provides several opportunities for you to begin the process of being washed by God's Word. The following are some ways you can allow God the opportunity to cleanse your mind with His Word.

✱ Read through the following list. Check the box beside the items you do already. Circle any item that you sense God wants you to devote more time and attention to.

- ❑ Carefully evaluate the books and magazines you read in your leisure time. Are they pulling you away from God's Word?
- ❑ Do the same with the movies and TV shows you watch, and the music you listen to. Are there thoughts, images, and ideas you need to be cleansed from?
- ❑ Daily read a part of God's Word.
- ❑ Study certain passages closely to see what God may want you to do in response to His Word.
- ❑ Study related topics in Scripture to understand more clearly what God is saying on a particular subject.
- ❑ Memorize verses, passages, chapters, and even books of the Bible.
- ❑ Meditate on God's Word. Think about what He is saying to you through it. Pray through passages of the Scripture and consider what it means for your life.
- ❑ Discuss God's Word with other believers. God may give you insight through a fellow believer.

✳ Pray as you conclude today's study. Ask God to use the reading, studying, and memorizing of Scripture in this course as a time of cleansing of your mind. If you sense God calling you to devote more time to His Word (instead of TV, movies, sports, or other reading), tell Him so.

DAY 2

Today's Bible Meditations

Finally, brethren, whatever is true, whatever is honorable, whatever is right, whatever is pure, whatever is lovely, whatever is of good repute, if there is any excellence and if anything worthy of praise, let your mind dwell on these things.

Philippians 4:8

Pure

✳ Begin today's lesson by reading the Bible verses and the name of Christ for today. Work on your memory verse. Then use the suggested prayer to begin your study.

I'd like us to look again at the virtues described in *James 3:17*. This is your memory verse for this week. Do you remember it? *The wisdom from above is first pure, then peaceable, gentle, reasonable, full of mercy and good fruits, unwavering, without hypocrisy (Jas. 3:17).* So, beginning today, we're studying the virtues one by one. There are three aspects of each virtue.

1. What it is (Christlike Virtue).
2. What it isn't (Satanic Opposite).
3. How it can be distorted (Perversion).

See, for every virtue, there is an opposite that Satan uses to pull us away from developing the qualities. For example, the opposite of purity is lust. And, if left on its own, the human mind tends to adopt the opposite quality. But even more dangerous is the perversion of each virtue. While this is not the opposite of the virtue, you might say that the perversion is the virtue stretched to an unhealthy limit. A Christian is more susceptible to perverting a virtue than to acting on its opposite. For example, if you are trying to develop purity in your own life, you can easily get sidetracked into being prudish or "holier-than-thou."

That's why the mental quality of discernment is so important. Imagine yourself walking a tightrope of virtue. If you fall off on one side, you're developing the opposite quality of the virtue. If you fall off on the other side, you pervert the virtue. *Discernment,* the spiritual quality of knowing right from wrong, helps you keep your balance.

Name of Christ for Today
A Refiner and Purifier
(Mal. 3:3)

Prayer to Begin the Lesson
Lord Jesus, You are my example of perfect purity. There is nothing impure in You at all. I want to be pure as You are pure. You are a refiner and a purifier. Refine and purify me so I can be like You. Burn away anything in my life that is impure. Amen.

✱ Look at the chart below. Ask God to guide you to the virtue He wants to work on first in your life. Circle the one you sense God wants you to work on first.

SATANIC OPPOSITE	CHRISTLIKE VIRTUE	PERVERSION
Lustful	*Pure*	Self-Righteous
Fussy	*Peaceable*	Compromising
Harsh	*Gentle*	Unkind Restraint
Unapproachable	*Reasonable*	Yes-Person
Merciless	*Merciful*	Indulgent
Lazy	*Fruitful*	Fruit-Obsessed
Wavering	*Steadfast*	Inflexible
Lying	*Honest*	Brutal

At the back of this book, there is a special tool for helping you develop these virtues. Titled "Lifelong Helps for Developing the Mind of Christ," they aren't by any means complete, they serve as a starting point for you to allow God to bring these virtues into your life.

✱ Turn to pages 192-202 and find the page for the virtue you circled. Place a marker there, or fold down the page so you can refer to it this week. Write the page number here: ___________.

✱ Now, turn to the Mind of Christ cards section at the back of the book. Tear out the card that relates to the virtue you selected. Carry it with you this week to help you focus your attention on this virtue, its opposites, and perversions.

Pure

✱ Read through the list of words in the right margin to help you understand what purity is and what it isn't. Below, write your definition of purity.

____

____

Pure:
blameless, clean, chaste, spotless, unblemished, innocent, stainless, uncontaminated, above reproach

Opposites of Pure:
lustful, carnal, fleshly, lewd, impure, dirty, tainted, stained, corrupt, immoral, depraved

Perversions of Pure:
puritanical, rigid, overly strict, self-righteous, holier-than-thou, prudish, severe, pharisaical

Susan was active in her youth group, and she was a sincere, committed Christian. She had been having a daily quiet time for over a year, and was almost finished reading through the entire Bible. She had joined a small-group discipleship study, and really felt like she was making progress in getting closer to God.

One Wednesday night during Bible study, Susan's youth leader was going through a study on moral purity. As the group discussed temptation and impurity, Susan felt pleased that a lot of the discussion didn't seem to apply to her. But she began to look around at other members of her youth group. She thought of a joke Andy had told at the last lock-in that offended her. Immediately, she prayed, "Lord, purify his mind. I pray that he'll really listen to this part about impure speech." Then, she thought of some rumors she had heard about Melissa at school. "Lord," she prayed, "the way she's been acting lately, those rumors are probably true. Please help her to get her life straightened out."

When Susan went home that night, she thought some more about the whole subject of impurity. The more she thought about it, the more she seemed to find impurity in the people she knew. Her list of people she was praying for got long, and the kinds of impurity she sensed in them got more and more complicated. But slowly, gently, the Holy Spirit led her to realize that maybe the problem was with her. She asked the Lord to show her if the sin was with her, and not with all the people on her "impure" list.

Susan knew that a Satanic opposite of purity is lust. As a Christian, she had tried to avoid lust. She didn't go to many movies, and she switched channels when a suggestive video came on. But Satan also has a perversion of purity. Susan had overshot her goal of being pure and had become self-righteous.

Christians encounter many degrees of this perversion. Almost all of them involve pride, and may involve looking down on others. Susan was not quite that bad. She felt genuine affection for them. Nevertheless, God showed her that she was judging them.

Where did Susan go wrong? She really was trying to grow in Christ. She was faithfully reading her Bible. But remember the Pharisees? They knew their Bible, the *Torah,* backwards, forwards, and sideways. Yet, Jesus saved His harshest rebukes for this group. Look at this story He told about them in *Luke 18:9-13:*

> *He also told this parable to certain ones who trusted in themselves that they were righteous, and viewed others with contempt:*
>
> *"Two men went up into the temple to pray, one a Pharisee, and the other a tax-gatherer.*
>
> *"The Pharisee stood and was praying thus to himself, 'God, I thank Thee that I am not like other people: swindlers, unjust, adulterers, or even like this tax-gatherer. I fast twice a week; I pay tithes of all that I get.'*
>
> *"But the tax-gatherer, standing some distance away, was even unwilling to lift up his eyes to heaven, but was beating his breast, saying, 'God, be merciful to me, the sinner!' "*

The only standard for behavior is Jesus' own purity. The problem with the Pharisees (and Susan's problem), was that they were using themselves as a measuring stick for others' behavior.

✱ **Read the list of words in the right margin of page 65 to help you understand the perversions of purity. Can you think of an experience when you have observed this kind of behavior? If so, who was involved, and when?**

____

____

Jesus Is the Standard

There's a reason the Bible tells us to *consider Jesus (Heb. 3:1),* and to *fix our eyes on Jesus (Heb. 12:2b).* While it's important to read the biblical passages on purity, if you try to understand purity apart from how Jesus lived it out, you'll end up perverting the virtue.

Jesus was absolutely pure. Was He ever tempted to lust? No doubt He had the opportunity. We read in *Luke 8:3* that there was a group of women who followed Jesus and helped support His ministry financially. Few men have had more adoring women around them than Jesus. But Jesus also had 12 men who watched His every move for three and a half years. One of those disciples, Peter, described Jesus as *a Lamb unblemished and spotless (1 Pet. 1:19).* Another disciple, John, said that *in Him there is no sin (1 John 3:5).* The ones who knew Jesus best report that Jesus was absolutely pure.

But He also was never puritanical. Puritanical, prudish, holier-than-thou people tend to be narrow in their selection of friends, surrounding themselves with "good" people. Jesus hung out with so many tax-collectors, prostitutes, and other "lowlifes" that He earned the nickname Friend of Sinners. He accepted dinner invitations with self-righteous Pharisees and sinful tax-collectors the same. Jesus kept His balance between the opposite of purity and its perversions.

✱ What is one virtue of the mind of Christ?

P ____________	Peaceable	Gentle	Reasonable
Merciful	Fruitful	Steadfast	Honest

Jesus was able to live such a pure life because He constantly measured His behavior by God's standard. He was always aware of the presence of the Father (see *Luke 2:49; John 4:34; 5:19-23; 6:38;* and *17:4*). In the same way, you can be constantly conscious of the presence of Christ. He is with you always, according to *Matthew 28:20.* Jesus is your reference point.

✱ Turn to pages 192-193 and scan the Pure list in the Lifelong Helps. Notice some practical suggestions for being constantly aware of Christ's presence. Conclude your study today by asking God to enable you to be more aware of His presence in your life moment by moment.

Today's Bible Meditation
"It is not so among you, but whoever wishes to become great among you shall be your servant, and whoever wishes to be first among you shall be your slave."
Matthew 20:26-27

Name of Christ for Today
Prince of Peace
(Isa. 9:6)

Prayer to Begin the Lesson
Prince of Peace, my world doesn't know much about peace. And sometimes, I don't feel very peaceful myself. I ask You to shape my life to be peaceable like You. Then, as You see fit, put me around people who need a peacemaker. Work through me to show peace to my world.
Amen.

Peaceable

✳ Begin today's lesson by reading the Bible verse and the name of Christ for today. Work on your memory verse. Then use the suggested prayer to begin your study.

Peaceable

One of the most popular titles for Jesus, especially around Christmas, is "Prince of Peace." *Peaceable,* our second virtue, describes a way of acting. Trying to go too far as a peacemaker can pervert the virtue into compromising, while the opposite of peaceable is argumentative. Jesus had some things to say about peace which might surprise you:

> *"Do not think that I came to bring peace on the earth; I did not come to bring peace, but a sword. For I came to set a man against his father, and a daughter against her mother, and a daughter-in-law against her mother-in-law; and a man's enemies will be the members of his household" (Matt. 10:34-36).*

In all of Jesus' peacefulness, Jesus also knew where to draw the line. He never compromised His beliefs or His expectations to maintain peace. We must not distort His teachings in order to maintain peace with someone. That's when we pervert the virtue.

✳ Read through the list of words in the left margin to help you understand what peaceable is and what it isn't. Below, write your definition of peaceable.

____

____

✳ Read the list of words in the right margin to help you understand the perversions of peaceable. Can you think of an experience when you have observed this kind of behavior? If so, who was involved, and when?

____

____

Jesus Was Peaceable

Have you ever fought with your brother or sister? Well, so did Jesus' disciples. One day, James and John started fighting over who would get the top spot in the Kingdom. We see this same scenario happen time and time again in history. Our human pride makes us compete for position, power, fame, money, or territory. Look how Jesus acted as a peacemaker in this situation.

> *Then the mother of the sons of Zebedee came to Him with her sons, bowing down, and making a request of Him.*
>
> *And He said to her, "What do you wish?" She said to Him, "Command*

that in Your kingdom these two sons of mine may sit, one on Your right and one on Your left."

But Jesus answered and said, "You do not know what you are asking for. Are you able to drink the cup that I am about to drink?" They said to Him, "We are able."

He said to them, "My cup you shall drink; but to sit on My right and on My left, this is not Mine to give, but it is for those for whom it has been prepared by My Father."

And hearing this, the ten became indignant with the two brothers. But Jesus called them to Himself and said. "You know that the rulers of the Gentiles lord it over them, and their great men exercise authority over them. It is not so among you, but whoever wishes to become great among you shall be your servant, and whoever wishes to be first among you shall be your slave; just as the Son of Man did not come to be served, but to serve, and to give His life a ransom for many" (Matt. 20:20-28).

Jesus set an example for us. Jesus certainly had the right to lord His power over His followers. But instead, He came to serve, and to give His life for all of us. Our world is full of fighting because nobody wants to serve. We all want to be served instead of serving. Peace comes when we make up our minds to be servants instead of masters, following Jesus' example.

Peaceable:
peaceful, friendly, harmonious, orderly, quiet, content, reconciling, calm, agreeable, compatible

Opposites of Peaceable:
fussy, nit-picking, picky, contentious, argumentative, ornery, controversial, disagreeable, mean, obstinate, bad-tempered

Perversions of Peaceable:
compromising, wishy-washy, people-pleaser

✳ What are two virtues of the mind of Christ?

P __________	P __________	**Gentle**	**Reasonable**
Merciful	**Fruitful**	**Steadfast**	**Honest**

Competition in the body of Christ does not reflect this quality of being peaceable. Whether it's jealousy over who gets the biggest part in the youth drama group or competition for spots on the youth council, we are least like Jesus when we forget about being servants to one another.

✳ Yesterday, I asked you to identify one virtue in your life that God wants to work on. You marked the Lifelong Helps in the back of the book for that particular virtue. As you conclude today's lesson, turn to that page, and prayerfully read throughout the section, "Becoming ______________." Ask God to show you any attitudes or actions that are not like this virtue. Seek forgiveness. Then, ask God to renew your mind and actions so that you may reflect that virtue more closely in your life.

DAY 4

Today's Bible Meditation
(to be selected at the end of today's lesson)

____

____

____

____

Name of Christ for Today
Merciful and Faithful High Priest
(Heb. 2:17)

Prayer to Begin the Lesson
Lord Jesus,
You are holy enough
to be my High Priest, but
You are also merciful
enough for me to be able to
approach You.
How I love You for Your
mercy and faithfulness!
Please help me to be
merciful and faithful to
others.
Amen.

Gentle, Reasonable, and Merciful

✳ Begin today's lesson by reading the Bible verse and the name of Christ for today. Work on your memory verse. Then use the suggested prayer to begin your study.

Gentle

The third virtue of *James 3:17* is *gentle.* When I think of the word *gentle,* I think of images such as a mother with a newborn baby, a favorite teacher giving me the extra tenth of a point that will move me from a *C* to a *B,* or the sound of water lapping on the shores of a peaceful lake. *Matthew 16:15-23* describes gentleness in action. Jesus showed a lot of gentleness in His dealings with the disciples, especially hot-headed Peter. He could gently beckon Peter to get out of the boat and walk on water, and minutes later gently reprimand Peter's lack of faith (see *Matt. 14:28-32).* He could heap praise on Peter for his insight, then sharply rebuke him for trying to squeeze Jesus into Peter's own agenda:

> *He said to them, "But who do you say that I am?"*
>
> *And Simon Peter answered and said, "Thou art the Christ, the Son of the living God."*
>
> *And Jesus answered and said to him, "Blessed are you, Simon Barjona, because flesh and blood did not reveal this to you, but My Father who is in heaven. And I also say to you that you are Peter, and upon this rock I will build My church; and the gates of Hades shall not overpower it. I will give you the keys of the kingdom of heaven; and whatever you shall bind on earth shall be bound in heaven, and whatever you shall loose on earth shall be loosed in heaven."*
>
> *Then He warned the disciples that they should tell no one that He was the Christ. From that time Jesus Christ began to show His disciples that He must go to Jerusalem, and suffer many things from the elders and chief priests and scribes, and be killed, and be raised up on the third day. And Peter took Him aside and began to rebuke Him, saying, "God forbid it, Lord! This shall never happen to You."*
>
> *But He turned and said to Peter, "Get behind Me, Satan! You are a stumbling block to Me; for you are not setting your mind on God's interests, but man's" (Matt. 16:15-23).*

For Jesus, gentleness didn't always mean sweetness and warm fuzzies. There was room in Jesus' dealings with people for sharp rebuke. But Jesus often balanced His sharp rebukes with gentleness.

✳ What are three virtues of the mind of Christ?

P __________	**P** __________	**G**__________	**Reasonable**
Merciful	**Fruitful**	**Steadfast**	**Honest**

The opposite of gentle is harsh, and the perversion of it is negligence. Think again about a teacher at school. She can deal gently with her students by recognizing hard work even when the grades don't measure up. But suppose, in trying to be gentle, she allows you to get away with not studying at all. She would be too lax for your own good.

Gentle:
fair, moderate, considerate, approachable, pleasant, nurturing, tender, tactful, delicate, gracious, considerate, kindhearted

Opposites of Gentle:
harsh, caustic, rough, abusive, hard, stiff, bitter, cruel, fierce, violent, blunt, brash, rude, snappy, short, snippy, grating

Perversions of Gentle:
unkind restraint, negligent, spoiling, careless, neglectful, inattentive, reckless

✱ **Read through the list of words in the right margin to help you understand what gentle is and what it isn't (opposites). Below, write your definition of *gentle*.**

Gentle is____

____

✱ **Read the list of words in the right margin to help you understand the perversions of gentle. Can you think of an experience when you have observed this kind of behavior? If so, who was involved, and when?**

____

____

Reasonable

The next virtue in *James 3:17* is *reasonable.* A reasonable person is approachable. They are happy to do a favor for someone. The opposite of this virtue is unapproachable. You probably know some people who back off from every opportunity to do something for someone else. The perversion of this virtue is to say "yes" to everything. In the business world, you would call this kind of person a yes-man or a yes-woman. You might call him or her a brown-noser.

Reasonable:
approachable, cordial, helpful, accessible, available, open, reachable, cooperative, willing, inclined, accommodating, responsive

Opposites of Reasonable:
unapproachable, cold, cool, distant, uncooperative, inaccessible, closed, frigid, introverted

Perversions of Reasonable:
yes-person, brown-noser, pushover, sucker

✱ **Read through the list of words in the right margin to help you understand what reasonable is and what it isn't (opposites). Below, write your definition of *reasonable*.**

Reasonable is ______________________________________

____

✱ **Read the list of words in the right margin to help you understand the perversions of reasonable. Can you think of an experience when you have observed this kind of behavior? If so, who was involved, and when?**

____

____

Jesus was approachable. One day, He was on His way to heal the daughter of a man named Jairus, when He was interrupted to deal with another woman who came to Him for healing. He could have said, "Look, lady, there's a 12- year-old girl who needs me right now. Come back some other time." Instead, look how He responded:

> *A woman who had had a hemorrhage for twelve years, and had endured much at the hands of many physicians, and had spent all that she had and was not helped at all, but rather had grown worse, after hearing about Jesus, came up in the crowd behind Him, and touched His cloak. For she thought, "If I just touch His garments, I shall get well."*
>
> *And immediately the flow of her blood was dried up; and she felt in her body that she was healed of her affliction. And immediately Jesus, perceiving in Himself that the power proceeding from Him had gone forth, turned around in the crowd and said, "Who touched My garments?"*
>
> *And His disciples said to Him, "You see the multitude pressing in on You, and You say, 'Who touched Me?'"*
>
> *And He looked around to see the woman who had done this. But the woman fearing and trembling, aware of what had happened to her, came and fell down before Him, and told Him the whole truth. And He said to her, "Daughter, your faith has made you well; go in peace, and be healed of your affliction" (Mark 5:25-34).*

Jesus never turned down a request for healing. He tested a woman's faith on one occasion *(Matt. 15:21-28)*, and He delayed going to Lazarus in order to perform a greater miracle *(John 11:4)*. But Jesus always was responsive to people. By the way, the girl whom Jesus was on the way to heal when the woman with the hemorrhage interrupted Him eventually died. But Jesus went to her house and raised her from the dead (see *Mark 5:35-43*). The whole story of Jesus is of His constant availability. If Jesus were alive in the flesh today, you could imagine Him as someone who never looked at His watch while He talked to you.

Merciful:
caring, forgiving, gracious, decent, noble, sympathetic, tolerant, compassionate, charitable, benevolent

Opposites of Merciful:
merciless, unmerciful, unsympathetic, compassionless, hardened, pitiless, spiteful, sadistic

Perversions of Merciful:
indulgent, lenient, permissive

Merciful

The fifth virtue is *merciful*. The opposite of merciful is merciless, and the perversion is indulgent. You don't meet too many merciless Christians (hopefully!), but we often are tempted to be indulgent.

✷ **Read through the list of words in the left margin to help you understand what merciful is and what it isn't (opposites). Below, write your definition of merciful.**

Merciful is ____

____

✷ **Read the list of words in the left margin to help you understand the perversions of merciful. Can you think of an experience when you have observed this kind of behavior? If so, who was involved, and when?**

____

____

Imagine yourself in a courtroom, facing the judge. You've been caught speeding. No argument—the radar gun didn't lie. The judge looks at you and says, "I'm going to let you off this time, since it's your first offense. Just don't let it happen again."

You have just experienced mercy. The judge had every right to make you pay the fine, but allowed you to go free instead. Mercy involves a person who has a right to punish but chooses not to do so. Mercy can also involve a person who has no obligation to someone else doing something good for them.

Jesus is our supreme example of mercy. The numerous healings Jesus performed clearly demonstrate intense compassion and sympathy for the hurt and suffering. The feeding of the five thousand happened as a result of Jesus having compassion on the hungry multitudes who had followed Him for days without food (see *Matt. 9:36)*. When Jesus wept at Lazarus' tomb, it was partially out of empathy for Mary and Martha (see *John 11:35)*. Through Jesus we know the great, compassionate heart of God.

The greatest demonstration of mercy is the act of forgiveness. Forgiveness involves a person who has been offended pardoning the offender. Sin is an offense against God's absolute holiness. When God forgives our sins, He is exercising mercy. The greatest single act of mercy was when Jesus prayed for our forgiveness from the cross. After enduring all the pain and suffering that our sins caused Him, some of Jesus' final words were *"Father, forgive them; for they do not know what they are doing"* (see *Luke 23:33-34)*.

✱ What are five virtues of the mind of Christ?

P __________ P __________ G__________ R __________

M __________ Fruitful Steadfast Honest

✱ Turn in the Lifelong Helps to the virtue you're working in this week. Read the Scriptures for Meditation and select one that is especially meaningful. Write it in the space under Today's Bible Meditation at the beginning of today's lesson. Spend time with God seeking understanding of this verse and the virtue. Ask God to help you in making that virtue evident in your living.

DAY 5

Today's Bible Meditation
"We must work the works of Him who sent Me, as long as it is day; night is coming, when no man can work."
John 9:4

Name of Christ for Today
A Sure Foundation
(Isa. 28:16, KJV*)*

Prayer to Begin the Lesson
Jesus, You are steadfast—
a Sure Foundation,
and a Solid Rock.
I waiver so often
in my practice of faith.
Please plant my feet firmly
on Your solid foundation
so that I can be strong and
productive in my faith.
Amen.

Fruitful, Steadfast, and Honest

✱ **Begin today's lesson by reading the Bible verse and the name of Christ for today. Work on your memory verse. Then use the suggested prayer to begin your study.**

Fruitful

The sixth virtue in *James 3:17* is *fruitful.* The opposite is fruitless, and the perversion is to be fruit-obsessed. The term can apply both to the fruit of the Spirit in *Galatians 5:22-23,* or to bearing fruit for God's kingdom by bringing other people to the Lord. In that second sense, fruitfulness is the most easily demonstrated of all the virtues in *James 3:17.* Look how fruitful Jesus was! In two thousand years, millions of people have had their lives changed because of His ministry. Here is one example:

> *And they brought to Him one who was deaf and spoke with difficulty, and they entreated Him to lay His hand upon him. And He took him aside from the multitude by himself, and put His fingers into his ears, and after spitting, He touched his tongue with the saliva; and looking up to heaven with a deep sigh, He said to him, "Ephphatha!" that is, "Be opened!"*
>
> *And his ears were opened, and the impediment of his tongue was removed, and he began speaking plainly. And He gave them orders not to tell anyone; but the more He ordered them, the more widely they continued to proclaim it. And they were utterly astonished, saying, "He has done all things well: He makes even the deaf to hear, and the dumb to speak" (Mark 7:32-37).*

✱ **Read through the list of words in the right margin to help you understand what fruitful is and what it isn't (opposites). Below, write your definition of fruitful.**

Fruitful is ______________________________

____

✱ **Read the list of words in the right margin to help you understand the perversions of fruitful. Can you think of an experience when you have observed this kind of behavior? If so, who was involved, and when?**

____

____

✱ What are six virtues of the mind of Christ?

P __________ P __________ G__________ R __________

M __________ F__________ Steadfast Honest

Steadfast

The seventh virtue in *James 3:17* is without wavering, or *steadfast.* The opposite would be wavering, and the perversion would be inflexible. Jesus was neither of these. Once He set His face toward the cross, nothing kept Him from carrying out His plan. Even when faced with the horror of His own death, He didn't waver:

> *He went a little beyond them, and fell on His face and prayed, saying, "My Father, if it is possible, let this cup pass from Me; yet not as I will, but as Thou wilt."*
>
> *He went away again a second time and prayed, saying, "My Father, if this cannot pass away unless I drink it, Thy will be done" (Matt. 26:39, 42).*

Jesus was steadfast, but He wasn't inflexible. Because Jesus is also approachable, you remember from yesterday, He can be interrupted. In *Mark 1:35-37,* Jesus' prayer time was interrupted by Simon and his companions.

✳ **Read through the list of words in the right margin to help you understand what steadfast is and what it isn't (opposites). Below, write your definition of steadfast.**

Steadfast is____

____

✳ **Read the list of words in the right margin to help you understand the perversions of steadfast. Can you think of an experience when you have observed this kind of behavior? If so, who was involved, and when?**

____

____

Honest

The last virtue in *James 3:17* is probably the first one that we all learn as children. It's *honest,* without hypocrisy, or sincere. The opposite is lying, or hypocritical, and the perversion is being brutal.

Let's say your best friend wears an outfit that doesn't flatter her at all. How do you handle it? Do you lie to her and say it looks wonderful on her? That would be the opposite of this virtue. Or do you say, "You look awful in that! I've never seen anything quite so ugly in my life! If you go out in public in that thing, you're going to scare away small children!" That would be the perversion of the virtue. To tell your friend that much would be brutal and cruel.

How did Jesus live out this virtue? We know that Jesus is Truth (see *John 14:6),* and that there is nothing two-faced or hypocritical in His nature. But we also know that He was gentle. For example, He dealt honestly with the woman at the well, but wasn't brutal with her when talking with her about her immoral lifestyle:

> *He said to her, "Go, call your husband, and come here."*
>
> *The woman answered and said, "I have no husband." Jesus said to her, "You have well said, 'I have no husband'; for you have had five husbands,*

Fruitful:
productive, fertile, prolific, constructive, high yield

Opposites of Fruitful:
fruitless, unproductive, non-productive, ineffective, worthless, waste of time, empty, hollow, profitless

Perversions of Fruitful:
fruit-obsessed, success-driven, workaholic, obsessed with numbers, vain, showy

Steadfast:
firm, unshakable, sure, never-failing, enduring, long-lasting, resolute, constant, devoted, steady, immovable, resolved, uncompromising

Opposites of Steadfast:
wavering, waffling, unsure, weak, unstable, wobbly, fickle, flimsy, shaky, faltering, halting, hesitant, indecisive, reluctant, wayward

Perversions of Steadfast:
inflexible, rigid, narrow-minded, obstinate, stubborn, unbendable, bullheaded, hardheaded, authoritarian, tyrannical, severe

and the one whom you now have is not your husband; this you have said truly" (John 4:16-18).

Jesus didn't call her a two-bit floozy, but He also didn't ignore her sin. He was totally honest with her. Real honesty can be courageous and bold with genuine integrity. Jesus insisted on inner perfection and confronted hypocrisy with crisp honesty *(Luke 11:37-54)*. The spirit of discernment allows us to integrate honesty, integrity, and confrontation. Look at how Jesus confronted the hypocrisy of the scribes and Pharisees:

> *Now when He had spoken, a Pharisee asked Him to have lunch with him; and He went in, and reclined at the table. And when the Pharisee saw it, he was surprised that He had not first ceremonially washed before the meal. But the Lord said to him, "Now you Pharisees clean the outside of the cup and of the platter; but inside of you, you are full of robbery and wickedness. You foolish ones, did not He who made the outside make the inside also? But give that which is within as charity, and then all things are clean for you.*
>
> *"But woe to you Pharisees! For you pay tithe of mint and rue and every kind of garden herb, and yet disregard justice and the love of God; but these are the things you should have done without neglecting the others. Woe to you Pharisees! For you love the front seats in the synagogues, and the respectful greetings in the market places. Woe to you! For you are like concealed tombs, and the people who walk over them are unaware of it."*
>
> *And one of the lawyers said to Him in reply, "Teacher, when You say this, You insult us too." But He said, "Woe to you lawyers as well! For you weigh men down with burdens hard to bear, while you yourselves will not even touch the burdens with one of your fingers. Woe to you! For you build the tombs of the prophets, and it was your fathers who killed them. Consequently, you are witnesses and approve the deeds of your fathers; because it was they who killed them, and you build their tombs. For this reason also the wisdom of God said, 'I will send to them prophets and apostles, and some of them they will kill and some they will persecute, in order that the blood of all the prophets, shed since the foundation of the world, may be charged against this generation, from the blood of Abel to the blood of Zechariah, who perished between the altar and the house of God; yes, I tell you, it shall be charged against this generation.' Woe to you lawyers! For you have taken away the key of knowledge; you did not enter in yourselves, and those who were entering in you hindered."*
>
> *And when He left there, the scribes and the Pharisees began to be very hostile and to question Him closely on many subjects, plotting against Him, to catch Him in something He might say (Luke 11:37-54).*

Honest:
sincere, true, genuine, ethical, sound, trustworthy, upright, straightforward, factual, candid, real

Opposites of Honest:
lying, dishonest, hypocritical, fake, phony, fraudulent, crooked, deceitful, scheming, shady, corrupt

Perversions of Honest:
brutal, cruel, callous, pitiless, ruthless, spiteful, unrelenting, vicious, unkind, indifferent

✱ **Read through the list of words in the left margin to help you understand what honest is and what it isn't (opposites). Below, write your definition of honest.**

Honest is ____

____

✱ Read the list of words in the left margin to help you understand the perversions of honesty. Can you think of an experience when you have observed this kind of behavior? If so, who was involved, and when?

____

____

✱ What are eight virtues of the mind of Christ?

P ________ P ________ G________ R ________

M ________ F________ S________ H________

✱ Conclude this unit of study by asking God to continue molding and shaping your life to discard every attitude and behavior that does not measure up to the standard set by Christ. Ask God to perfect these virtues in your life.

UNIT 5

Day 1
Love

Day 2
Joy and Peace

Day 3
Patience and Kindness

Day 4
Goodness and Faithfulness

Day 5
Gentleness and Self-Control

Scripture Memory Verse
The fruit of the Spirit is love, joy, peace, patience, kindness, goodness, faithfulness, gentleness, self-control; against such things there is no law.
Galatians 5:22-23

Fruit of the Spirit

Hymn Part 2—Christ's Lifestyle
Who, although He existed in the form of God, did not regard equality with God a thing to be grasped (Phil. 2:6).

What Is in This Unit for Me?

The nine virtues in *Galatians 5:22-23* are the fruit of the Holy Spirit, who dwells in you. The more you develop the mind of Christ, the less you will display your old nature, because you will allow the Holy Spirit to display more of His nature. This week you will display more of the qualities of Christ. God will continue working on developing discernment in you. As you measure your thoughts against the perfection of Christ, God will continue to renew your mind with the virtues of Christ.

Lifelong Objective

In Christ, you will develop the mental quality of discernment and use it to display love, joy, peace, patience, kindness, goodness, faithfulness, gentleness, and self-control.

How God Will be Working in You

Christ's lifestyle in you is a result of developing the mental quality of discernment. God's goal is your virtue. Your growth in Christ's character can only be measured by your perfection. Christ enables your virtue in His position as Model. He makes your virtue possible.

Unit Learning Goals

- You will understand the difference between the nine virtues in *Galatians 5:22-23* and their opposites and perversions.
- You will know the nine virtues that are the fruit of the Spirit.
- You will demonstrate a spiritual hunger for Christ to establish these virtues in your mind.

What You Will Do to Begin Developing the Virtues of Godly Wisdom

- You will study nine virtues, their opposites and perversions.
- You will become familiar with the Lifelong Helps on pages 189-220.
- You will focus your attention on one of the virtues and begin using the Helps to move toward maturity in that virtue.

Lifelong Helps Related to This Unit

Christlike Virtues (pp. 192-202)

The Mind of Christ Cards Related to This Unit

4A. Unit 5: Scripture Memory—*Galatians 5:22-23*

7B. Fruit of the Spirit	12A-B. Love	15B. Kindness
13A-B. Love Is—*1 Cor. 13*	16A. Goodness	14A. Joy
16B. Faithfulness	14B. Peace	17A. Gentleness
15A. Patience	17B. Self-Control	

Love

DAY 1

✳ **Begin today's lesson by reading the Bible verses and the name of Christ for today. Work on your memory verse. Then use the suggested prayer to begin your study.**

We're going to begin this week with a review of last week. Remember the virtues we studied from *James 3:17*? For each of the virtues, we looked at three aspects:

1. What it is (Christlike Virtue).
2. What it isn't (Satanic Opposite).
3. How it can be distorted (Perversion).

✳ **This is a test. Below, we've jumbled up the virtues, opposites, and perversions from last week. See if you can place them in the right categories. Circle the virtues, cross out the opposites, and underline the perversions.**

brutal	approachable	gentle	harsh
honest	indulgent	lustful	lying
merciful	merciless	pure	self-righteous
unapproachable	spoiling	yes-person	

After you finish, check your answers with the chart on page 65.

The Holy Spirit will help you understand the difference between the virtues, their opposites, and their perversions as He continues to develop the spiritual quality of discernment in your life.

This week's format will be the same as last week's, only we'll be looking at *Galatians 5:22-23* instead of *James 3:17*. This passage is referred to as the Fruit of the Spirit. Jesus described His life's mission in terms of the leadership of the Holy Spirit. In Week Ten, we'll be looking more closely at the relationship between Jesus and the Holy Spirit, but keep in mind that Jesus is God. The Holy Spirit is also God. They are not two Gods, but different persons of the Trinity. God has expressed Himself to us in three persons, Father, Son, and Holy Spirit. Thus, the Fruit of the Spirit is also an expression of the mind of Christ.

✳ **Pray as you read the chart of the virtues in *Galatians 5:22-23*. Ask God to guide you to one virtue He would like you to work on this week. Circle it.**

Satanic Opposite	Christlike Virtue	Perversion
Hate, Fear	*Love*	Possessive, permissive
Pain	*Joy*	Frenzy
War	*Peace*	Neutral
Impatient	*Patience*	Lenience
Hard	*Kindness*	Soft
Badness	*Goodness*	Finicky Nice
Unbelief	*Faithfulness*	Presumption
Arrogance	*Gentleness*	Weakness
Undisciplined	*Self-Control*	Fleshly Effort

Today's Bible Meditation
God demonstrates His own love toward us, in that while we were yet sinners, Christ died for us.
Romans 5:8

Name of Christ for Today
The Bridegroom
(John 3:29)

Prayer to Begin the Lesson
Jesus, You love the church like a bridegroom loves his bride. You gave us a new commandment—that we love each other the way You love us. Teach me to love others that way.
Amen.

✳ Now turn to pages 192-202 and fold down the corner of the page corresponding to the virtue you selected. Then, turn to the back and tear out the card that relates to this virtue. Carry it around with you this week and refer to it often to focus your attention on this virtue.

Love

The first fruit of the Spirit is *love.* Jesus' entire life was love. *Having loved His own who were in the world, He loved them to the end (John 13:1).* The ultimate expression of love is unlimited giving of oneself to others. Jesus lived (and died) this expression. Look how He describes it in John:

> *"Greater love hath no one than this, that one lay down his life for his friends" (John 15:13).*

Paul tells us that there is nothing in the entire universe that can separate us from God's love in Jesus Christ (see *Rom. 8:38-39).* There are no human words that can describe the depth of Christ's love for us. Paul says that this love *surpasses knowledge (Eph. 3:19).* No wonder Christ's love controls us *(2 Cor. 5:14).* The love of Christ is the motivating factor in the Christian life.

✳ What is one virtue of the mind of Christ?

L ____________	Joy	Peace
Patience	Kindness	Goodness
Faithfulness	Gentleness	Self-Control

Love:
affection, compassion, benevolence, adoration, fondness, commitment

Opposites of Love:
hate, animosity, dislike, enmity, hostility, ill-will, malice, fear, vindictiveness

Perversions of Love:
possessive, overly protective, permissive, smothering love, manipulative

The obvious opposite of love is hate. There are numerous perversions of love, such as permissiveness, protectiveness, and possessiveness. Remember that the perversion of a virtue is that virtue carried to an unhealthy extreme. Think of an overprotective mother who never lets her child play on the swing set because she's afraid he'll get hurt, and you've got a visual image of the perversion of love.

✳ Read through the list of words in the left margin to help you understand what love is and what it isn't (opposites). Below, write your definition of *love.*

Love is ____

✳ Read the list of words in the left margin to help you understand the perversions of love. Can you think of an experience when you have observed this kind of behavior? If so, who was involved, and when?

____

____

Love is probably the greatest virtue of all. Loving God and loving others are the essence of the two greatest commandments *(Mark 12:30-31).* We will look at love more closely in Week 11.

" 'You shall love the Lord your God with all your heart, and with all your soul, and with all your mind, and with all your strength.' The second is this, 'You shall love your neighbor as yourself.' There is no other commandment greater than these" (Mark 12:30-31).

✱ If you still have time, read the Scriptures for Meditation under Love in the Lifelong Helps (p. 198). Then close your study by asking God to show His love through you to a watching world. Ask God to give you specific opportunities to demonstrate love toward someone else.

Joy and Peace

DAY 2

Today's Bible Meditation
"If you keep My commandments, you will abide in My love; just as I have kept My Father's commandments, and abide in His love. These things I have spoken to you, that My joy may be in you, and that your joy may be made full.
John 15:10-11

Name of Christ for Today
Our Peace
(Eph. 2:14)

✱ Begin today's lesson by reading the Bible verse and the name of Christ for today found in the margin. Work on your memory verse. Then use the suggested prayer to begin your study.

Joy

How many portraits of Jesus do you see in which He's smiling? Have you ever seen a stained-glass window rendition of Christ in which He didn't have a somber, serious expression? We sometimes have a hard time picturing Jesus as joyful. Yet, since it is listed as a fruit of the Spirit, and since Jesus was full of the Holy Spirit *(Luke 4:1)*, we know that joy is a Christlike virtue. Jesus took joy in His fellowship with His friends, such as Mary, Martha, and Lazarus *(Luke 10:38-39; John 11:3,5)*. He was filled with joy when His disciples returned from their preaching mission *(Luke 10:21)*. But for Jesus, joy did not depend on outside circumstances. Joy was a constant experience that resulted from being in close fellowship with the Father. Jesus wanted His disciples to have the same kind of joy He had: *"These things I have spoken to you, that My joy may be in you, and that your joy may be full" (John 15:11)*. Later, He promised that their joy after His resurrection would be indestructible—a permanent feature in their lives *(John 16:22)*.

Can you imagine an indestructible joy? Happiness in our lives usually depends on circumstances. Just as the mercury in a thermometer goes up and down depending on the outside temperature, our level of happiness rises and falls according to what's going on around us. But if happiness is a thermometer, joy is a thermostat. A thermostat controls the temperature in a room, while a thermometer just responds to it. Indestructible, God-given joy can sustain a person regardless of surrounding circumstances.

That's why, even on His way to the cross, Jesus was able to be joyful. His joy came

Prayer to Begin the Lesson
*Lord Jesus,
the angels proclaimed Your joy when You came into the world. You are the Prince of Peace. You are my Peace. Guide me to live in such a way that I will know Your joy and Your peace.
Amen.*

from glorifying the Father. *Who for the joy set before Him endured the cross (Heb. 12:2).* On the last night of His life, Jesus prayed:

> *"Father, the hour has come; glorify Thy Son, that the Son may glorify Thee, even as Thou gavest Him authority over all mankind, that to all whom Thou hast given Him, He may give eternal life. And this is eternal life, that they may know Thee, the only true God, and Jesus Christ whom Thou hast sent. I glorified Thee on the earth, having accomplished the work which Thou hast given Me to do" (John 17:1-4).*

Even when facing that hideous death, Jesus' thermostat of joy was set on high. In the parable of the talents, the master commands the faithful servants to *"enter into the joy of your master" (Matt. 25:21-23).* We can enter into the same joy—the joy of Jesus.

✱ What are two virtues of the mind of Christ?

L ____________	J ____________	Peace
Patience	Kindness	Goodness
Faithfulness	Gentleness	Self-Control

The opposite of joy is sadness or hurt. The perversion of joy is frenzy. Like all emotions, joy is under control in the Christlike personality. While it is not controlled by outside circumstances, circumstances can produce a particular expression of joy. Often people settle for pleasure instead of experiencing true joy. There's nothing wrong with pleasure. Jesus took pleasure in being with His friends. But joy is bigger than pleasure. Pleasure comes and goes, but joy remains constant.

✱ Read through the list of words in the left margin to help you understand what joy is and what it isn't (opposites). Below, write your definition of *joy*.

Joy is ____

____

Joy:
delight, gladness, calm, cheerfulness, bliss, enjoyment, contentment, radiance

Opposites of Joy:
pain, hurt, agony, anguish, distress, misery, torment, woe, sadness

Perversions of Joy:
frenzy, maniacal, crazed excitement, hysteria

✱ Read the list of words in the left margin to help you understand the perversions of joy. Can you think of an experience when you have observed this kind of behavior? If so, who was involved, and when?

____

____

Peace

We looked last week at the virtue of being peaceable, which deals with how you relate to others. Today, we're talking about the virtue of peace, which deals with a state of being. Since Jesus is the Prince of Peace *(Isa. 9:6)*, peace is His to give, and He gives it to His disciples *(John 14:27)*.

Jesus warned against worry *(Matt. 6:25,34)*. Worry and insecurity are the same thing. When you're feeling insecure about something, you can't act decisively. (When was the last time you asked someone out when you were feeling insecure?) But Jesus always acted decisively. When He healed somebody, they were healed for good. Jesus never went backwards in the phases of His life. He had peace with who He was, what He was doing, and where He was going. Wouldn't it be nice to have that kind of peace? He has given it to us!

✱ What are three virtues of the mind of Christ?

L ____________	J ____________	P____________
Patience	**Kindness**	**Goodness**
Faithfulness	**Gentleness**	**Self-Control**

Jesus was able to give this kind of peace to His disciples. This gift was given at the end of His life after the disciples had observed Him for about three and a half years. Jesus talked with them extensively about important information they would need after His death:

- the Holy Spirit
- remaining in Him
- the treatment they would receive
- His departure and how it would effect them at the hands of the world

Then, He wrapped it up:

> *"Behold, an hour is coming, and has already come, for you to be scattered, each to his own home, and to leave Me alone; and yet I am not alone, because the Father is with Me. These things I have spoken to you, that in Me you may have peace. In the world you have tribulation, but take courage; I have overcome the world" (John 16:32-33).*

This is one of the greatest promises we have as Christians. The world will always give us trouble, but we are in Christ. And Christ has overcome the world!

Peace is resting on the character and achievements of Christ.

The opposite of peace is war. If you remember back in Week Two, we talked about how lusts produce war within us. The mind of Christ, however, does not conflict, or war, with itself. Peace is to be whole, not fragmented by warring inner factions.

✱ Read through the list of words in the margin to help you understand what peace is and what it isn't (opposites). Below, write your definition of *peace*.

Peace is ____

____

The perversion of peace is being neutral. One of the most graphic rebukes of Jesus was for lukewarm, halfway, neutral, people. Look at *Revelation 3:15-16:*

Peace:
rest, quietness, tranquility, harmony, serenity

Opposites of Peace:
war, rage, havoc, discord, conflict, strife, rivalry, clash, feud, brawl, rift, worry

Perversions of Peace:
neutrality, lukewarmness, indifference, detached, uncommitted, uninvolved

> *"I know your deeds, that you are neither cold nor hot; I would that you were cold or hot. So because you are lukewarm, and neither hot nor cold, I will spit you out of My mouth."*

A lukewarm person rides the fence between hot and cold, "playing it cool" to impress certain people, and "being on fire" for God at other times to impress other people. Jesus has little use for this kind of hypocritical compromising.

Neutrality can also paralyze people from fighting against injustice. We've all heard stories about people who have ignored cries for help during a big-city mugging. Their excuse was that they "didn't want to get involved." This kind of bland neutrality has nothing to do with peace.

✱ **Read the list of words in the left margin to help you understand the perversions of peace. Can you think of an experience when you have observed this kind of behavior? If so, who was involved, and when?**

____

____

Yesterday, I asked you to pick out one virtue in your life that God wanted you to work on. You marked the section of Lifelong Helps that talked about that virtue. As you conclude today's study, turn to that page, and prayerfully read through the section, "Showing _________." Ask God to show you any actions or attitudes that are not like this virtue. Seek forgiveness, and ask God to renew your mind and actions so that you can more closely reflect that virtue in your life.

Patience and Kindness

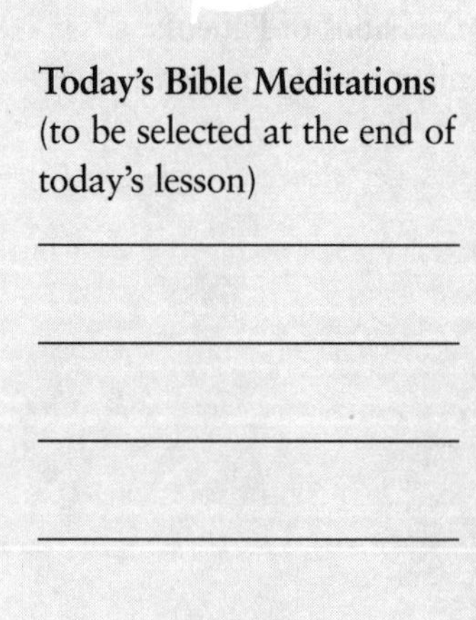

✱ **Begin today's lesson by reading the Bible verses and the name of Christ for today. Work on your memory verse. Then use the suggested prayer to begin your study.**

Patience

The next virtue in Galatians is *patience*. We're going to start off today looking at an example of how Jesus showed patience. Even when He was under incredible stress, He was patient with His disciples:

> *Then Jesus came with them to a place called Gethsemane, and said to His disciples, "Sit here while I go over there and pray."*
>
> *And He took with Him Peter and the two sons of Zebedee, and began to be grieved and distressed. Then He said to them, "My soul is deeply grieved, to the point of death; remain here and keep watch with Me."*
>
> *And He went a little beyond them, and fell on His face and prayed, saying, "My Father, if it is possible, let this cup pass from Me; yet not as I will, but as Thou wilt."*
>
> *And He came to the disciples and found them sleeping, and said to Peter, "So, you men could not keep watch with Me for one hour? Keep watching and praying, that you may not enter into temptation; the spirit is willing, but the flesh is weak."*
>
> *He went away again a second time and prayed, saying, "My Father if this cannot pass away unless I drink it, Thy will be done." And again He came and found them sleeping, for their eyes were heavy.*
>
> *And He left them again, and went away and prayed a third time, saying the same thing once more. Then He came to the disciples and said to them, "Are you still sleeping and taking your rest? Behold the hour is at hand and the Son of Man is being betrayed into the hands of sinners. Arise, let us be going; behold, the one who betrays Me is at hand!" (Matt. 26:36-46)*

The opposite of *patient* is, obviously, *impatient*. Impatience reveals anxiety, intolerance, irritability, and many other un-Christlike qualities. The perversion is lenience.

✱ **Read the list of words in the margin (p. 86) to help you understand what patient is and what it isn't (opposites). Below, write your definition of patient.**

Patient is ____

____

✱ **Read the list of words in the margin (p. 86) to help you understand the perversions of patient. Can you think of an experience when you have observed this kind of behavior? If so, who was involved, and when?**

____

____

Today's Bible Meditations
(to be selected at the end of today's lesson)

____

____

____

____

Name of Christ for Today
A Life-Giving Spirit
(1 Cor. 15:45)

Prayer to Begin the Lesson
*Jesus, You are alive in me!
You are a life-giving spirit.
You've given me life,
both eternal and abundant.
Thank You for the life
You've given me. Thank
You for being kind and
patient with me when I
don't measure up to Your
standards. Continue Your
life in me that I may be
patient and kind with others.
Amen.*

Patient:
endurance, constancy, hanging in there, steadfastness, perseverance

Opposites of Patient:
impatient, edgy, chafing, crabby, touchy, hotheaded, rash, impulsive

Perversions of Patient:
lenient, indulgent, permissive

Jesus was patient, but He was never lenient with His disciples. There were many times when His disciples just didn't seem to get it. Jesus would be talking about His impending death, and they would be arguing over which of them would be the greatest in Heaven! (See *Mark 9:34; 10:35-45; Luke 22:24-27.)* The disciples didn't learn humility in spite of Jesus' efforts to teach them. They were not chosen for how quickly they caught on to things!

But Jesus put up with them, and often retaught material He had covered with them already. For example, *Mark 8* records a feeding of the four thousand shortly after the feeding of the five thousand. You might say that the disciples needed a refresher course on how God could provide for their physical needs! But shortly after the miracle, Jesus overhears a discussion the disciples are having on the boat. It seems they had forgotten to bring any bread for the boat ride.

> *And Jesus, aware of this, said to them, "Why do you discuss the fact that you have no bread? Do you not yet see or understand? Do you have a hardened heart? Having eyes, do you not see? And having ears, do you not hear? And do you not remember, when I broke the five loaves for the five thousand, how many baskets full of broken pieces you picked up?" They said to Him, "Twelve."*
>
> *"And when I broke the seven for the four thousand, how many large baskets full of broken pieces did you pick up?"*
>
> *And they said to Him, "Seven." And He was saying to them, "Do you not yet understand?" (Mark 8:17-21)*

✻ What are four virtues of the mind of Christ?

L ____________	J ____________	P____________
P____________	**Kindness**	**Goodness**
Faithfulness	**Gentleness**	**Self-Control**

Kindness

The fifth fruit of the Spirit is *kindness.* We usually imagine a kindly old grandparent when we think of this word. The word in Galatians that is translated "kindness" describes an attitude or disposition that goes beyond just doing kind deeds for people. Jesus displayed kindness. He dealt tenderly with children, with the helpless, with the lame and impaired. With those that needed firmness, Jesus was uncompromising and firm. With the vulnerable, Jesus dealt sympathetically. We see one of the kindest actions from Jesus when He healed the leper after the Sermon on the Mount.

> *And when He had come down from the mountain, great multitudes followed Him. And behold, a leper came to Him, and bowed down to Him, saying, "Lord, if You are willing, You can make me clean." And He stretched out His hand and touched him, saying, "I am willing; be cleansed." And immediately his leprosy was cleansed. And Jesus said to him, "See that you tell no one; but go, show yourself to the priest, and present the offering that Moses commanded, for a testimony to them" (Matt. 8:1-4).*

✻ **What are five virtues of the mind of Christ?**

L __________	**J __________**	**P __________**
P __________	**K __________**	**Goodness**
Faithfulness	**Gentleness**	**Self-Control**

The opposite of *kindness* is "hardness of heart." The perversion of it is "to do good deeds for others in order to win their approval." Kindness is not rewarded by how people will pay you back. Kindness is its own reward, because the person who is demonstrating kindness is becoming more like Christ.

✻ **Read through the list of words in the margin to help you understand what kindness is and what it isn't (opposites). Below, write your definition of *kindness.***

Kindness is ____

____

✻ **Read the list of words in the margin to help you understand the perversions of kindness. Can you think of an experience when you have observed this kind of behavior? If so, who was involved, and when?**

____

____

✻ **Turn to the Lifelong Helps to the virtue you are focusing on this week. Read the Scriptures for Meditation and select one that is especially meaningful. Write it in the left margin under "Today's Bible Meditation" at the beginning of today's lesson. Spend some time with God to seek understanding of the verse and the virtue. Ask God to help you in making that virtue evident in your life.**

Kindness:
goodness of heart, integrity, goodness in deeds or actions

Opposites of Kindness:
hard, severity, harsh, rough, abusive, bitter, cruel, violent, fierce, blunt, brash, rude, short, unkind

Perversions of Kindness:
mushy, sappy, negligence, inattentive, careless, unchecked, coddling, indulgent

Today's Bible Meditation
Now it is required that those who have been given a trust must prove faithful.
1 Corinthians 4:2

Name of Christ for Today
The Good Shepherd
(John 10:11)

Prayer to Begin the Lesson
Jesus, Good Shepherd,
guide me in the paths
of righteousness.
Feed me on the riches
of Your truth.
Quench my thirst
for fellowship with You!
Amen.

Goodness and Faithfulness

✷ **Begin today's lesson by reading the Bible verses and the name of Christ for today. Work on your memory verse. Then use the suggested prayer to begin your study.**

Goodness

Ben glanced at his watch. A look of irritation came across his face as he tapped on the watch's face repeatedly.

"What's wrong?" asked Stacy.

"Oh, it's this watch. It's no good," said Ben.

The next virtue in the list from Galatians is *goodness.* As it's used here, and as Jesus used it, good is talking about whether or not something is working, like Ben's watch. In the parable of the talents, for example, the master called the servants who had invested well "good and faithful" servants (see *Matt. 25:23).* They were called "good" because they worked, or produced. In the same way, Jesus said that a "good" tree produces "good" fruit (see *Matt. 7:17).* Something is good when it works.

Please don't confuse this with any idea that you have to "work" your way to God's approval. The Bible is very clear that it is by the grace of God that we're saved, not by anything that we do or produce (see *Eph. 2:8-9).* God's love for you is not based on how productive you are. What we are talking about here is a fruit of the Spirit. When the Holy Spirit is active in your life, you will be productive for Him.

Jesus obviously produced. After one particular healing of a deaf man, the crowds *were utterly astonished, saying, "He has done all things well; He makes even the deaf to hear, and the dumb to speak" (Mark 7:37).* He had a success rate of 100 percent! His can't-miss ratio showed that God the Father was endorsing all His works. In this way, Jesus was good.

✷ **What are six virtues of the mind of Christ?**

L ____________	**J** ____________	**P** ____________
P ____________	**K** ____________	**G** ____________
Faithfulness	**Gentleness**	**Self-Control**

Jesus was also good in the way we more often think of good—wholesome and pure. He loved His friends, and He worked hard at building good, wholesome friendships. He enjoyed human life. It was good to Him, and worthy of His blessing. Jesus showed goodness at its best.

The opposite of *goodness* is *badness.* One perversion of it is to be a "goody-two-shoes." While Jesus was absolutely good, He was never seen as a "goody-goody." As I mentioned, He loved His friends, and we can tell from the Scriptures that He loved to eat with His friends. So much so that the Pharisees (who were seen as "goody-goodies") accused Him of being a glutton and a drunkard (see *Matt. 11:19).* Jesus was neither one. Though He obviously loved eating, He knew when to stop.

Think about the humanness of Jesus. Would a bunch of rough, burly fisherman follow a goody-goody? Yet the Bible says that James and John left their nets and followed Jesus (see *Mark 1:18)*. Would children be attracted to an uptight, persnickety personality? Yet the Bible says that little children often came to Jesus (see *Mark 10:13-14)*. Goodness does not mean being a finicky, uptight, goody-two-shoes.

Goodness:
uprightness of heart and life, moral, wholesome, productive, functioning, working order

Opposites of Goodness:
badness, unwholesome, evil, corruption, depravity, immorality, spoiled, wickedness, non-functioning, non-productive

Perversions of Goodness:
goody-two-shoes, self-righteous

✷ Read through the list of words in the margin to help you understand what goodness is and what it isn't (opposites). Below, write your definition of *goodness*.

Goodness is ____

____

✷ Read the list of words in the margin to help you understand the perversions of goodness. Can you think of an experience when you have observed this kind of behavior? If so, who was involved, and when?

____

____

Faithfulness

The seventh fruit of the Spirit is *faithfulness*. Jesus was faithful in His love for His disciples (see *John 13:1)*. Jesus is faithful in His promises:

> *"If you ask Me anything in My name, I will do it" (John 14:14).*
> *"I will not leave you as orphans; I will come to you" (John 14:18).*
> *"After a little while the world will behold Me no more; but you will behold Me; because I live, you shall live also" (John 14:19).*

Jesus was faithful to the work that God had called Him to until His dying breath:

> *After this, Jesus, knowing that all things had already been accomplished, in order that the Scripture might be fulfilled, said, "I am thirsty." A jar full of sour wine was standing there; so they put a sponge full of the sour wine upon a branch of hyssop, and brought it up to His mouth. When Jesus therefore had received the sour wine, He said, "It is finished!" (John 19:28-30).*

Jesus is our faithful High Priest, according to *Hebrews 3:1*. He is the *faithful witness* in *Revelation 1:5*. And in *Hebrews 13:8*, the Bible says that *Jesus Christ is the same yesterday and today, yes and forever.*

There aren't many examples of faithfulness in our world today. Almost all of us have been affected by divorce, either in our own families or in others' that we know. Every week at school, it seems like another "perfect couple," who had claimed "true love always" to each other, breaks up. Someone who is the same yesterday, today, and forever is hard to come by. But Jesus is the standard for faithfulness by which we measure ourselves.

Faithfulness:
trustworthiness, integrity, reliability, loyalty, dependability, consistency

Opposites of Faithfulness:
faithlessness, fickleness, untrustworthiness, inconsistency, unreliability, uncertainty

Perversions of Faithfulness:
legalism, workaholism, over-committed, fanatical, overly zealous, extremism

✱ **What are seven virtues of the mind of Christ?**

L ____________	**J** ____________	**P** ____________
P ____________	**K** ____________	**G** ____________
F ____________	**Gentleness**	**Self-Control**

The opposite of *faithfulness* is *faithlessness* or *fickleness*. All of us, in some measure, are fickle in our faith. We don't measure up to the high standard of Jesus for faithfulness. The perversion of *faithfulness* is *legalism*—doing the right things for the wrong reason. Jesus constantly battled against the Pharisees, who were very faithful to the law, but their hearts were a million miles away from Christ (see *Matt. 15:8)*.

✱ **Read through the list of words in the margin (p. 89) to help you understand what faithfulness is and what it isn't (opposites). Below, write your definition of *faithfulness.***

Faithfulness is ____

____

✱ **Read the list of words in the margin (p. 89) to help you understand the perversions of faithfulness. Can you think of an experience when you have observed this kind of behavior? If so, who was involved, and when?**

____

____

✱ **Pray as you close today's study. Ask God to wash away those things in your life that don't measure up to His standards of goodness and faithfulness. Ask Him to make you a more faithful disciple, as well as a more faithful friend to others. Invite God to complete His work in you.**

Gentleness and Self-Control

✱ **Begin today's lesson by reading the Bible verses and the name of Christ for today. Work on your memory verse. Then use the suggested prayer to begin your study.**

Gentleness

The next virtue we come to is *gentleness.* Now, before you start feeling a sense of deja vu from last week's lesson, let me say that the word for gentleness here is different from the word in *James 3:17.* Here, the word may be thought of more as the King James Version translates it—meekness. But be careful! Oftentimes, when you start talking about "meek" people start imagining little timid mice. That is a perversion of meekness, or gentleness. There was nothing mousy about Jesus when He said:

> *"Come to Me, all who are weary and heavy-laden, and I will give you rest. Take My yoke upon you, and learn from Me, for I am gentle and humble in heart; and you shall find rest for your souls. For My yoke is easy, and My load is light" (Matt. 11:28-30).*

✱ **What are eight virtues of the mind of Christ?**

L ____________	J ____________	P ____________
P ____________	K ____________	G ____________
F ____________	G ____________	**Self-Control**

The word Paul uses here is best thought of as "strength under control." Imagine a caged lion. Very strong, but able to be controlled. That's the kind of gentleness Paul had in mind when he was writing to the Galatians, and that's what God desires to develop in you. This is a subject we will look at more closely when we study servanthood next week, and the Beatitudes in week 7.

✱ **Read through the list of words in the margin (p. 92) to help you understand what gentleness is and what it isn't (opposites). Below, write your definition of *gentleness.***

Gentleness is ____

____

____

✱ **Read the list of words in the margin (p. 92) to help you understand the perversions of gentleness. Can you think of an experience when you have observed this kind of behavior? If so, who was involved, and when?**

Today's Bible Meditation
"Take My yoke upon you, and learn from Me, for I am gentle and humble in heart; and you shall find rest for your souls."
Matthew 11:29

Name of Christ for Today
The True Vine
(John 15:1)

Prayer to Begin the Lesson
Heavenly Father,
You are the Gardener, and Jesus is the True Vine. Help me to be fruit on that vine, taking my nourishment from You, and growing in You. Prune away things and activities in my life so I can be most fruitful. Holy Spirit, please bear your fruit through me.
Amen.

Gentleness:
meekness, humility,
accepting God's dealings with us as good without resisting Him,
a fruit of power,
lowly before God and humble before people

Opposite of Gentleness:
arrogance, haughtiness, pride, cockiness, egotism,
vanity, conceit

Perversions of Gentleness:
weakness, wimpy, cowardly, spinelessness,
timidity

Self-Control:
strength, discipline, restraint, willpower under the direction and operation of the Holy Spirit, mastery over sinful desires

Opposites of Self-Control:
undisciplined, self-indulgent, slothful, compulsive,
lazy, sluggish

Perversions of Self-Control:
Stoic, fleshly effort,
self-effort, obsessive

____

____

____

Self-Control

The last virtue is *self-control.* Notice in the word the most important element of self-control: *self.* Self-control is a discipline that can't be imposed by an outside source. It can't be achieved by energy or training. No, self-control is a fruit of the Spirit. The spiritual Christian has this quality not because of anything he or she does but because the Holy Spirit is at work in his or her life. And the more we allow the Spirit to be active in our lives, the more self-control develops.

Self-control is another easily observable virtue. You can see it developing in your life as you get into the habits of prayer, Bible study, and witnessing. We see self-control in the life of Jesus in His discipline of prayer. For example, He prayed all night before choosing the disciples *(Luke 6:12).* Frequently, He rose early in the morning to pray (see *Mark 1:35).* It's obvious that Jesus was a disciplined scholar of Scripture from His enormous knowledge of it. Look at the self-control Jesus displayed in His trial before Pilate:

> *Now Jesus stood before the governor, and the governor questioned Him, saying, "Are You the King of the Jews?" And Jesus said to him, "It is as you say." And while He was being accused by the chief priests and elders, He made no answer. Then Pilate said to Him, "Do You not hear how many things they testify against You?" And He did not answer him with regard to even a single charge, so that the governor was quite amazed (Matt. 27:11-14).*

✱ **What are nine virtues of the mind of Christ?**

L __________	J __________	P __________
P __________	K __________	G __________
F __________	G __________	S__________

The opposite of *self-control* is to be *undisciplined.* The perversion is *Stoicism.* The Stoics were a group of Greek philosophers who believed that by adopting a rigorously self-denying lifestyle, they could reach intellectual perfection. Maybe the best modern day example of a perversion of self-control is with eating disorders. People suffering from anorexia have pushed self-control to such an absurd extreme that it is killing them. Their self-control is an illusion: they are no more in control over the compulsion not to eat than others can control the compulsion to eat. Self-control and self-effort are not the same thing. The spiritual Christian always remembers that *It is God* [not self] *who is at work in you, both to will and to work for His good pleasure (Phil. 2:13).* Self-control is dependent on God's work in our lives.

✱ **Read through the list of words in the left margin to help you understand what self-control is and what it isn't (opposites). Write your definition of *self-control.***

Self-control is ____

____

✱ Read the list of words in the margin **(p. 92)** **to help you understand the perversions of self-control. Can you think of an experience when you have observed this kind of behavior? If so, who was involved, and when?**

____

____

The idea of self-control is carefully taught in the poetry and wisdom literature of the Bible (see *Ps. 141:3; Prov. 16:32;* and *25:28).* When we allow God's Spirit to rule in our lives, we know that the outcomes are in God's hands (see *Prov. 3:5-6; 20:24,* and *Jer. 10:23).*

✱ Conclude this week's study by looking back over the nine Fruit of the Spirit. Pray and ask God to do whatever is necessary in you so that your life will bear this fruit on every occasion.

UNIT 6

Day 1
Two Reasons for Servanthood

Day 2
Serving God and Others

Day 3
The Servant's Job Description, Part 1

Day 4
The Servant's Job Description, Part 2

Day 5
The Servant's Job Description, Part 3

Scripture Memory Verse
"It is enough for the disciple that he become as his teacher, and the slave as his master."
Matthew 10:25

The Servant Mind

Hymn Part 3—Christ's Servanthood
[Jesus] *made himself nothing, taking the very nature of a servant (Phil. 2:7, NIV).*

What Is in This Unit for Me?

Having the servant mind of Christ frees God to do great things through you. You will discover a power and a peace of God you've never experienced in your life before as you allow Him to be the Master.

Lifelong Objective

In Christ, you will take on the form of a servant and serve God and others with the heart and mind of a servant.

How God Will be Working In You

This week, God is working on the mental quality of willingness. God's goal is the business of the Kingdom. You will be measuring your growth in servanthood against the example of Christ. Christ will lead you in His role as Master.

Unit Learning Goals

- You will know two reasons for being a servant.
- You will demonstrate your lowliness before God.
- You will understand the importance of serving God and others.
- You will know 14 characteristics of servanthood.
- You will indicate your willingness for God to develop these characteristics in your life.
- You will submit to God as your Master.

What You Will Do to Begin Developing the Servant Mind

- You will ask God to mold you into the image of His Son, the perfect servant.
- You will look at 14 characteristics of servanthood and how Jesus demonstrated them.
- You will see how the characteristics of servanthood free God to do His work in and through you.
- You will give God permission to give you any assignment as His servant.

Lifelong Helps Related to This Week

Servanthood Instrument (p. 203)

The Mind of Christ Cards Related to This Week

4A. Unit 6: Scripture Memory—*Matthew 10:25*
18A. The Servant Mind 1
18B. The Servant Mind 2
19A. The Servant Mind 3
19B. The Servant Mind 4

Two Reasons for Servanthood

DAY 1

✱ **Begin today's lesson by reading the Bible verse and the name of Christ for today. Work on your memory verse. Then use the suggested prayer to begin your study.**

Job Description

Imagine this: It's summertime, you're out of school, and you're looking through the want ads for a summer job, so you can make a little extra cash to put gas in the car. You come across this ad:

> Servant: Needed immediately: servants to help build a kingdom of enormous proportions. Must be willing to work long hours with no recognition whatsoever for yourself. Must be willing to leave everything behind, including, family, friends, reputation, and possibly own life. No experience necessary; in fact, everything you have done up to this point will be counted as rubbish. Compensation: eternal reward, recognition by the Master as a good and faithful servant.

✱ **Would you take this job? Check your response:**

- ❑ **Yes. In a heartbeat.**
- ❑ **You must be joking. No way.**

In today's world, the qualifications for a servant seem ludicrous. Who would want a job like that? No glory for yourself? Nothing but a pat on the back from the Master—a "Well done, good and faithful servant?" You would be hard-pressed to find applicants for this job by the world's standards. Yet, the Bible is full of stories of people who signed up for this duty. Abraham, Isaac, Jacob, Moses, Samuel, David, Job, Simeon, Paul, Peter, Timothy, James, Jude, and others. They were servants because they chose to worship the one true God.

Of course, the ultimate example of servanthood is Jesus Himself. Jesus' entire life was about servanthood. This week, we will be looking at how Jesus demonstrated the qualities of a servant.

The Lost Concept of Servanthood

We've pretty much lost the concept of servanthood in America today. When domestic servants were common, the aspects of servanthood—humility, subjection to someone else's authority, and obedience—were easily understood. We no longer have a need for human servants today—now that we've got computers, microwave ovens, and washing machines.

Democracy and servanthood don't exactly complement one another, either. As Americans, we are accustomed to the idea that everyone is equal. Servanthood is about a servant being less than equal to his or her master.

So in human terms, we don't really understand servanthood. Slavery has been abolished, as it should have been. Dictatorships in which rulers have absolute authority, are looked down upon as morally unacceptable. Many social institutions that were

Today's Bible Meditations

[Jesus] made himself of no reputation, and took upon him the form of a servant.

Philippians 2:7

From everyone who has been given much shall much be required; and to whom they entrusted much, of him they will as all the more.

Luke 12:48

Name of Christ for Today

Righteous Servant

(Isa. 53:11, NIV*)*

Prayer to Begin the Lesson

Lord Jesus,
It seems like no one in the world wants me to be a servant except for You. Everyone seems to say, "Look out for yourself! Do what it takes to get to the top." You have such a different message, Jesus, and it's You that I want to follow. This week, teach me what it means to be a servant, and remind me of servanthood's rewards.
Amen.

based on inequality have been done away with, and the world is generally better off without them.

The problem is, we've lost a concept of biblical servanthood. Since we've grown up saying the Pledge of Allegiance every morning ("with liberty and justice for all"), we usually refuse to submit ourselves to others. This often carries over into refusal to submit to other believers, the church, and even to God.

Now, the fact is, God is the only One who deserves to have any servants. Any human being who tries to exercise absolute authority over another human being will ultimately mess it up. God is the only One who can handle the responsibility. And if we can get over our resistance to the idea of servanthood, the rewards are incredible.

✳ Which of the following is true in your opinion? Check one:

- ❑ **Most Christians have a good view of servanthood and they regularly practice mutual submission to one another.**
- ❑ **Most Christians are clueless about biblical servanthood, and they resist submission to one another.**

Two Reasons for Servanthood

The Bible gives us two reasons for why we should be a servant. First, it's a command. *Philippians 2:7* tells us to think like Jesus, who *took upon him the form of a servant.* We are to think like servants. Many of Jesus' parables describe the relationships in God's kingdom as that of servants to a master or king. One truth that these parables emphasize over and over is that servants will be called to give an account of their servanthood. Likewise, Jesus will call His servants to give an account for their servanthood. He expects us to be His servants.

✳ What is one reason for being a servant?

____

✳ How would Jesus evaluate your servanthood today? Check one:

- ❑ **Well done. You've been a faithful servant and a good manager.**
- ❑ **Poorly done. You've been wicked and lazy in your service and a poor manager.**
- ❑ **Other** ______________________________

Another reason we should be servants is because Jesus is. Did you know that the term *Christian* literally means "little Christ"? That means that we are to imitate Jesus in everything we do. Before the Lord's Supper, Jesus washed His disciples feet. In Jesus' day, this was a duty done by the lowliest servant in a household. When He was finished, He told His disciples, *"If I then, the Lord and the Teacher, washed your feet, you also ought to wash one another's feet. For I gave you an example that you also should do as I did to you" (John 13:14-15).* Why did Jesus wash His disciple's feet? He wasn't as interested in clean feet as He was in the disciples learning about servanthood.

✳ What is a second reason you should be a servant?

____

Does God need us to be His servants? Of course not. He's the Creator of the Universe. There isn't anything He needs. He doesn't need our money, our talents, our intelligence, or our service. So if He doesn't need it, why does He demand our service? Simple. Servanthood isn't meant to meet God's needs, but our needs. Servanthood does more for us than it could ever do for the Lord.

✳ Conclude today's study by starting to learn your memory verse, *Matthew 10:25*. Can you find satisfaction in being like your Master? Pray that nothing else will satisfy you except serving the Lord. Ask God to help you develop an attitude of servanthood this week.

Serving God and Others

DAY 2

✳ Begin today's lesson by reading the Bible verse and the name of Christ for today. Work on your memory verse. Then use the suggested prayer to begin your study.

We talked a lot yesterday about the world's system, and how, according to the world's rules, servanthood is at the bottom. But there's a little-known secret to the Christian life, and I'm going to let you in on it now: The key to greatness is servanthood. It's not power, or position, or fame. One day, Salome, the mother of James and John, learned this lesson when she came to Jesus with an unusual request for her sons. She wanted her sons to be given thrones on the right and left side of Jesus when He came into His kingdom. When the other disciples heard about this, they were pretty ticked off (probably because they hadn't thought of asking the same thing). But Jesus explained to them the upside-down route to greatness in the kingdom of God.

✳ Read what Jesus said to the disciples in *Matthew 20:25-28*. Circle the world's ways to greatness. Then, underline God's way to greatness in the kingdom.

> *But Jesus called them to Himself, and said, "You know that the rulers of the Gentiles lord it over them, and their great men exercise authority over them. It is not so among you, but whoever wishes to become great among you shall be your servant, and whoever wishes to be first among you shall be your slave; just as the Son of Man did not come to be served, but to serve, and to give His life a ransom for many" (Matt. 20:25-28).*

Greatness, coming through lowly servanthood? Hard to believe, isn't it? Even most Christians have a hard time accepting this part of Jesus' teaching. The least shall be greatest and the last shall be first! Think how different theme parks would be if that's how they worked the lines for rides and attractions!

Today's Bible Meditation
"No servant can serve two masters; for either he will hate the one, and love the other, or else he will hold to one, and despise the other. You cannot serve God and mammon."
Luke 16:13

Name of Christ for Today
Our Passover
(1 Cor. 5:7)

Prayer to Begin the Lesson
Lord Jesus,
You came as a servant
of God in order to go to

the cross on my behalf. You were my Passover as you gave Yourself on the cross as the Lamb of God. I can't really understand that kind of love and service. Teach me to love in such a way that I would be willing to give myself in service to God and others.
Amen.

Jesus talked about "the rulers of the Gentiles" to describe the world's way of doing things. In the world, the elite are often determined by heredity or wealth. At school, the most popular students are athletic or have the most leadership skills. Nobody ever strives for greatness by offering to carry your school cafeteria tray. Jesus, however, says that the truly great in heaven, the servants, will be those who are humble.

✱ In God's kingdom, which is the most important for greatness? Check one.

- ❑ **High position of authority**
- ❑ **Influence of a dynamic personality**
- ❑ **Power backed by masses of supporters or intimidating force**
- ❑ **Servanthood**

This truth reverses many of the values you've learned. But when you think about it, this is the only way heaven can work. We imagine the kingdom of Heaven as being a place of perfect peace, where there is a real oneness of spirit. This is only possible when people are mutually submissive to each other, and when all the members of a society behave in this way. There is no competition, no rivalry, and no one who is trying to set himself or herself up as "the boss."

What Kind of a World Is This?

How could a society function if there was no leader? If no one is "the boss," wouldn't this little Utopia just be anarchy? Back up! I didn't say there would be no leader. I said that no one would try to set themselves up as a leader. There would still be a supreme authority. A society based on servanthood could have only one supreme authority, one Master. That Master must be God. Paul knew this lesson well. He wrote, *Am I now seeking the favor of men, or of God? Or am I striving to please men? If I were still trying to please men, I would not be a bond-servant of Christ (Gal. 1:10).* We must be servants of Christ. Our one driving force must be to please Christ and do His will. There can't be anything else in our lives competing for the role of Master. *"No servant can serve two masters; for either he will hate the one, and love the other, or else he will hold to one, and despise the other" (Luke 16:13).*

Serving Each Other

So, here's the order: Love Christ above all else, but serve other's needs above your own. *You were called to freedom, brethren; only do not turn your freedom into an opportunity for the flesh, but through love serve one another (Gal. 5:13).* Is this a contradiction? If we are to serve Christ, and if we can't serve two masters, how can we serve somebody else?

I've used the term *mutual submission* this week. What I mean is that we are not to serve one another as master. We are to serve each other on equal terms. Our obedience is to Christ as our Master; while our service is to one another.

✱ Draw a line matching the service on the left with the motive on the right.

Serve God •	**• In order to become great**
Serve Each Other •	**• Because He is Supreme**
	• Because of love

We serve God because He is supreme. He has the right and authority to demand our service. God is the sovereign Ruler of the universe. We serve each other, not out of a selfish desire to become great, but because God loves us and commands us to love one another. Love serves others by meeting needs.

✱ We're almost halfway through this 12-week introduction to the mind of Christ. Today's lesson is a little shorter than most. Take some time today to review.

- **Review all your memory verses.**
- **Read over your Bondage to Freedom Lists to see the progress you are making.**
- **Review the Lifelong Helps regarding Christlike virtues. Which one is God working on in your life? ____________**

✱ Conclude your study time in prayer. Let God guide your praying according to His desires for you. The Holy Spirit can help you pray when you do not know what to ask for (see *Rom. 8:26-27*). Ask Him to guide you now.

The Servant's Job Description, Part 1

✱ Begin today's lesson by reading the Bible verse and the name of Christ for today. Work on your memory verse. Then use the suggested prayer to begin your study.

Today's Bible Meditation
"So you too, when you do all the things which are commanded you, say, 'We are unworthy slaves; we have done only that which we ought to have done.' "
Luke 17:10

Name of Christ for Today
An Offering and a Sacrifice
(Eph. 5:2)

There is a businesswoman who does a lot of work out of her home. She has two young children who, like all small children, require a lot of attention. So, she hired a nanny to be at the house during the day. She cleans the house, cooks the meals, and takes care of the children.

Now, think about this: for every bed the nanny makes, that's one less bed the businesswoman has to make. For every meal she cooks, that's extra time the businesswoman has to get her work done. You see, when the nanny does her work, that frees the businesswoman to do her work.

The New Testament gives us a picture of what a servant is like. From these passages, we get 14 characteristics that describe the servant mind. You might think of this as elements of the servant's job description. Just as the businesswoman's nanny frees her to get her work done, when we fulfill this job description, we free God to do His work. Now, this job description doesn't really reflect what the servant is supposed to do. It's more a reflection of the kind of person God is looking for to fill the job.

Prayer to Begin the Lesson
Jesus,
You paid it all.
Your perfect offering and sacrifice of Your life make my spiritual life possible.
Thank You. I love You!
I exalt Your name as an offering and Sacrifice to God.
Amen.

THE SERVANT'S JOB DESCRIPTION
(Characteristics of the Servant Mind)

1. Humble	5. Faithful	9. Gentle	13. Good
2. Obedient	6. Watchful	10. Able to Teach	14. Wise
3. Willing	7. Courageous	11. Patient	
4. Loyal	8. Not Quarrelsome	12. Meek	

✳ Which of the following is first in importance for a servant of God? Check One.
- ❏ **Work: What the servant does.**
- ❏ **Character: What the servant is.**

✳ Turn to the back of the book and tear out the Mind of Christ Cards 18 and 19. Review these characteristics during the next few days.

God can train anyone for the job of servant. He's not looking for specific talents and abilities; He'll take care of those. God's first desire for your servanthood is your character. Jesus said, *"A disciple is not above his teacher, nor a slave above his master. It is enough for the disciple that he become as his teacher, and the slave as his master" (Matt. 10:24-25).* Remember, *being* is a lot more important than *doing*. So we're going to take a closer look at these 14 characteristics that need to be true of your mind.

Each of these characteristics was true in Jesus' life. As you seek to develop the mind of Christ, pay attention to His role as the righteous Servant.

✳ Who is your standard and model for these qualities of servanthood?

____

Humble
A proper attitude toward the Master's work in others.
- Fleshly attitude: "Who do you think you are?"
- Humility frees God to manifest Himself in you and through you *(Isa. 57:15).*

1. Humble

The most basic servant characteristic is humble *(Acts 20:19).* The servant must be humble before God in order to obey God, and must be humble before others to fit in with their works of service. Humble people don't seek recognition for their work. They would rather advance the Kingdom than look good to others. They see their work as part of a bigger picture, and that bigger picture is more important to them than their piece of it. Humble people do all they can to learn from other people, and they seek to make others' work easier.

✳ Write one characteristic of the servant mind.

1. ______________ **3. Willing** **5. Faithful**

2. Obedient **4. Loyal**

The quality of humility establishes the fact that we really are members of the body of Christ. Think about the body analogy Paul uses in *1 Corinthians 12: 14-21.*

> *For the body is not one member, but many. If the foot should say, "Because I am not a hand, I am not a part of the body," it is not for this reason any the less a part of the body. And if the ear should say, "Because I am not an eye, I am not a part of the body," it is not for this reason any the less a part of the body. If the whole body were an eye, where would the hearing*

be? If the whole were hearing, where would the sense of smell be? But now God has placed the members, each one of them, in the body, just a He desired. And if they were all one member, where would the body be? But now there are many members, but one body. And the eye cannot say to the hand, "I have no need of you"; or again the head to the feet, "I have no need of you."

Paul paints a pretty ridiculous picture, doesn't he? Imagine all your body parts refusing to cooperate, because each one wanted to lead the body! As ridiculous as it sounds, though, chances are your own youth group has behaved in exactly the same way! But when we demonstrate humility, we free God to manifest Himself as the Leader. God won't take leadership where He's not invited, whether it's in an individual's life or in the life of a youth group. When we humbly step aside, we free God to reveal Himself.

✳ When you are humble, what does that free God to do?

Humility frees God to ______________________________

Jesus was humble. His friends were lowly, common people. He did not normally seek out friendships with influential people. Jesus humbly washed the disciple's feet, and encouraged them to do the same (see *John 13:14-17).* Jesus showed a humble spirit of servanthood.

2. Obedient

Obedience is our second servant characteristic. Obedience is an attitude which sets no limits on what the Master can order. True obedience is instant, not delayed. Once God's will is known, the obedient servant doesn't question it. We obey God because He's God, no matter what. To be obedient means you understand the nature of God's authority. It's like being a private in the army: You don't question an order from a superior officer; you just obey it. Obedience is more important to God than the amount of money you put into the offering plate, the amount of time you spend at church, or even how much of the Bible you read. *1 Samuel 15:22* says, *"To obey is better than sacrifice, and to heed [pay attention] than the fat of rams."* Obedience is the sign of true servanthood, and it is always the best thing you can do in any situation.

Obedient
Understanding the authority of the Master over my time and life.
- Fleshly attitude:
  "In a minute."
  "I'll get around to it."
- When you are an obedient servant *(Eph. 6:5)*, you free God to do mighty acts *(Judg. 7)*.

✳ Write two characteristics of the servant mind.

1. ______________ 3. **Willing** 5. **Faithful**

2. ______________ 4. **Loyal**

Obedience frees God to act in mighty ways. In the Book of Judges, God told Gideon to reduce his army from 32,000 to 300. Gideon did it, and the defeat of the Midianites was one of the greatest in Israel's history. And by cutting back the army from thousands to just a few hundred, there was no doubt in anyone's mind that God had acted in a mighty way (see *Judg. 7:2-7).* Imagine if Gideon had stuck with his original army. Even if he had won (which isn't likely), it wouldn't have been a very memorable battle. God may require strange things. No doubt bystanders thought it was strange when

Joshua marched around and around the city of Jericho *(Josh. 6:1-20)*. But God's grand intentions can only be realized when we are obedient.

✱ When you are obedient, what does that free God to do?

Obedience frees God to ______________________________

Jesus was obedient. His obedience was evident throughout His entire life. He was obedient to His earthly parents *(Luke 2:51)*, and He was obedient to His Heavenly Father. At the end of His life, Jesus declared, *"That the world may know that I love the Father, and as the Father gave Me commandment, even so I do" (John 14:31)*. Jesus obeyed perfectly.

Willing
Identification with the Master's attitudes.

- Fleshly attitude: "You've got to look out for yourself."
- When you are a willing child *(Eph. 6:7)*, you free God to reward divinely.

3. Willing

The third servant characteristic is *willing* (see *Eph. 6:7)*. Our service must be with a whole heart. Sometimes, our behavior depends more on our feelings than our will. But feelings are often confusing. Only the will can be single-minded. Only the will can overcome feelings.

There are days when you may not "feel" like being a Christian. There are days when married people don't "feel" like they're "in love." But married people who are committed to each other look past their feelings and obey their marriage vows. And Christians who are committed to Christ will behave like Christians no matter what they are feeling like at a particular time.

You see, continuing obedience cannot be a result of feelings, but of the will. Even when feelings are out of control, you can still give your will to God. You are to do the will of God with *sincerity of your heart (Eph. 6:5)*.

The will can exist in one of three ways: weak-willed, self-willed, or God-willed. A God-willed person identifies her will with God's. A weak-willed person identifies his or her will with others. This is the source of all peer pressure. A self-willed person (also known as a strong-willed person) rarely submits to anybody. Both weak-willed and self-willed persons are independent of God.

The will is what defines the personality. If your will is independent of God, then your entire personality is independent. When your will identifies with Jesus, and becomes dependent on Christ, that is what having the mind of Christ is all about. Christ's will becomes your will.

✱ Most frequently I am (check one):
❑ Weak-willed. I follow the crowd so easily!
❑ Self-willed. Nobody's gonna tell me what to do!
❑ God-willed.

✱ Write three characteristics of the servant mind.

1. ______________ **3.** ______________ **5. Faithful**

2. ______________ **4. Loyal**

Willingness frees God to reward divinely. You are to obey with all your heart, *knowing that from the Lord you will receive the reward of your inheritance (Col. 3:24)*. Identifying your will with that of God establishes a spiritual likeness.

✻ **When you are willing, what does that free God to do?**

Willingness frees God to ______________________________

Jesus was willing. Christ's identification of His will with that of the Father is one of the striking aspects of His life. Already, we have seen that the dominating desire of Jesus' life was to do the will of His Father. His passion was the Father's will. Most likely, Jesus didn't "feel" like going to the cross. But in the Garden that night, Jesus remained consistent in seeking the Father's will: *"My Father, if this cannot pass away unless I drink it, Thy will be done" (Matt. 26:42).* If the will of the servant is not the same as the will of the Master, the work won't get done.

✻ **Are you willing to obey God and follow Him? How's your humility? Is pride making you more self-willed than God-willed? Ask God to remove any pride that is keeping you from obeying Him.**

DAY 4

The Servant's Job Description, Part 2

✻ **Begin today's lesson by reading the Bible verse and the name of Christ for today. Work on your memory verse. Then use the suggested prayer to begin your study.**

✻ **Let's review from yesterday. Write three characteristics of the servant mind.**

1. ______________ 3. ______________ **5. Faithful**

2. ______________ **4. Loyal**

4. Loyal

The next servant characteristic is *loyal* (see *Luke 16:13).* A loyal person has an undivided heart. When someone is loyal to someone or something, he is truly dependable. Loyalty is a nonnegotiable in the job description for a servant. Obedience to the Master may require sacrifice and even death. Only loyalty remains devoted no matter what the cost. Loyalty is also exclusive. By definition, a person cannot be loyal to more than one thing, because partial loyalty is no loyalty at all. God demands our loyalty. Exodus describes Him as a jealous God (see *Ex. 20:5).* Lordship, like loyalty, cannot be divided. You cannot say no to God and still call Him Lord.

Today's Bible Meditation
"Has the Lord as much delight in burnt offerings and sacrifices as in obeying the voice of the Lord? Behold, to obey is better than sacrifice, and to heed than the fat of rams."
1 Samuel 15:22

Name of Christ for Today
A Teacher Come From God
(John 3:2)

Prayer to Begin the Lesson
Teacher,
You know what will allow me to experience life to the fullest. You came to give me that abundant life.

Teach me the ways of a servant, and I will follow them.
Amen.

Loyal
Unswerving devotion to the Master.
- Fleshly attitude: "You scratch my back, I'll scratch yours."
- When you are a loyal citizen *(Luke 16:13)*, you free God to promote you *(Gen. 39-41)*.

Faithful
Confidence that the Master will continue His plan.
- Fleshly attitude: "I'm tired of this."
- When you are faithful *(1 Cor. 4:2)*, you free God to expand His ministry through you *(Matt. 25:21)*.

✳ What is a fourth characteristic of the servant mind?

1. Humble **3. Willing** **5. Faithful**

2. Obedient **4.** ______________

In 1993, a movie came out called Rudy. It was the true story of a mediocre football player who dreamed of playing for the great Notre Dame football team. He was absolutely loyal to the Fighting Irish. When he finally made the team, he never amounted to much more than a tackling dummy for the first string players. Yet, because of his absolute loyalty, the coach finally allowed him to run a play in the last game of his senior year.

In the same way, loyalty frees God to promote you within Kingdom work. In *Genesis 37-41,* Joseph was betrayed by his brothers, Potiphar's wife, and the cupbearer, yet he remained faithful to his brothers, to Potiphar, and to God. Because he was loyal to God, God was free to promote Joseph. He eventually became the prime minister of Egypt.

✳ When you are loyal, what does that free God to do?

Loyalty frees God to ____

Jesus was loyal. His loyalty to the Father is seen in the dedication of His life to the Father's will. He was also loyal to His disciples. On His last night with them, He prayed, *"While I was with them, I was keeping them in Thy name" (John 17:12)*. Jesus was loyal to death on the cross.

5. Faithful

The fifth qualification for a servant is *faithful (1 Cor. 4:1-2)*. Through Moses, God commanded His people to be faithful: *"You shall fear the Lord your God; you shall serve Him and cling to Him, and you shall swear by His name" (Deut. 10:20)*. When we are faithful, we are reflecting God's own nature, for God is absolutely faithful to us. He says to us, in *Judges 2:1, "I will never break my covenant with you."* When Peter was facing persecution in the early church, his response to the persecutors was *"We must obey God rather than men" (Acts 5:29)*. Time and time again, Jesus praised faithfulness in His parables.

Jesus described us as branches who remain on the True Vine, Himself (see *John 15:1-7)*. A branch that is cut off from the vine shrivels up and dies. But a branch that is faithful to the vine gets nourishment, grows, and bears fruit. In faithfulness, we establish our "branchhood." We can't be faithful just in big things, either. Faithfulness applies to all matters, big and small *(Luke 16:10)*.

✳ Write five characteristics of the servant mind.

1. ______________ 3. ______________ 5. ______________

2. ______________ 4. ______________

Faithfulness frees God to expand His ministry through you. Think back on the parable of the talents. The servant with five talents and the servant with two talents were *"faithful with a few things"* and so the master put them *"in charge of many things" (Matt. 25:21,23).* The more we show ourselves trustworthy, the greater trust God rewards us with.

✳ When you are faithful, what does that free God to do?

Faithfulness frees God to ______________________________

Jesus was faithful to the Father, even to death. He was also faithful to His disciples: *"Having loved His own who were in the world, He loved them to the end" (John 13:1).* Jesus is faithful to us now. His last words to all His disciples (ourselves included) before He ascended into Heaven were, *"I am with you always, even to the end of the age" (Matt. 28:20).* One of Jesus' names is *Faithful and True (Rev. 19:11).*

6. Watchful

The sixth item on the job description is *watchful* (see *Luke 12:35-48).* A watchful servant is always on the alert, prepared for the return of the master. Let's say you had a baby-sitting job, and the people you were baby-sitting for come home an hour early and find you stretched out on their sofa, talking to your boyfriend on the phone, eating their potato chips, while their child is swinging from the dining room chandelier. Do you think you would be asked to baby-sit for that family again? Not likely, because you didn't prove yourself to be a watchful servant! Watchfulness indicates an attitude toward the master. It means you want to know what God says, and what He wants you to do. In Jesus' parables, good servants spent a lot of time waiting. A servant in Jesus' day was expected to be alert at all times.

Watchful
Attentiveness to the Master's voice.
- Fleshly attitude: "I wish I had not said that."
- When you are watchful, you free God to speak *(Hab. 2:1).*

✳ Write one characteristic of the servant mind.

6. ______________	**8. Not Quarrelsome**
7. Courageous	**9. Gentle**

Watchfulness frees the Lord to speak. It reminds me of my third grade teacher, who wouldn't speak until everyone in the class was paying attention to her. In the same way, God speaks when we are alert to His voice. The Old Testament prophet Habakkuk demonstrated the quality of being watchful when he wrote, *I will stand on my guard post....I will keep watch to see what He will speak to me (Hab. 2:1).* Those who are alert for action will hear God's voice.

✳ When you are watchful, what does that free God to do?

Watchfulness frees God to ______________________________

Jesus was watchful. He was always on the lookout for what God wanted Him to do next. He said to His disciples, *"Truly, truly, I say to you, the Son can do nothing of Himself, unless it is something He sees the Father doing; for whatever the Father does, these things the Son also does in like manner" (John 5:19).* Christ always depended on God for direction. The night before He chose His disciples, He stayed up all night in prayer *(Luke 6:12).* A watchful servant remains alert to the Master.

Courageous
Conviction about the Master's priorities.
- Fleshly attitude: "I'm not taking any chances."
- When you are a courageous soldier, you free God to protect you (*Dan. 6:23*).

7. Courageous

Our next servant characteristic is *courageous*. Before Jesus was born, Zechariah's son proclaimed that the Messiah would *"grant us that we... might serve Him without fear, in holiness and righteousness before Him all our days" (Luke 1:74-75)*. David was God's servant, and he fought the giant Goliath without fear (see *1 Sam. 17)*. The servant Daniel defied the king's decree in order to pray to God (see *Dan. 6:10)*. And the Apostle Paul, on a boat that was about to be shipwrecked, told the crew, *"This very night an angel of the God to whom I belong and whom I serve stood before me, saying, 'Do not be afraid....' Therefore, keep up your courage, men, for I believe God" (Acts 27:23-25)*. Courage is a servant quality that demonstrates conviction.

✳ Write two characteristics of the servant mind.

6. ____________________	**8. Not Quarrelsome**
7. ____________________	**9. Gentle**

Courage proves that you are a soldier of God, and it frees God to protect you. When David fought Goliath, he claimed, *"The battle is the Lord's" (1 Sam. 17:47)*. When Daniel was thrown into the lion's den, no wound was found on him the next morning *because he had trusted in his God (Dan. 6:23)*. Paul's faith in God was justified as the entire crew made it safely to shore *(Acts 28:1)*.

✳ When you are courageous, what does that free God to do?

Courage frees God to ____

Jesus was incredibly courageous! He knew from the beginning of His ministry what kind of death He would die. He knew what would happen to Him when He got to Jerusalem. So He headed resolutely toward His own death, with His disciples like scared rabbits behind Him: *They were on the road, going up to Jerusalem, and Jesus was walking on ahead of them; and they were amazed, and those who followed were fearful (Mark 10:32)*. Jesus was courageous.

Not Quarrelsome
Peace that looks for the Master's work in others.
- Fleshly attitude: "Why do they always pick on me?"
- When you are not quarrelsome *(2 Tim. 2:24)*, you free God to focus on the main thing *(Luke 10:41-42)*.

8. Not Quarrelsome

There are five servant qualifications in *2 Timothy 2:24-25: And the Lord's bond-servant must not be quarrelsome, but be kind to all, able to teach, patient when wronged, with gentleness correcting those who are in opposition.* The first of these is a negative: the servant of the Lord must not be quarrelsome.

Have you ever been assigned to a project at school with people that you just didn't get along with? Did you get much work done? Oftentimes, personalities get in the way of efficiency. It happens in the church, too. As servants of God, we are called to work together to build up the Kingdom. As we have seen in past weeks, the true callings and gifts from God complement and enhance one another. Since not everyone has the same gifts (see *1 Cor. 12)*, it is crucial that God's servants not quarrel with each other.

✱ **Write three characteristics of the servant mind.**

6. ____________________ **8.** ____________________

7. ____________________ **9. Gentle**

A servant who possesses the quality not to be quarrelsome is a peacemaker. This frees the lord to focus on the main thing. We lose our focus when we start bickering over picky things, and I always appreciate the person in a meeting who says, "Okay, let's get focused again, folks." That person is a peacemaker.

✱ **When you are not quarrelsome, what does that free God to do?**

Not being quarrelsome frees God to ______________________________

Jesus was not quarrelsome. He never picked a fight or started an argument, although He was quick to reply when confronted. Once, Jesus was asked by a man in the crowd, *"Teacher, tell my brother to divide the family inheritance with me."* Jesus replied, *"Man, who appointed Me a judge or arbiter over you?"* Then He warned, *"Beware, and be on your guard against every form of greed; for not even when one has an abundance does his life consist of his possessions" (Luke 12:13-15).* Jesus refused to get drawn into someone else's quarrel. Instead, He acted as a peacemaker.

✱ **Close this lesson by spending time with Jesus. Continue throughout today in an attitude of watchful prayer. Wait. Listen. Prepare to obey.**

DAY 5

Today's Bible Meditation
"Truly, truly, I say to you, the Son can do nothing of Himself, unless it is something He sees the Father doing; for whatever the Father does, these things the Son also does in like manner."
John 5:19

Name of Christ for Today
The Only Wise God
(1 Tim. 1:17)

Prayer to Begin the Lesson
Only Wise God,
I don't completely understand why servanthood is the way to greatness in Your kingdom.
But You are in control.
Give me the wisdom I lack.
Help me to be as wise as a serpent and as harmless as a dove.
Amen.

The Servant's Job Description, Part 3

✳ Begin today's lesson by reading the Bible verse and the name of Christ for today. Work on your memory verse. Then use the suggested prayer to begin your study.

✳ To review from yesterday, write three characteristics of the servant mind.

6. W________________ **8. N________________**

7. C________________ **9. Gentle**

9. Gentle

This is now the third week in a row that we've emphasized some aspect of gentleness. Do you get the feeling it's pretty important?

Many hair care products and soaps advertise that they are "Gentle Enough to Use Everyday." This means that the shampoo won't be harsh or damaging on your hair. A servant must have that same, gentle, soothing quality. Servants are often called on to be peacemakers. A peacemaker can't be harsh or damaging. Many of our tasks as servants require gentleness.

✳ Write the ninth characteristic of the servant mind.

6. Watchful **8. Not Quarrelsome**

7. Courageous **9. ________________**

Just as courage frees God to protect you, gentleness frees God to strengthen you. When Jesus predicted that Peter would deny Him, He was gentle: *"Simon, Simon, behold, Satan has demanded permission to sift you like wheat; but I have prayed for you, that your faith may not fail; and you, when once you have turned again, strengthen your brothers" (Luke 22:31-32).* Maybe that prayer was what enabled Peter to stand so strong before the Sanhedrin in *Acts 4:8-12.* Gentleness and strength must go together. Gentleness without strength is wimpiness. Strength without gentleness is brutality.

✳ When you are gentle, what does that free God to do?

Gentleness frees God to____

Jesus was gentle. One of the most tender pictures we have of Jesus is His declaration, *"I am the door of the sheep… if anyone enters through Me, he shall be saved, and shall go in and out, and find pasture" (John 10:7-9).* Here is a case of gentleness growing out of great strength.

10. Able to Teach

Paul's next servant job qualification from *2 Timothy 2:24* is ability to teach. This may scare you. Isn't teaching a spiritual gift *(Rom. 12:6-7)?* Not everyone has every spiritual gift, and teaching isn't mine! That's what my youth minister and pastor do.

You are partly right. There is a specific spiritual gift of teaching. But that isn't what Paul is talking about here.

The other day, I was at a restaurant, and the waitress that served me was being followed by another person in a waiter's uniform. He was watching everything the waitress did. I soon realized that he was in training as a waiter, and she was teaching him what to do by her example.

All of us have the responsibility of teaching our faith and our servanthood in this way. This doesn't always mean standing in front of people with a piece of chalk. But as people watch us, we are teaching them what it means to be a Christian.

Able to Teach
Understanding of the Master's work
- Fleshly attitude: "I don't have time for Bible study."
- When you are able to teach *(2 Tim. 2:24)*, you free God to establish His authority *(Matt. 7:28-29)*.

✳ Write one characteristic of the servant mind.

10. ______________ 12. Meek 14. Wise

11. Patient 13. Good

Christians are light for this world, because the light of the World dwells in us *(Matt. 5:14)*. When we teach others by our lives what it means to be a follower of God, we free God to establish His divine authority in their lives. Peter tells us, *Always being ready to make a defense to everyone who asks you to give an account for the hope that is in you (1 Pet. 3:15).*

✳ When you are able to teach, what does that free God to do?

Being able to teach frees God to ________________________________

Jesus was the greatest teacher who ever lived, both by His example and by His words. Early in His ministry, *He came down to Capernaum, a city of Galilee. And He was teaching them on the Sabbath; and they were amazed at His teaching, for His message was with authority (Luke 4:31-32)*. At the close of the Sermon on the Mount, the Bible says that *the multitudes were amazed at His teaching; for He was teaching them as one having authority, and not as their scribes* (*Matt. 7:28-29*). On occasion Jesus' wise teaching silenced those who opposed Him.

11. Patient

The next servant characteristic is *patient*. In God's Kingdom, waiting time is never wasted time. There are two types of patience that a servant needs to keep in mind. The first is being patient with God, and allowing God to answer you on His timetable (which, by the way, is always perfect timing). The second is being patient with others, both non-Christians and fellow Christian servants. It is especially tempting to lose your patience with unbelievers who are slow to respond to your witness. But the true servant realizes that, just as the Lord is patient with us, we also must be patient with others: *The Lord is not slow about His promise, as some count slowness, but is patient toward you, not wishing any to perish but for all to come to repentance (2 Pet. 3:9).*

Patient
Forbearance that values the Master's purpose for others.
- Fleshly attitude: "Enough is enough!"
- When you are patient, you free God to answer prayer *(John 14:8-14)*.

Meek
Disciplined sensitivity to the Master.
- Fleshly attitude: "I'll get even with them!"
- When you are meek as a sheep *(2 Tim. 2:24)*, you free God to guide you.

✻ **Write two characteristics of the servant mind.**

10. ______________	**12. Meek**	**14. Wise**
11. ______________	**13. Good**	

Patience frees the Lord to answer prayer in His way and in His time. God is never in a rush, even though we usually are. Waiting on God allows Him to provide the best answer. We are to become like God, who is infinitely patient with us.

✻ **When you are patient, what does that free God to do?**

Patience frees God to ______________________________

Jesus was patient. We've already talked about Jesus' patience with His disciples. Time and time again, though they were slow to understand, Jesus repeated His teachings to them. Look back on Week Five for more about Jesus' patience.

12. Meek

The last servant characteristic *2 Timothy 2:23-25* talks about is *meek*. In the entire Bible, only two people are called meek. Moses was one of them. *Numbers 12:3* tells us that Moses was more meek than anyone else on earth. Then, in *Matthew 11:29,* Jesus uses the word to describe Himself.

Last week, I warned you about associating meekness with mousiness. Here's another reason why. Moses and Jesus are the two strongest figures in the Bible. There was nothing mousy about Moses confronting Pharaoh, or of Jesus clearing out the Temple. No weakness is found in either of these characters. A servant can recognize his or her lowly position before God without being weak. The greatest show of strength is to voluntarily submit to someone else. Involuntary submission has nothing to do with meekness.

✻ **Write three characteristics of the servant mind.**

10. ______________	**12.** ______________	**14. Wise**
11. ______________	**13. Good**	

I have a dog whom I take out on walks every once in a while. He's a strong little dog, and sometimes its not clear who's walking whom! Little by little, he's learning that if he doesn't try to pull against me on the leash, we'll have a lot more fun on our walks. I'll keep him safe from the traffic, we'll run more, and we'll go further than we will if he's fighting against me the whole time.

Our meekness before God is a lot like that. Meekness frees the Lord to guide you. *Psalm 25:9* says, *The meek will he guide in judgment: and the meek will he teach his way* (KJV).

✻ **When you are meek, what does that free God to do?**

Meekness frees God to ______________________________

Think about Jesus' meekness again. Think how He came to earth. He could have come as a king, a high priest, or a great military general. Instead, He came as a lowly carpenter, but with great spiritual strength.

13. Good

The parable of the talents gives us another characteristic: *"Well done, good and faithful slave" (Matt. 25:21).* Jesus uses the word to imply that the servant has produced and has accomplished Kingdom work (See the discussion of *good* in Week Five). A good servant has practical worth.

Good
Applied trust in the Master's excellence.
- Fleshly attitude: "It was just a little mistake!"
- When you are a good servant *(Matt. 25:21),* you free God to produce fruit *(Matt. 7:17).*

✻ Write four characteristics of the servant mind.

10. ______________ 12. ______________ 14. Wise

11. ______________ 13. ______________

Goodness frees the Lord to produce fruit in you. It proves that you really are the servant God saved you to be. *"You will know them by their fruits" (Matt. 7:20).* A good servant produces fruit.

✻ When you are good, what does that free God to do?

Goodness frees God to ________________________________

In all that Jesus is, He is productive. He is good. Two thousand years of Christian history and billions of Christians throughout the centuries have shown the fruit that Jesus' ministry bore. He claimed *"I am the good shepherd" (John 10:11).* You can apply goodness to every one of His roles and titles: He is the Good Teacher, the Good Savior, the Good Brother, the Good Priest, and all the others.

14. Wise

The last servant characteristic is closely identified with watchfulness, which we talked about yesterday. It is *wise.* In *Matthew 24:45-47,* Jesus describes the servant who is ready for his Master's return in this way: *"Who then is the faithful and sensible slave whom his master put in charge of his household to give them their food at the proper time? Blessed is that slave whom his master finds so doing when he comes. Truly I say to you, that he will put him in charge of all his possessions."*

Wise
Dependence on the Master's method.
- Fleshly attitude: "I don't know what to do."
- When you are a wise disciple *(Matt. 24:42-47),* you free God to invest you with authority.

The words in the above verse in the *New American Standard Version* say "faithful and sensible" and is translated "faithful and wise" in the *King James Version* of the Bible. Jesus is not talking about intellectual wisdom in this passage. He is talking about practicality, or what we would call common sense. *Common sense* means being aware enough of the world's way of doing things that we are able to resourcefully build the kingdom. When Jesus sent out the 12 disciples on their preaching mission, He said to them, *"Behold, I send you out as sheep in the midst of wolves; therefore be shrewd as serpents, and innocent as doves" (Matt. 10:16).*

We can be childlike and yet resourceful. The servant must use good judgment, keen discernment, and, at times, intelligent discrimination.

✻ Write five characteristics of the servant mind.

10. ______________ 12. ______________ 14. ______________

11. ______________ 13. ______________

Wisdom frees God to invest you with authority. Wisdom establishes that you are a disciple, learning from Jesus and becoming like Him. The authority of the shrewd, practical, sensible, wise servant will be greatly increased.

✱ When you are wise, what does that free God to do?

Wisdom frees God to ______________________________

Jesus was wise. Although He was totally innocent, He was always keenly perceptive. Whenever anyone tried to trap Him with a question that would get Him in trouble with the religious leaders, He could always see right through him. Most of Jesus' great works were accomplished in Galilee. Little is recorded of miracles in Judea, compared to what He did in Galilee. This shows a lot of wisdom on Jesus' part. He wisely chose to do most of His work away from where the religious leaders lived. Practicality and sensibility placed His work where it would do the most good— among the poor and the lowly.

✱ Conclude this week's study by praying this prayer:

> **Heavenly Father, the qualities of a servant are attainable, and I thank You for that. Being a servant goes against the grain of everything I am taught in my culture. They tell me at school to look out for number one in everything I do. You teach me that I am at my best when I am stooping to serve. It's hard for me to believe that.**
>
> **But I do believe You, Lord. You're always right, no matter how strange Your Word may seem by the standards of the world. Lord, there is such a huge distance between who I am and what Jesus lived out in His human life. Make me like Him, no matter what it takes. In Jesus' name.**
>
> **Amen.**

The Beatitudes

UNIT 7

Day 1
Two Halves of a Whole, Part 1

Day 2
Two Halves of a Whole, Part 2

Day 3
Poor in Spirit, Mourn, Meek

Day 4
Hungry, Merciful, Pure in Heart

Day 5
Peacemakers, Persecuted for Righteousness

Scripture Memory Verse
"Blessed are the poor in spirit, for theirs is the kingdom of heaven."
Matthew 5:3

Hymn Part 4—Christ's Humanity
[Jesus] was made in the likeness of men... And... found in appearance as a man (Phil. 2:7-8).

What Is in This Unit for Me?

This week, you will realize that God uses circumstances, even painful ones, to develop qualities in you that He will, in turn, bless. God will be working on developing the qualities He describes in the Beatitudes. God will also work through you to manifest Himself to others as you give of yourself.

Lifelong Objective

You will become a reflection of Christ's perfect humanity as you develop and manifest the qualities described in the Beatitudes.

Unit Learning Goals

- You will understand some of the differences between the first four and the second four Beatitudes.
- You will understand ways God uses circumstances to develop the Beatitudes in your life.
- You will understand what the Beatitudes are and what they are not.
- You will understand eight ways you can worship God because of what He does in you and through you.
- You will demonstrate an openness to God's work of developing the Beatitudes in your life.

What You Will Do to Begin Developing the Beatitudes

- You will contrast the first four Beatitudes with the second four to understand what they mean and how God uses them.
- You will begin using the LifeLong Helps and the Mind of Christ Cards for this week to guide you in the process of developing the Beatitudes in your life.
- You will look at your life to identify past and present circumstances that God uses to mold you into the image of His Son.
- You will surrender yourself to allow God to work in and through you to reflect the qualities of Christ's humanity.

Lifelong Helps Related to This Week

Beatitudes (pp. 204-211)

The Mind of Christ Cards Related to This Unit

4B. Unit 7: Scripture Memory—*Matthew 5:3*
6A-B. Scripture Memory—*Matthew 5:3-10*

20. A-1: Poor in Spirit	24. B-1: Merciful
21. A-2: Mourn	25. B-2: Pure in Heart
22. A-3: Meek	26. B-3: Peacemakers
23. A-4: Hungry	27. B-4: Persecuted

Today's Bible Meditations
And be kind to one another, tender-hearted, forgiving each other, just as God in Christ also has forgiven you.
Ephesians 4:32

[Jesus] was made in the likeness of men... And being found in appearance as a man.
Philippians 2:7-8

Name of Christ for Today
An Advocate with the Father
(1 John 2:1)

Prayer to Begin the Lesson
Jesus,
an advocate is someone who speaks on behalf of someone else. Thank You for speaking for me. Because of You, the Father has forgiven me. I don't deserve what You do for me, but I thank You for doing it. Because I have been given much, I, too want to give.
Amen.

Two Halves of a Whole, Part 1

✳ Begin today's lesson by reading the Bible verse and the name of Christ for today. Work on your memory verse. Then use the suggested prayer to begin your study.

Hymn Part 4: Christ's Humanity

This week, we begin to look at the fourth part of the hymn in *Philippians 2. Verses 7* and *8* say that Jesus *was made in the likeness of men: and ... found in appearance as a man.* So, Jesus was completely God, but He was also completely human. Why would Jesus give up His place in heaven in order to live as a human being? Well, for one reason, He did it so He could show us how to live. Jesus gave us an idea of what God had in mind when He created us. In Weeks 7-10, we'll look at the humanity of Jesus and how He lived His life. Jesus gives us the ground rules for how to live. We can learn a lot from Him.

Right Living: What a Blessing!

The greatest sermon ever preached, and the largest single body of Jesus' teachings, is the Sermon on the Mount, in *Matthew 5-7.* Here, Jesus lays down the program for human conduct. The first few verses of the Sermon on the Mount give us the description of a Kingdom person. These eight blessings are called The Beatitudes, which literally means "beautiful attitudes." They are crucially important to God's program for life.

✳ There are many Lifelong Helps in the back of this book that will assist you in following God's pattern for blessed living. We're going to introduce you to them. Put a check beside each item as you complete it.

- ❑ **First, tear out Scripture Memory Cards 4A and 6A/6B. Notice that your memory verse for this week is the first of the eight Beatitudes. The others are found on Card 6. Don't worry—you're not expected to memorize all of them this week. But begin to hide these verses away in your mind and heart so that God can call attention to them any time He wants.**
- ❑ **Next, tear out the Mind of Christ Cards related to the Beatitudes (cards 20-27). Notice that you have one card for each Beatitude. This will allow you to focus on them one at a time as God develops them in your life.**
- ❑ **Finally, turn to pages 204-211. Notice that we've given you detailed information on each Beatitude. Fold down the corner of the page, or put a bookmark there so you can turn to it easily.**

The eight Beatitudes are a great description of a complete person. Now, if you look carefully at them, you'll see a difference between the first four and the second four. Basically, the first four deal with how God makes you a better person. The second four deal with how God uses you to make a difference to other people. The first four focus on the inside; the last four with the outside.

✳ The Lifelong Helps on page 204 look more closely at the contrasts between the first four and last four Beatitudes. Turn there and spend a few minutes studying the differences. Then, complete this exercise. Identify which one of the items in each pair goes with the first four, and mark it with an *A*. Mark the item that goes with the second four with a *B*.

Basis for Happiness:	____ Your Giving
	____ Your Need
Keys to:	____ God's Heart
	____ Christ's Character
Focus:	____ Turn your mind toward others
	____ Turn your mind toward God
Command:	____ Love God
	____ Love Others
Object:	____ God gives based on your need to be conformed to the image of Christ
	____ God works through you to reveal Himself to a watching world
Greatness:	____ The practice
	____ The door
Worship:	____ You bring glory to God by revealing Christ's character to others
	____ You give praise God as He meets your needs

Basis for Happiness

"Blessed." Each Beatitude starts off with this word. Another translation of *Matthew 5* uses the word *happy*. Let's look at the difference between the first four and the second four Beatitudes as they give the basis for blessedness. The first four say that you are blessed when a need is met. The poor in spirit need God. The mourners need comfort. The meek need others. Those who hunger for righteousness need satisfaction.

The second four Beatitudes focus on giving. The merciful give God's grace to the world. The pure in heart give holiness. The peacemakers give wholeness. The persecuted give their lives.

Maybe you know of the artist M.C. Escher. In one of his most famous paintings, there is a set of steps that connects to itself, in a circle. Yet, it appears that every step goes up. That's a lot like the Beatitudes. God gives of Himself because of our desperate need for Him (the first four). The greater our need, the more His giving. As we receive from Him, we can give to others (the second four). What's amazing is that, as we climb higher in serving others, we realize with each step that we need God more, cycling back to the beginning.

✳ As you look at your own spiritual life, where are you in the cycle? Are you needy? Are you giving? Where would you put yourself on the staircase?

____

The Keys

Each Beatitude has the same format: "Blessed are the ______, for they shall ______." Think of the first half of the Beatitude as a key, and the second half as the door that key opens. There's also a bigger picture. The first four Beatitudes are the keys to God's heart. The second four are the keys to Christ's character.

✳ **End today's study by thanking God for His work in you. Ask God to show you which qualities He wants to work on in your life. Read the eight Beatitudes on page 204. If God directs your attention toward one in particular, circle it.**

DAY 2

Today's Bible Meditation
Consider it all joy, my brethren, when you encounter various trials, knowing that the testing of your faith produces endurance. And let endurance have its perfect result, that you may be perfect and complete, lacking in nothing.
James 1:2-4

Name of Christ for Today
A Man of Sorrows
(Isa. 53:3)

Two Halves of a Whole, Part 2

✳ **Begin today's lesson by reading the Bible verse and the name of Christ for today. Work on your memory verse. Then use the suggested prayer to begin your study.**

✳ **As you read the following contrasts between the first four Beatitudes and the second four, circle key words for each topic. Then, write a *1* or *2* beside each word to indicate the group of Beatitudes to which it belongs.**

Focus

The first four Beatitudes turn the mind to God. When a person experiences poverty of spirit, brokenness, meekness, or hunger, that person instinctively turns to God. The second four Beatitudes turn the mind toward others. Think about it. The Beatitude says, "Blessed are the merciful." Can you show mercy to God? No! We can only show mercy to others. In the same way, we demonstrate peace, purity, and grace under persecution to those around us.

Remember what Jesus said the two greatest commandments are? The most important: love God above everything else, and the second is to love our neighbor (see *Mark 12:29-31*). Sound familiar? The Beatitudes follow the same pattern! First, turn the mind to God, and second, turn the mind to others.

Greatness

The first four Beatitudes are the door to greatness. They produce those qualities that Jesus said make us the greatest in the Kingdom (see *Mark 9:35; 10:43; Luke 22:26-27*). When you look at them, they aren't exactly what the world considers keys to greatness, are they? God's standard is different.

The second four Beatitudes are the practice of greatness. As we practice these Beatitudes we give the world a picture of what grace and holiness looks like. How do we live out the Beatitudes? By studying the examples of people who practiced them—Abraham, Joseph, Moses, David, Daniel, and Paul.

Prayer to Begin the Lesson
*Lord Jesus,
every time I read about the sorrows You experienced for me, I realize how precious I am to You. You experienced great suffering for great purposes. My human side would prefer an easy road. Please help me to be willing to experience the trials of life as the Father develops these qualities in my life. Like James says, I want to be "perfect and complete, lacking nothing."
Amen.*

God's Goal

What does God hope to achieve by developing the Beatitudes in your life? In the first four, He is working on your inner life. The more we apply them to our lives, the more our need for God and our need for others grows. In the second four Beatitudes, God uses our outer life to affect the world around us.

In the first four Beatitudes, God uses circumstances to show us our need for Him and how He can meet that need. For example, we might find ourselves brokenhearted (mourning). At that time, God can make Himself more real to us than ever before and we become more aware of His presence because of our brokenheartedness. Instead of blaming God, we can see that God is using our problems to grow us up in the image of His Son. In the second four Beatitudes, however, God allows us to use circumstances to bring glory to Him in others' lives. For instance, if you are acting as a peacemaker between two of your friends, you are bringing God's presence into their lives.

✳ When was a time that God used a difficult or painful experience in your life to help you grow spiritually. Write a brief reminder to yourself about that experience.

Starting with tomorrow's lesson, you'll be using the Lifelong Helps on the Beatitudes. Read the instructions on pages 204-205 in preparation for tomorrow. Underline any ideas you may want to refer to later or that you want to ask your small group leader about. Based on this page of instructions, answer this question:

✳ God uses circumstances to develop the Beatitudes in your life. For what is He training you?

End today's study by asking God to open your mind to understand His activity in your life. Ask Him to reveal when and how He has worked in your life in the past and how He is working in the present to develop these qualities. Record insights God reveals to you in your journal.

DAY 3

Today's Bible Meditation
"God be merciful to me, the sinner!"
Luke 18:13

Name of Christ for Today
All
(Col 3:11)

Prayer to Begin the Lesson
All that I need is You, Jesus
All that I need is You
From early in the morning
till late at night
All that I need is You.
Amen.

Poor in Spirit, Mourn, Meek

✱ **Begin today's lesson by reading the Bible verse and the name of Christ for today. Work on your memory verse. Then use the suggested prayer to begin your study.**

Get ready to flip. You're going to be flipping a lot in the next few days! We're changing our pattern of study today. You'll be using the Lifelong Helps at the back of the book to help you in your study of the Beatitudes. We'll give you assignments that call for you to use the Helps on pages 206-213. So, tear two little strips of paper—one for this page and one for the back of the book. Oh, one more thing: you'll also need the Mind Of Christ Cards 20-27.

The Poor in Spirit

✱ Read Poor in Spirit (p. 206) and answer the following:

What is the principle for this Beatitude? ______________________

What is this Beatitude a key to? ______________________

How would you define *poor in spirit*? ______________________

____

Has God used a circumstance to develop this Beatitude in you? Write a brief reminder to yourself of the situation.

____

✱ How does this Beatitude make you respond to God? ______________________

____

Mourn

✱ Read Mourn (pp. 206-207) and answer the following:

What is the principle for this Beatitude? ______________________

What is this Beatitude a key to? ______________________

How would you define *mourn*? ______________________

Has God used a circumstance to develop this Beatitude in you? Write a brief reminder to yourself of the situation.

____

____

How does this Beatitude make you respond to God? ____________________

____

Meek

✳ Read Meek (pp. 207-208) and answer the following questions.

What is the principle for this Beatitude? ______________________________

What is this Beatitude a key to? ____________________________________

How would you define *meek*? ______________________________________

____

Has God used a circumstance to develop this Beatitude in you? Write a brief reminder to yourself of the situation.

____

____

How does this Beatitude make you respond to God? ____________________

____

✳ End today's lesson in prayer. What has God done in your life today? Talk to Him about it. Ask Him how you should respond to what you've learned in today's study.

DAY 4

Today's Bible Meditation
O God, Thou art my God; I shall seek Thee earnestly; my soul thirsts for Thee, my flesh yearns for Thee, in a dry and weary land where there is no water.
Psalm 63:1

Name of Christ for Today
Head of the Church
(Eph. 5:23)

Prayer to Begin the Lesson
Lord Jesus, I hunger and thirst after You. You satisfy my needs the way water quenches my thirst after football practice, or a snack satisfies me when I come home from school. Lord, there is a need for my youth group to hunger and thirst for You even more. You are working on that desire in me. As Head of the Church, please build that desire in others, too. Use me in that work! You have my permission! Continue to fill me up today!
Amen.

Hungry, Merciful, Pure in Heart

✳ **Begin today's lesson by reading the Bible verse and the name of Christ for today. Work on your memory verse. Then use the suggested prayer to begin your study.**

Get ready to flip some more! Today, we'll continue using the Lifelong Helps at the back of the book.

Hungry for Righteousness

✳ **Read *Hungry* (p. 208) and answer the following:**

What is the principle for this Beatitude?______________________________

What is this Beatitude a key to? ______________________________

How would you define *hunger and thirst for righteousness*?

____

____

Has God used a circumstance to develop this Beatitude in you? Write a brief reminder to yourself of the situation.

____

____

How does this Beatitude make you respond to God? ____________________

Merciful

✳ **Read Merciful (pp. 208-209) and answer the following:**

What is the principle for this Beatitude? ______________________________

What is this Beatitude a key to? ______________________________

How would you define *merciful*? ______________________________

____

Has God used a circumstance to develop this Beatitude in you? Write a brief reminder to yourself of the situation.

____

____

How does this Beatitude make you respond to God? ____________________

____

Pure in Heart

✳ Read Pure in Heart (pp. 209-210) and answer the following:

What is the principle for this Beatitude? ______________________________

What is this Beatitude a key to?______________________________________

How would you define *pure in heart*? ________________________________

____

Has God used a circumstance to develop this Beatitude in you? Write a brief reminder to yourself of the situation.

____

____

How does this Beatitude make you respond to God? ____________________

____

✳ What has God done in your life today? Talk to Him about it. Ask Him how He wants you to respond to what you've learned about these three Beatitudes.

DAY
5

Today's Bible Meditation
Now all these things are from God, who reconciled us to Himself through Christ, and gave us the ministry of reconciliation.
2 Corinthians 5:18

Name of Christ for Today
Righteous Judge
(2 Tim. 4:8)

Prayer to Begin the Lesson
Righteous Judge,
the history books are full of stories about people who have been condemned for serving You. Even today, people are still persecuted for claiming Your name. I ask You to judge such actions with Your righteous justice. People all around me are in strife. Help me to be the peacemaker You want me to be. Help me carry out the ministry of reconciliation you have given me.
Amen.

Peacemakers, Persecuted for Righteousness

✻ Begin today's lesson by reading the Bible verse and the name of Christ for today. Work on your memory verse. Then use the suggested prayer to begin your study.

Continue using the Lifelong Helps for the Beatitudes and complete these assignments.

✻ Read Peacemaker (p. 210) and answer the following:

What is the principle for this Beatitude? ______________________

What is this Beatitude a key to? ______________________

How would you define *peacemaker*? ______________________

____

Has God used a circumstance to develop this Beatitude in you? Write a brief reminder to yourself of the situation.

____

____

How does this Beatitude make you respond to God? ______________________

____

Persecuted for Righteousness

✻ Read Persecuted (p. 211) and answer the following:

What is the principle for this Beatitude?______________________

What is this Beatitude a key to? ______________________

How would you define *persecuted for righteousness*? ______________________

____

____

Has God used a circumstance to develop this Beatitude in you? Write a brief reminder to yourself of the situation.

____

____

How does this Beatitude make you respond to God? ____________________

____

* Review the eight Beatitudes using the Mind of Christ Cards 20-27. Pick out one that you feel God is really dealing with you about. Spend some extra time (this lesson was a lot shorter!) meditating on the Scriptures in the Lifelong Helps for that Beatitude.

* Conclude your study of the unit praying for God to use any circumstance He wants to develop the first four Beatitudes in your life. Give Him permission to call on you to demonstrate the second four qualities whenever or wherever He needs to show the world what He is like. Pray for the other members of your small group, and then pray for your youth group as a whole, as you seek to develop the mind of Christ.

UNIT 8

Day 1
Jesus Relates to Us

Day 2
Jesus and "Negative" Emotions

Day 3
Jesus and "Positive" Emotions

Day 4
Controlling Emotional Impulses

Day 5
Jesus and Wisdom

Scripture Memory Verse
And the Word became flesh, and dwelt among us, and we beheld His glory, glory as of the only begotten from the Father, full of grace and truth.
John 1:14

Jesus and Emotions

Hymn Part 4—Christ's Humanity
[Jesus] was made in the likeness of men... And... found in appearance as a man (Phil. 2:7-8).

What Is in This Unit for Me?

Jesus was able to express emotions without sinning. As a teenager, that's a challenge sometimes. You will discover ways to control emotional impulses and show godly wisdom in your everyday world. God will be working on you helping you to accomplish His will in your life.

Lifelong Objective

In Christ, you will express your emotions in ways that honor God.

Unit Learning Goals

- You will understand why you should imitate Jesus' humanity.
- You will understand that "negative" emotions are appropriate also, and you will identify some negative and positive emotions Jesus expressed.
- You will demonstrate your desire for being able to express emotions in Christ-honoring ways.
- You will understand one way you can miss experiencing the mind of Christ as it relates to joy.
- You will find ways you can demonstrate the mind of Christ by showing compassion.
- You will understand how to control emotional impulses with godly wisdom and the exercise of your will.
- You will understand the importance of biblical wisdom for right living.
- You will demonstrate a renewed commitment to be a faithful student of God's Word.

What You Will Do to Begin Godly Expression of Emotions

- You will study the way Jesus expressed His emotions—not only positive emotions, but what we would call negative emotions.
- You will seek God's help in developing godly wisdom for right living.
- You will go back over your Bondage to Freedom lists to see areas God is still working on to set you free.
- You will review the Lifelong Helps for Christlike Virtues and The Beatitudes for the purpose of letting God continue to mold you into the image of His Son.

Lifelong Helps for Review in This Unit

Bondage to Freedom Lists (pp. 189-191)
Christlike Virtues (pp. 192-202)
The Beatitudes (pp. 204-213)

The Mind of Christ Card Related to This Unit

4B. Unit 8: Scripture Memory—*John 1:14*

Jesus Relates to Us

DAY 1

Today's Bible Meditation
For you have been called for this purpose, since Christ also suffered for you, leaving you an example for you to follow in His steps, who committed no sin, nor was any deceit found in His mouth.

1 Peter 2:21-22

Names of Christ for Today
Son of Man
(Matt. 12:8)
The Last Adam
(1 Cor. 15:45)
The Second Man
(1 Cor. 15:47)

Prayer to Begin the Lesson
Son of Man,
thank You for deciding to be human for me. Your life gives me a perfect example of what human life should be. There's no temptation that I go through that You didn't deal with, yet You didn't sin. You've showed us what perfect humanity looks like. You were holy, spotless, and blameless. Help me to follow in Your steps. I want to be like You.
Amen.

✱ **Begin today's lesson by reading the Bible verse and the name of Christ for today. Work on your memory verse. Then use the suggested prayer to begin your study.**

You just don't understand! How many times have you thought that, or even said it, as you've talked to your parents, your brothers or sisters, or your friends? The fact is, as a teenager you can often feel like no one in the world understands you. You're dealing with a lot of changes, and one of the biggest parts of the roller-coaster ride of adolescence is your emotions. It's normal, it's natural, and to tell the truth, you would be weird if you didn't feel weird sometimes. Emotions are part of being human. Still, when you're dealing with your emotions, do you ever feel like saying to Jesus, "You just don't understand"?

But Jesus does understand, because Jesus was human! This week, we're focusing on Jesus' emotions. Jesus expressed a broad range of emotions, yet He never sinned in the way He expressed them. Not like us. We express emotions inappropriately sometimes. We blow up at people, or we keep things so bottled up it stresses us out. Our emotions sometimes lead us into sinful acts. We want you to learn how to control your emotions by following the example of Jesus.

God's Emphasis on the Inner Person

What's more important to God—the inside or the outside? To God, the mind has always been more important than outward actions. In Old Testament thinking, the emphasis was on the heart, and they often used the word *heart* in the same way we use mind. Check out *Proverbs 23:12: Apply your heart to discipline.* Or *Proverbs 23:7* (KJV)—*As he thinketh in his heart, so is he.* Jesus used the word the same way. *Jesus, knowing their thoughts said, "Why are you thinking evil in your hearts?" (Matt. 9:4).*

✱ **Which is more important to God? Check one.**

_____ My inner being **____ My outward actions**

Lots of times, we're satisfied if our outer, visible actions fulfill the expectations of society and the requirements of God. If you've ever shoved everything into your closet when your mother told you to clean your room, you know what I'm talking about! But just hiding something out of the way doesn't cut it with God. God told Samuel, *"God sees not as man sees, for man looks at the outward appearance, but the Lord looks at the heart" (1 Sam. 16:7).* You could say today that God looks at the mind. God is a lot more concerned with who you are on the inside than with outer appearances.

Suppose you are obedient to your parents when they are around, but as soon as they are out of the room you start to bad-mouth and criticize them. The Bible would say that you have sinned against your parents. Jesus applied that standard to adultery. He said that if anyone who looked at a woman with a lustful attitude had already committed adultery with her in his heart (see *Matt. 5:28).* All outer behaviors begin with inner thoughts. Cain was first guilty of the invisible sin of jealousy before he committed the visible sin of murdering his brother Abel (see *Gen. 4:5).* God knows your heart and your thoughts—even when you think you've kept them from everyone. His main concern is your mind.

✳ Which comes first? Check one:

___ Thoughts / emotions ___ Outer actions

We know Jesus came to earth to die for our sins. But Jesus also came to earth to teach us how to live. We learn a lot from the way Jesus lived His life.

Jesus intentionally identified with ordinary, everyday people, just like us, even when it rankled the fur of the religious establishment. He said, *"The Son of Man came eating and drinking, and they say, 'Behold, a gluttonous man and a drunkard, a friend of tax-gatherers and sinners!' " (Matt. 11:19)*. Jesus hung out with tax-collectors, adulterous women, and fisherman—not exactly the upper crust of society. He went out of His way to relate to the most humble and insignificant people, and opened up the door for us to be able to relate to Him.

He even submitted to baptism—an act normally reserved for sinners. John didn't want to perform the baptism, but Jesus convinced him by saying, *"Let it be so now; it is proper for us to do this to fulfill all righteousness" (Matt. 3:15,* NIV). Jesus wasn't baptized for His own sins, He was baptized so He could identify with sinners. Jesus became what we are so that we can become what He is.

✳ Why should you want to be like Jesus in His humanity?

____

____

✳ There aren't any additional Lifelong Helps this week. So go back over the Helps related to Christ's virtues (pp. 192-202) and the Beatitudes (pp. 204-213). Ask God to identify the area in your life He wants to work on. Spend time this week studying and praying through the Lifelong Help that deals with the area God identifies.

✳ Finish up today in prayer. As you pray, use the Name of Christ for today—Son of Man. Thank Jesus for His example of perfect humanness. Tell Jesus of your desire to be like Him. Ask Him to prepare your mind and heart for the upcoming study of emotions.

Jesus and "Negative" Emotions

DAY 2

✱ Begin today's lesson by reading the Bible verse and the name of Christ for today. Work on your memory verse. Then use the suggested prayer to begin your study.

If you were to make a list of emotions you occasionally felt but didn't necessarily like, what would be on the list? Anger? Hate? Fear? Sadness? Jealousy? All of these are part of the normal human range of emotions. Unlike love, happiness, or generosity, however, none of them make us feel very good. So, for lack of a better term, let's call them "negative" emotions.

Now, which of these emotions do you think Jesus expressed? With the exception of hate and fear, which are contrary to God's nature (see *1 John 4:8* and *4:18),* I think that we can find examples throughout the Bible of God and Jesus expressing "negative" emotions. God can be angry *(Num. 25:3),* and jealous *(Ex. 20:5).* Since Jesus is the exact representation of God's nature *(Heb. 1:3),* we can find examples of Jesus showing the same kind of emotions.

Three times in the New Testament, Jesus is described as being angry. The Gospel of John shows Jesus throwing the money changers out of the Temple at the beginning of His ministry. The other three Gospels record this action in the last week of Jesus' earthly life (see *Matt. 21:12-13; Mark 11:15-17; Luke 19:45-46).* As you read the following account from John, notice how Jesus didn't just throw a temper tantrum. He showed zeal for His Father's house. He carefully planned out His response, taking the time to make a whip before displaying His anger for desecration of the Temple.

> *And He found in the temple those who were selling oxen and sheep and doves, and the moneychangers seated. And He made a scourge of cords, and drove them all out of the temple, with the sheep and the oxen; and He poured out the coins of the moneychangers, and overturned their tables; and to those who were selling the doves He said, "Take these things away; stop making My Father's house a house of merchandise" (John 2:14-17).*

Jesus' anger is recorded again in *Mark 3:1-5.* One Sabbath day, a man with a shriveled hand came to Jesus for healing. The Pharisees were watching to see what Jesus would do. They were ready to pounce on Jesus for breaking the law—they didn't care at all about the man with the hand. So Jesus, *looking around at them with anger,* [was] *grieved at their hardness of heart (v. 5).* We all know how anger can be expressed inappropriately. But Jesus used these violations of holiness and justice to demonstrate appropriate expressions of anger. As human beings, it is probably best if we don't try to imitate holy anger. Holy anger, as Jesus demonstrated it, comes from an absolutely pure source. Likely we're not going to have the purity it takes to pull off holy anger.

✱ What is a "negative" emotion that Jesus expressed in an appropriate way?

____

Today's Bible Meditation
Jesus wept.
John 11:35

Names of Christ for Today
The Exact Representation of [God's] Nature
(Heb. 1:3)

Prayer to Begin the Lesson
Jesus,
sometimes my emotions are destructive to my relationships with others. Let me learn today by Your example how to express emotions in positive ways. You are the perfect image of God. Teach me to be a reflection of Your nature, so that You will be honored in my life.
Amen.

One day, Jesus expressed indignation with His disciples. Remember yesterday's study, when we talked about how Jesus related to ordinary, humble human beings? One of the groups Jesus related to especially well was children. So, on this particular day, Jesus' disciples were trying to keep people from bringing children to Him for blessing. Jesus was usually patient with His disciples when they were slow to catch on to His way of doing things. But this time, the Bible says that *He was indignant (Mark 10:14)*. It was important for Jesus to connect with children, so this offense was pretty serious for Jesus!

Another time, the Pharisees came up to Jesus and asked for a sign from heaven. Believe it or not, this came right after Jesus had fed the four thousand. What bigger sign could they want? It was sort of like your parents saying "I sure hope you can pull your grades up" after you show them your straight *A* report card! Mark tells us that Jesus sighed *deeply in his spirit (Mark 8:12)*, a rare example of exasperation. Even God's patience is limited by His own perfect holiness.

Four times the New Testament portrays Jesus as being "troubled." Although it means slightly different things in each context, they all come down to Jesus feeling deeply bothered. The first of these occurred at the death of Lazarus. On this occasion, Jesus was *deeply moved in spirit, and was troubled* at the sight of Mary's weeping *(John 11:33)*. Jesus was *troubled in spirit* when He announced the betrayal of Judas *(John 13:21)*. The idea of being betrayed by a close friend was no doubt bothersome and deeply troubling. In Gethsemane the night before His death, Jesus *began to be very distressed and troubled (Mark 14:33)*. Jesus even talked about His overwhelming sadness: *"My soul is deeply grieved to the point of death" (Mark 14:34)*. Later in Gethsemane, He was *in agony* and probably sweated blood *(Luke 22:44)*. No doubt Jesus was capable of deep human emotion. He expressed it openly and straightforwardly.

✻ What are some other "negative" emotions Jesus expressed?

____

Jesus also expressed deep grief. At Lazarus' tomb, we know that *Jesus wept (John 11:35)*. You can almost hear the grief in His voice when He weeps over Jerusalem. It is the grief of someone who has been deeply wounded: *"O Jerusalem, Jerusalem, the city that kills the prophets and stones those sent to her! How often I wanted to gather your children together, just as a hen gathers her brood under her wings, and you would not have it!" (Luke 13:34)*.

✻ We've looked at Jesus' "negative" emotions. What are some negative emotions you have expressed?

____

✻ How would you evaluate the way you normally express negative emotions? Check one, or write your own response.

- ❑ **I always act in appropriate ways.**
- ❑ **Sometime I do OK; other times I just explode.**
- ❑ **People describe me as hotheaded. I usually express negative emotions in bad ways.**

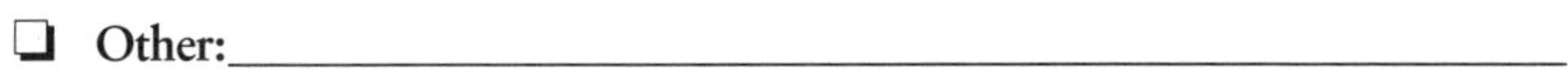

❑ Other:____

✳ Pray about the way you express negative emotions. Ask Jesus to help you in responding to your negative emotions in ways that would honor Him and never displease Him.

Jesus and "Positive" Emotions

✳ Begin today's lesson by reading the Bible verse and the name of Christ for today. Work on your memory verse. Then use the suggested prayer to begin your study.

Yesterday, we defined negative emotions as being the ones that you didn't enjoy having, but are still a healthy part of being human. But don't get the idea that by "negative" emotions, we mean emotions that you shouldn't have. Today, we're dealing with "positive" emotions—those that make you feel good. Did you know that the New Testament names more positive emotions of Jesus than negative ones? Let's try to identify some of them.

✳ Read the following paragraphs and underline the definition of *hope.*

What are some things you hope for? "I hope I do OK on this final;" "I hope I meet the right person to marry;" "I hope I don't get in trouble for being late last night." Often our expressions of hope carry an element of uncertainty or desperation to them—sort of like when you pass a police officer, knowing you were going too fast. You keep looking in the rearview mirror, hoping that the police car doesn't pull out behind you.

Jesus' expressions of hope weren't like this, however. In the New Testament, *hope* is "the present enjoyment of a future blessing." It's more like anticipation—the feeling of "I can't wait"—your youth camp is coming up, and you're so excited, you just can't wait. Jesus expressed desire and anticipation prior to the Lord's Supper. He told His disciples, "*I have earnestly desired to eat this Passover with you before I suffer" (Luke 22:15)*. Hope is a rare virtue. Because Jesus knew the ultimate outcome of His life and His suffering, He looked forward to His last supper with the disciples. It was a happy time.

✳ Name two positive emotions of Jesus: ____________________________

____

Once Jesus said He was glad. *Gladness* is the celebration of continuing inner joy. Gladness occurs when joy expresses itself on a particular occasion. *Joy* is the constant

DAY 3

Today's Bible Meditation
And seeing the multitudes, He felt compassion for them, because they were distressed and downcast like sheep without a shepherd.

Matthew 9:36

Names of Christ for Today
A Righteous Man
(Luke 23:47, KJV)

Prayer to Begin the Lesson
Lord Jesus,
in Your life You were righteous. You were always right in the way You acted. I want to do what is right, also. Teach me how and when to show positive emotions. Don't let me miss Your mind in these areas. Clothe me in Your righteousness.
Amen.

expression; gladness comes and goes according to circumstance. When Jesus left for Bethany to raise Lazarus from the dead, He told the disciples, "*Lazarus is dead, and I am glad for your sakes that I was not there, so that you may believe" (John 11:14-15)*. Throughout His ministry, Jesus had been disappointed by the disciples' lack of faith. Lazarus' resurrection would give the disciples an opportunity to have their struggling faith strengthened. Jesus was glad about that.

Jesus expressed joy a number of times. When the 70 returned from their preaching mission, Jesus *rejoiced greatly in the Holy Spirit (Luke 10:21)*. Jesus even expressed joy on the night of the Lord's Supper, knowing that He would be dead 24 hours later. After Jesus told His followers that their obedience would cause them to remain in His love, He said: *"These things I have spoken to you, that My joy may be in you, and that your joy may be made full" (John 15:11)*.

I know what you're thinking. What could possibly be joyful about the last night of Jesus' life? He was about to be betrayed, arrested, tried, and executed. What did Jesus have to be joyful about?

Jesus was joyful because He was concentrating on that moment, not on what was to come. We often miss the mind of Christ in the area of joy because we take tomorrow's hurt and pain and apply it to today. Of course Jesus felt dread and sorrow; we see that in the Garden of Gethsemane. But He deliberately didn't express it until He got to the garden. In the Upper Room, He was actually cheerful. Jesus felt joy!

✻ How do we miss the mind of Christ as it applies to experiencing joy?

____

✻ Can you think of a time when you took tomorrow's hurt and applied it to today? Briefly describe it:

____

____

There are five times when the Gospels record Jesus having compassion. In three of them, the compassion is for a multitude (see *Matt. 14:14; 9:36; Mark 8:2)*. Jesus was moved with compassion for large crowds. He saw a great need among the people. If you can imagine being at one of your school football games, and in one instant being overwhelmed with a stadium full of lost people, that's how Jesus saw the crowds.

Jesus also had compassion for individuals. Once, as He began to heal a leper, Jesus was *moved with compassion (Mark 1:41)*. Once, Jesus interrupted a funeral procession in which a widowed mother had lost her son. In those days, when there was no state welfare system, a widow's children were her only means of support. Jesus was moved with compassion for this woman's deep need (see *Luke 7:13)*. In all of these cases, Jesus met needs and healed hurts.

✻ Based on Jesus' example, what are some of the reasons you might demonstrate the mind of Christ by showing compassion?

____

More than anything else, Jesus felt love. The love of Jesus is mentioned more times than any other emotion. When the rich young ruler came to Jesus, Jesus looked at him and *felt a love for him (Mark 10:21).* When Lazarus got sick, the message came to Jesus from Mary and Martha, *"Lord, behold, he whom You love is sick" (John 11:3).* Two verses later, John tells us that *Jesus loved Martha, and her sister, and Lazarus.* At the beginning of the Lord's Supper, *having loved His own who were in the world, He loved them to the end (John 13:1).* Later in the meal, Jesus said to them, *"As the Father has loved Me, I have also loved you" (John 15:9).* John referred to himself repeatedly as the disciple *whom Jesus loved (John 13:23; John 19:26).* Love is the central emotion in the mind of Christ.

✱ Turn to Love (pp. 197-198) and review the ways you can show love. Watch for opportunities this week to show the love of Christ.

✱ Close today's time by asking God to develop in you the perfect expression of positive emotions. Ask God to reveal to you opportunities throughout the day for you to express these emotions.

Controlling Emotional Impulses

DAY 4

Today's Bible Meditation
For it is God who is at work in you, both to will and to work for His good pleasure. Do all things without grumbling or disputing; that you may prove yourselves to be blameless and innocent, children of God above reproach in the midst of a crooked and perverse generation, among whom you appear as lights in the world.
Philippians 2:13-15

✱ Begin today's lesson by reading the Bible verse and the name of Christ for today. Work on your memory verse. Then use the suggested prayer to begin your study.

✱ As you read the following paragraphs, circle some of the emotions that Jesus did NOT display.

We've spent the last two days talking about the emotions that Jesus displayed, both "negative" and positive. (You do understand what we mean by "negative" emotions, don't you? If not, you might want to look back over the past two days to make sure you get it, or talk to your small group leader about it this week.) But there are some emotions that Jesus did not express—emotions that are not only negative, but also destructive. For example, Jesus never expressed pessimism, discouragement, doubt, cynicism, suspicion, or gloom. All of these are contrary to the nature of an all-knowing God. Jesus also had no phobias. He never worried about the problems of His life, such as the frequent failures of His disciples, His relationship with the religious authorities, His rejection in His own home town, or the dread of the cross.

We know from Jesus' example that emotions are normal, and typical of God's most perfect creation, humanity. Emotions are dangerous, however, when they are impulsive or uncontrolled. They are expressed as particular occasions call them out. Human emotions are also subject to change. Maybe, if you've got a younger brother or sister, they may do something one day that makes you smile and laugh, but that

Names of Christ for Today
Wonderful Counselor
(Isa. 9:6)

Prayer to Begin the Lesson
Wonderful Counselor,
I get into so much trouble when my emotional impulses get out of control. Sometimes, it just seems like I can't get a grip on them. I need Your counsel today. Teach me by Your example how to express my emotions correctly. I want to honor You and to shine as a light in a dark world. Thank You that You will help me want the right things, and enable me to do them.
Amen.

same thing may really get on your nerves on another day. That's because your emotions are subject to change. Sometimes we call that "moodiness."

Jesus' emotions weren't like that. He was never moody; He never got mad. A person knew when dealing with Jesus that the same behavior would get the same emotional response from Him every time. We've already seen, for example, that Jesus expressed anger when the money changers were violating the sacredness of the Temple. Would Jesus have given them more slack on another day? Was He just in a bad mood? No! Because holy anger was a permanent, unchanging part of Jesus' make-up, we know that the same situation would get the same response from Jesus every time. His emotions were controlled and not subject to change.

✳ **Which of the following best describes Jesus' emotions?**
- ❑ **Jesus was moody. His emotions were changeable and He expressed them impulsively.**
- ❑ **Jesus' emotions were a consistent part of His make-up. He expressed emotions thoughtfully and deliberately.**

Think back to the story of the casting out of the money changers. This was not an unthoughtful, impulsive action on the part of Jesus. He took the time to make a whip! Coolly and deliberately, Jesus expressed the righteous wrath of unchanging holiness.

Do you see why we cautioned you yesterday about trying to express righteous anger? Until we are at the point where absolute holiness consumes our entire being, it is best for us not to attempt it, Jesus could handle it. His emotions were unchanging.

The greatest danger to those who want the mind of Christ is acting from impulse.

What emotions are subject to impulse? Impulsive emotions are nearly always negative—anger, lust, revenge. Think of all the things you wished you hadn't said in an argument! These are the hardest emotions to control. But they are controllable! The Bible strongly emphasizes the will when it talks about the mind. Take revenge, for example. The spiritual mind places revenge in the hands of God *(Heb. 10:30)*. The mind of Christ has both "negative" and positive emotions, but they are always subject to the will. Their public display is subject to godly wisdom, which is the focus of tomorrow's lesson.

✳ **What is the best way for you to avoid impulsive expression of negative emotions? Check one:**
- ❑ **I'll wait until I feel an emotion coming on and pray for the strength to do the right thing.**
- ❑ **I set, renew, and prepare my mind so I can use my will to choose the right action when a negative emotion arises.**

Emotions fall into place when we find freedom (Weeks 2 and 3) and after learning to interpret circumstances according to the blessings of the Sermon on the Mount (Week 6). More mature emotions result from applying these lessons to your life. As you continue to apply them, you will be able to control emotional impulses using godly wisdom and the exercise of your will to do the right thing.

✱ Take a few minutes to review your Bondage to Freedom Lists. Does God want to set you free in some other areas? Continue working on your lists until you sense Christ has set you free indeed.

✱ Continue working on the Lifelong Helps (Virtues and Beatitudes) that God calls to your attention. Let God continue His work in these areas. Keep praying that God will mold you into the image of His Son Jesus Christ.

Jesus and Wisdom

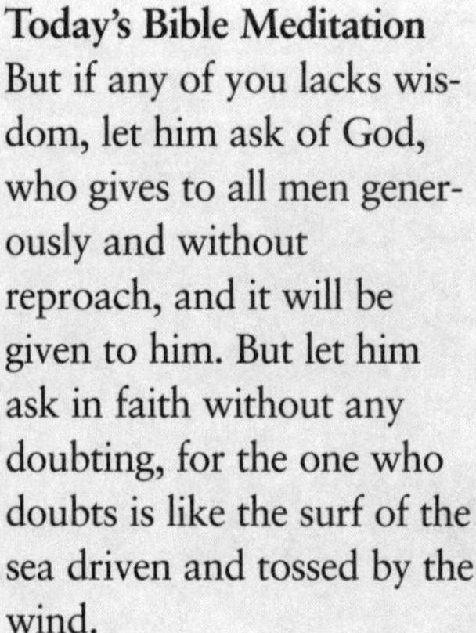

Today's Bible Meditation
But if any of you lacks wisdom, let him ask of God, who gives to all men generously and without reproach, and it will be given to him. But let him ask in faith without any doubting, for the one who doubts is like the surf of the sea driven and tossed by the wind.

James 1:5-6

Name of Christ for Today
Wisdom of God
(1 Cor. 1:24)

Prayer to Begin the Lesson
Lord Jesus, Wisdom of God,
I confess to You that I need Your wisdom. I can't handle all the problems I face

✱ Begin today's lesson by reading the Bible verse and the name of Christ for today. Work on your memory verse. Then use the suggested prayer to begin your study.

Jesus never failed to use His intellect to the advantage of God's cause. Even before He was a teenager, He was going about the work of His Father. When He was 12, He was in the Temple, listening to the teachers. The teachers questioned Jesus and were *amazed at His understanding and His answers (Luke 2:47).* Jesus had an unbelievable knowledge of the Old Testament, and He knew how to use it.

✱ As you read the following paragraph, circle the way Jesus responded to those who questioned Him. To what did He point them?

When people questioned Jesus, He always pointed them back to God's intent. For example, when the chief priests, scribes, and elders demanded that Jesus identify His authority, He referred them to John's baptism and God's divine purpose (see *Luke 20:3-4).* Jesus answered the question about paying taxes to Caesar by saying that both civil and heavenly authority should receive their due *(Luke 20:22-25).* He baffled the Sadducees by pointing out their failure to understand Scripture *(Luke 20:27-28).* In each case, God's purposes were the source of Jesus' answers.

You don't have to be a scholar, a seminary graduate, or a pastor to get a grasp on biblical wisdom. It's available to anyone who can read. There is a section of the Old Testament designated "wisdom literature"—Job, Psalms, Proverbs, Ecclesiastes, and Song of Solomon. As a child, Jesus grew in wisdom *(Luke 2:52).* The depth of His teaching amazed His hearers *(Matt. 7:28-29; Luke 4:32, 36).* Speaking of His own teaching, Jesus claimed, *"The words that I have spoken to you are spirit and are life" (John 6:63).* He often referred to the Scriptures as the reason for His actions. He quoted the Scriptures as a means to resist Satan during His temptation in the wilderness. The Bible is a valuable source of wisdom for those willing to take the time to study it.

✱ How important were the Scriptures to Jesus?________________________

If you are to have the mind of Christ, how important should the Scriptures be to you? ________________________________

by just relying on my own wisdom. I'm so thankful that You know all things and understand all things. Help me to increase in Your wisdom so that You can be glorified in my life. Continue to develop in me the virtues of godly wisdom. Make me pure, peaceable, gentle, approachable, merciful, fruitful, steadfast, and honest.

Amen.

✱ What are some practical ways you can allow the Scriptures to take their rightful place of importance in your mind?

- **❑ a. Carry my Bible with me everywhere so I can look up what I need anytime I need it. Maybe I need to get me one of those pocket sized ones.**
- **❑ b. Read and study the Scriptures.**
- **❑ c. Listen to pastors, youth ministers, and Sunday School teachers as they explain the Scriptures.**
- **❑ d. Meditate on the Scriptures by thinking about them day and night.**
- **❑ e. Memorize the Scriptures.**
- **❑ f. Trust that God will give me a Word from Him when the need arises; otherwise don't worry too much about knowing Scripture.**
- **❑ g. Talk about the application of Scripture with other believers.**

Of these possibilities *b, c, d, e,* and *g* make the most sense, and most closely reflect the pattern of Jesus' life. *A* is not bad, but it's not very practical. You can't always whip out your Bible in every situation, and if you don't have a good grasp on Scripture memory, you won't always find the verse you're looking for when you can. *F* is presumptuous, sort of like a preacher who comes to the pulpit, puts a finger down on the first verse the Bible falls open to, and starts preaching from there. God might give a word, but He isn't obligated to just because that preacher was too lazy to study. The best response is to *Study to shew thyself approved unto God, a workman that needeth not to be ashamed, rightly dividing the word of truth (2 Tim. 2:15,* KJV).
Paul said that in Christ *are hidden all the treasures of wisdom and knowledge (Col. 2:3).* Christ was so strongly identified with wisdom that Paul called Him *the wisdom of God (1 Cor. 1:24).* It is only by applying ourselves to God's wisdom as Christ did that we can develop the will, and control our emotional impulses.

✱ Reflect on how you are doing in becoming like Christ. Are you growing? Use the extra time gained from this shorter lesson to tell God what you are thinking and feeling right now. Use your journal to meditate on the progress you've made. As you pray, make a fresh commitment to God to be a faithful student of His Word.

Jesus' Relations with Things and People

UNIT 9

Hymn Part 4—Christ's Humanity
[Jesus] was made in the likeness of men... And... found in appearance as a man (Phil. 2:7-8).

What Is in This Unit for Me?

All of us who live in today's world need to know Jesus' radically different perspective on material things. Freedom from bondage to things is vital to abundant living. This week discover that you can trust God to provide for your needs so you do not have to worry about the needs of tomorrow. By examining the example of Jesus you also will develop appropriate relationships to God's agenda, friendships, and speech.

Lifelong Objective

You will become like Christ in your relation to material things, God's plan for your life, friendships, and control of your speech.

Unit Learning Goals

- You will understand what Jesus had to say about materialism and the way Jesus related to friends.
- You will demonstrate your commitment to lay up for yourself treasures in heaven.
- You will understand how God provides for our needs.
- You will demonstrate your confidence in how God can provide for you.
- You will see how Jesus based His actions on God's plan for His life.
- You will demonstrate your desire to follow God's plan for your life.
- You will demonstrate your gratitude for your friend Jesus.
- You will understand how Jesus controlled the things He said for divine purposes.
- You will show your commitment to developing self-control in the things you say.

What You Will Do to Develop Appropriate Relationships to People and Things

- You will evaluate your relationship to things according to the teachings of Christ, and you will seek freedom from possessions.
- You will study how God provides for His children, and work on developing a deeper trust in how He can provide for you.
- You will evaluate where you stand in relation to God's plan for your life.
- You will review the Christlike virtue of self-control and seek God's help as it relates to controlling your speech.

Lifelong Helps for Review in This Unit

Bondage to Freedom Lists—Possessions (p. 190)
Christlike Virtues—Self-Control (p. 202)

The Mind of Christ Card Related to This Unit

5A. Unit 9: Scripture Memory—*Matthew 6:20-21*

Day 1
Jesus and Material Things

Day 2
Trusting That God Will Provide

Day 3
Jesus' Sense of Timing

Day 4
Jesus' Friendship

Day 5
Jesus' Speech

Scripture Memory Verse
"But lay up for yourselves treasures in heaven, where neither moth nor rust destroys, and where thieves do not break in or steal; for where your treasure is, there will your heart be also."
Matthew 6:20-21

Today's Bible Meditation
And He said to them, "Beware, and be on your guard against every form of greed; for not even when one has an abundance does his life consist of his possessions."
Luke 12:15

"Do not lay up for yourselves treasures upon earth, where moth and rust destroy, and where thieves break in and steal. But lay up for yourselves treasures in heaven, where neither moth nor rust destroys, and where thieves do not break in or steal; for where your treasure is, there will your heart be also."
Matthew 6:19-21

Name of Christ for Today
Heir of All Things
(Heb. 1:2)

Prayer to Begin the Lesson
Lord Jesus, You are the Heir of All Things. I am amazed that You call me a joint-heir with You. I confess that I live like a poor person instead of a prince. I haven't learned to appreciate or understand the riches and treasures You make

Jesus and Material Things

✳ Begin today's lesson by reading the Bible verse and the name of Christ for today. Work on your memory verse. Then use the suggested prayer to begin your study.

Several years ago, a popular singer reminded us that "we are living in a material world." Few celebrities have made more of that fact than the singer of this song. She seems to be the epitome of wealth and material excess. Sadly, there is a lot of the "material girl" in all of us.

Jesus' Example

Both by example and by teaching, Jesus left no doubt that He didn't care much for material "stuff." Think about it. He was born in a stable. He lived as a working man (a carpenter). During His ministry, He didn't even have a permanent place to lay His head (see *Luke 9:58)*. At His death, the soldiers gambled for His only material possession—His seamless coat. His body was laid in a borrowed tomb because He didn't have a grave of His own.

✳ Which of the following best describes Jesus' attitude toward "stuff"? Check one:
- **❑ He was obsessed with stuff. He used His powers to get many things for His personal comfort and pleasure.**
- **❑ He was free from attachment to stuff. He chose a lowly life and saw no value in accumulating things.**

Jesus' Teaching

In *Luke 16:11,* Jesus contrasted true riches with unrighteous mammon (possessions). He warned against storing up earthly wealth, and advised His followers to store up *treasures in heaven, where neither moth nor rust destroys, and where thieves do not break in or steal" (Matt. 6:20)*. In connection to this warning, Jesus gave an important principle: *"Where your treasure is, there will your heart be also" (Matt. 6:21)*.

✳ Be completely honest with yourself. Where are most of your treasures? Check one:
- **❑ I don't have any treasures.**
- **❑ In heaven.**
- **❑ On earth.**

Many of Jesus' parables dealt with the concept of true riches. In one parable, a rich but stupid farmer kept storing his crops in larger and larger barns—accumulating "stuff" for himself. Then, he said, "You've done good for yourself. Kick back! Relax!" He died that same night, and his gathered wealth was worthless. How foolish (see *Luke 12:16-21)*.

Jesus said, *"No one of you can be My disciple who does not give up all his own possessions" (Luke 14:33)*. Many of the disciples' stories emphasize that they left everything in order to follow Jesus. Matthew *left everything behind and rose and began to follow Him (Luke 5:28)*. James and John left their fishing nets right there on the beach and took off after Jesus *(Matt. 4:20)*. Once, after Jesus was teaching on how hard it was for a rich person to enter the kingdom of God, Peter reminded Him, *"We have left everything and followed You: what then will there be for us?"* (see *Matt. 19:27)*. The Gospels never record any of the disciples going back to their former possessions or lives.

Jesus told the Rich Young Ruler to *"Go and sell all you possess, and give it to the poor, and you shall have treasure in heaven; and come, follow Me" (Mark 10:21)*. The young man was promised heavenly treasure if he would only give up his earthly treasure. But this young man had made wealth his god, and loved it even more than he loved God. The Bible says *he went away sad, because he had great wealth (Mark 10:22,* NIV). This is the only story in the Bible where it explicitly says that Jesus loved a would-be follower. His refusal must have been very painful for Jesus. He exclaimed, *"How hard it will be for those who are wealthy to enter the kingdom of God!" (Mark 10:23)*. When questioned about this, Jesus said, *"all things are possible with God" (Mark 10:27)*.

available to me. I also confess that I am too attached to the things of the world. Teach me to deny myself and give up my ownership to my things. I want to be completely free from attachment to things so I may follow You and Your example.

Amen.

✳ **Turn to the Lifelong Helps (p. 190) and review the Bondage to Freedom list related to possessions. Pray as you read through that list. Is there anything God is asking you to get rid of because it has become a false god to you? Respond in whatever way God directs you. You may want to go into more detail in your journal. But here, briefly describe how you feel about your material possessions.**

____

____

Jesus didn't compromise when it came to possessions. Notice that He didn't go running after the Rich Young Ruler (even though He loved him) to say "Wait! Come back! Maybe I made it sound a little harsh. Let's talk about this!" He said, *"No one can serve two masters; for either he will hate the one and love the other, or he will hold to one and despise the other. You cannot serve God and mammon* [money]*" (Matt. 6:24)*. One of the greatest rivals God has is worldly success. Does that mean that money itself is evil? No. We can have money and use it wisely, like the women who supported Jesus and His disciples. But it is a temptation to begin to worship material things. Jesus warned, *"That which is highly esteemed among men is detestable in the sight of God" (Luke 16:15)*.

The mind of Christ places God above everything else in the world.

A Remedy

Greed will cause us to hang on to things for our own use. Greed is described strongly in *Ephesians 5:5* as idolatry—worshiping a false god. The best remedy for materialism is cheerful giving.

Jesus repeatedly urged joyful giving. In the Sermon on the Mount, He commanded, *"Give to him who asks of you, and do not turn away from him who wants to borrow from you" (Matt. 5:42)*. Jesus warned that giving should be secret—no public announcements (see *Matt. 6:2-4)*. God is interested in the motivation of our heart.

✳ What is one way to get rid of a materialistic spirit?

____

Money can become a powerful god that demands allegiance in a subtle but effective way. Money itself is neither good nor evil. It can be used for worldly purposes or for God. We must be wise and heavenly minded in its use. We must be ready to give as faithful stewards of God's resources.

✳ Is there anything God wants you to give away as a way to be rid of your materialistic spirit? Pray about it. If God does reveal something, ask Him where or to whom you are to give it. You may need to set your mind and heart to give, and then watch for the opportunity God brings your way. If God guides you to give in a special way, describe below what, and to whom.

____

____

DAY 2

Today's Bible Meditation
"But if God so arrays the grass of the field, which is alive today and tomorrow is thrown into the furnace, will He not much more do so for you, O men of little faith? Do not be anxious then, saying, 'What shall we eat?' or 'What shall we drink?' or 'With what shall we clothe ourselves?' For all these things the Gentiles eagerly seek; for your heav-

Trusting That God Will Provide

✳ Begin today's lesson by reading the Bible verse and the name of Christ for today. Work on your memory verse. Then use the suggested prayer to begin your study.

If you are sitting in a place where you can look out a window, do it. Do you see any birds? Trees? Flowers? Even if you can't see outside right now, imagine that you are watching a nature show on one of those science cable channels. It seems like there's always one on, talking about how animals survive in the wild or something like that. You never see a wild animal worrying about where tomorrow's meal is coming from. They know, instinctively, that there will be food.

Jesus used animals to make a teaching point about how God provides for our needs. In two passages (see *Matt. 6:25-34* and *Luke 12:22-32)*, Jesus said that God provides for the birds and the lilies. Since God provides for them, certainly He will provide for His children, who are far more valuable. In Luke, Jesus promised to provide for more than food and clothing: *"Do not be afraid, little flock, for your Father has chosen gladly to give you the kingdom" (Luke 12:32).*

✳ Why should God's children not worry about food, drink, or clothing?

____

✳ **Go back over Today's Bible Meditation and look for the conditions of God's provision. What are the terms of the agreement? In other words, what should you seek first, after which God will provide?**

____

Although the Bible doesn't say anything about Jesus' teenage years, we assume that He worked in His earthly father's carpenter shop until He began His public ministry at age 30. He set an example, that a working profession is valid and useful. After He began His ministry, God supplied His material needs through the ministry of some women followers, *who were contributing to* [the disciples'] *support out of their private means (Luke 8:3)*. Jesus didn't require them to give away their wealth, as He did the Rich Young Ruler, because for them wealth was not a god. Their love and devotion was given to Jesus. Because of their support, Jesus and the disciples were freed to devote their entire time to ministry. Jesus never worried about having His daily needs met, because God took care of it. Our promise is that God will also do that for us.

Learning to Trust

When I was first asked to teach *The Mind of Christ* publicly, I developed a study guide to go with it. I was shocked, though, when I found out how much it would cost to print it. $1000.00! My wife and I checked our bank book: $37. I felt like God wanted me to print the study guide, but I couldn't see how. But I was convinced, based on my studies of Jesus' life, that if there was a genuine ministry need, God would supply the resources. My wife and I prayed for a miracle. It wasn't long before the treasurer of our church called with an unusual message. "T.W." he said, "We have a businessman in our church who just finished a major transaction. He came by this morning to tell us that he had an unexpected surplus, and that God told him to give it to you." Guess how much it was for? You guessed it—$1000.00!

We couldn't wait to take the study guide to the printer. Normally, I don't look forward to getting bills, but this time, I was practically waiting by the mailbox for the bill to come, because I was so excited about how God had met our needs. But the bill came, along with a stack of letters, and my heart sank. The printer underestimated the cost. The actual cost was $1097, and we didn't have the $97. Discouraged, I opened the rest of the mail. The third letter I opened was from a man who said he had been praying for my ministry. "God impressed on me that you had a need," his letter said, "and that I'm supposed to meet it." Inside was a check for $100.00. Once again, God had provided.

That story is not unique. Over the years, God has repeatedly supplied money that I have needed for ministry. The supply is usually exact, and it comes at the time of need—seldom early. You see, we are only able to please God when we walk with Him by faith (see *Heb. 11:6*). Jesus lived a life of faith, and He wants us to do the same.

✳ **When has there been a specific time in your life when God provided for you in a way that you knew it came from God? Write about the time in the margin, and prepare to share a summary with your small group this week.**

Don't Worry About Stuff

When you think about how big God is, and how small your needs are, worrying is pretty useless. Jesus told us not to worry about our daily needs, and He reminded us that only pagans (people without the understanding of God's work in their lives) con-

enly Father knows that you need all these things. But seek first His kingdom and His righteousness; and all these things shall be added to you."

Matthew 6:30-33

Names of Christ for Today
Leader and Commander of the People
(Isa. 55:4)

Prayer to Begin the Lesson
Lord Jesus,
not only are You head of the church; but You are also Leader and Commander of Your People. You have intended Your church to be an army that will follow You into battle against the enemy. Please help my youth group to follow Your leadership so that even the gates of hell will not prevail against Your church. I pledge my allegiance to You as my Commander in Chief. Give me so much confidence in Your provision that I won't worry about tomorrow. Give me the faith to trust that You will provide.
Amen.

sistently worry (see *Matt. 6:25-32).* As a teenager, you probably have a pretty good handle on not worrying about material needs. Chances are, you still live at home, and your parents take care of your basic needs of food, shelter, and clothing. If you remember that God provides for your needs in the same way, you'll save yourself a lot of stress as you get older. God is a loving Parent who wants to meet your needs.

Worry accomplishes nothing, is a waste of mental effort and is not characteristic of the mind of Christ.

✳ Which of the following best describes you? Check one.

- **❑ I've learned the lesson about God's provision and I seldom worry about my need for things. I trust God to provide for my needs.**
- **❑ I have desperate needs. My parents struggle financially. What if they can't take care of me?**
- **❑ I'm like a boat at sea. When my needs are met and it's smooth sailing, my confidence is high. But when things get tight, my worry meter kicks into overdrive.**
- **❑ Other: ______________________________**

✳ Be honest with God. Confess to Him that you are His child. Ask for the faith and confidence to trust His provision even in difficult times. Ask Him to develop your trust in Him so that you won't worry like pagans do. Pray that God will be honored in your life.

Jesus' Sense of Timing

DAY 3

✱ Begin today's lesson by reading the Bible verse and the name of Christ for today. Work on your memory verse. Then use the suggested prayer to begin your study.

Once I heard a youth preacher emphasize the point that Jesus never wore a watch. He was preaching on the story of Jesus healing Jairus' daughter in *Luke 8:43-48.* On His way to Jairus' house, He interrupted His trip to deal with the woman who had an issue of blood. He knew that the little girl would die if He delayed. You could imagine a normal person, say, a doctor on one of those prime-time hospital dramas, looking at his watch and saying, "Sorry, lady. I'd love to help you, but a little girl's life is at stake." Jesus didn't do that. He never seemed rushed; He never seemed worried about a schedule. Even when He got the news that His good friend Lazarus was sick, *He stayed then two days longer in the place where He was (John 11:6).* Jesus knew what He would do. He had a plan that would bring glory to God, and He was more concerned with that than with the momentary illness of Lazarus. By the way, the resurrection of Lazarus was the decisive factor in the Sanhedrin's decision to kill Jesus. So Jesus knew what He was doing. Today, we're going to look at the Jesus who never wore a watch.

✱ Check the words below that normally describe your feelings and thoughts about your schedule. Put an *I* next to the ones that seem to apply to you most of the time. Then, go back over the list. Put a *J* next to the ones that describe how you think Jesus felt most of the time.

❑ angry	❑ calm	❑ can't wait to get started
❑ confident	❑ cool	❑ excited
❑ frustrated	❑ hurried	❑ overloaded
❑ relaxed	❑ rushed	❑ stressed
❑ worried	❑ want to quit	❑ too much time

How did your thoughts and feelings compare to Jesus'? Jesus set His mind on the Kingdom, and He focused His attention on His purpose for ministry. Every miracle, every teaching, everything fit into a purposeful progression. Jesus was living His life according to His Father's plan. Jesus timed every phase of His ministry in relation to His crucifixion. Look at these examples:

- After Jesus' brothers tried to get Him to go to the Feast of Tabernacles so He could get the crowd's attention, He told them, *"My time is not yet at hand" (John 7:6).*
- Later, during that same Feast, Jesus was challenged by some of the religious leaders when He identified Himself as God. The leaders were furious with Him, but the Bible says, *no one seized Him, because His hour had not yet come (John 8:20).*
- After He raised Lazarus from the dead, *Jesus... no longer continued to walk publicly among the Jews, but went away from there (John 11:54).* Jesus didn't withdraw because He was afraid, or had "worn out His welcome." He knew that the people would try to make Him a king by force, and because this wasn't within the Father's time table, He left the region.

* Jesus *resolutely set His face to go to Jerusalem (Luke 9:51).*

Today's Bible Meditations

And He said, "Go into the city to a certain man, and say to him, 'The Teacher says, "My time is at hand; I am to keep the Passover at your house with My disciples." ' "

Matthew 26:18

Then He came to the disciples, and said to them, "Are you still sleeping and taking your rest? Behold, the hour is at hand and the Son of Man is being betrayed into the hands of sinners."

Matthew 26:45

Names of Christ for Today

King Eternal, Immortal, Invisible

(1 Tim. 1:17)

Prayer to Begin the Lesson

Jesus, thank You for focusing Your attention and living according to Your Father's plan. I'm glad You came to earth to save me. Thank You for going to the cross to pay my debt. I rejoice that the sealed tomb could not stop God's plan, but that you were raised to reign eternally. I praise you. Amen.

- On Monday of Holy Week, Jesus said, *"The hour has come for the Son of Man to be glorified" (John 12:23).*
- When Jesus sent the disciples to prepare the room for the Last Supper, He instructed them to say to the host, *"My time is at hand" (Matt. 26:18).*
- Jesus began His prayer for the disciples, *"Father, the hour has come" (John 17:1).*
- In Gethsemane, Jesus said to the sleeping disciples, *"The hour has come" (Mark 14:41).*

Jesus' entire life focused on that final week. That's where He put all His concentration.

✷ Check one of the responses below:

- **❑ Jesus was single-minded. He focused all His attention on the purpose His Father had for Him.**
- **❑ Jesus was scattered in His thinking. He had a million things to do and not enough hours in the day to do them.**

How do we imitate this kind of single-mindedness? While none of us knows our life's plan as well as Jesus did, we all have the same access to the Father that Jesus did! We know that Jesus spent extensive time in prayer. We've seen how much Jesus read, memorized, and studied God's Word. Jesus devoted Himself to knowing the Father. The more we apply these disciplines to our lives, the more we can have Jesus' focus and sense of timing.

✷ Turn to Unit 1 (pp. 14-15) and read again the description of single-minded. Would you describe yourself as single-minded or scatter-brained? Circle one.

✷ End today's lesson by spending time with God. Tell God about your desire to work His agenda for your life. Agree to follow God one day at a time using His timetable.

Jesus' Friendships

DAY 4

✳ **Begin today's lesson by reading the Bible verse and the name of Christ for today. Work on your memory verse. Then use the suggested prayer to begin your study.**

Your friendships are an important part of your life. During your teenage years, your relationship with friends your age become increasingly more important. Good news! Friendships were important to Jesus too.

We've talked about the Christlike virtue of being approachable. Jesus was approachable and faithful to His friends. He stood by them in times of need, and He ministered to their needs. For example, when He visited the house of His friend Simon Peter, He healed Peter's mother.

✳ **Name at least two virtues Jesus displayed in relationship to His friends.**

Jesus was __________________ and ________________.

As Jesus displayed faithfulness and approachability to His friends, His friends in turn were loyal to Him. Several of these friends we would consider to be coworkers of Jesus.

- Jesus sent 70 of His followers out on a preaching mission *(Luke 10:1)*.
- Many of His women friends supported Jesus' ministry out of their own pockets *(Luke 8:3)*, and several of them remained at the cross, even through terrifying circumstances *(Matt. 27:55)*.
- Those same women later went to the tomb *(Matt. 28:1; Luke 24:10)*.

Jesus had many friends, and He made them easily. The Bible describes Mary, Martha, and Lazarus as close acquaintances of Jesus, and He visited them often *(John 11)*. On one occasion, He was at a wedding of family friends *(John 2:1-11)*, and we know that He often accepted dinner invitations. Joseph of Arimathea requested permission to bury Jesus, and laid Him in his own tomb *(Matt. 27:57-58)*. Nicodemus participated in the burial *(John 19:39)*.

Have you ever wondered why Jesus had disciples? Sometimes they were so slow to understand things; they argued constantly with each other; and during Jesus' trial and crucifixion, they ran and hid. Why would God Himself choose to be around them? The fact is, Jesus' closest friends in His lifetime were His disciples, and the Bible says that He chose them *that they might be with Him (Mark 3:14)*. Jesus wanted and needed friendship just as much as you and I do. In *John 15:13*, Jesus said the greatest love a person can demonstrate is to lay down his life for his friends. Just a short time after He said this, Jesus would do exactly that. He told the disciples, *"No longer do I call you slaves, for the slave does not know what his master is doing; but I have called you friends, for all things that I have heard from My Father I have made known to you" (John 15:15)*.

✳ **Read Today's Bible Meditation, *John 15:13-15*, again, and answer these questions. Based on *verse 13*, what demonstrates supreme love of a friend?**

____

Today's Bible Meditation
"Greater love has no one than this, that one lay down his life for his friends. You are My friends, if you do what I command you. No longer do I call you slaves, for the slave does not know what his master is doing; but I have called you friends, for all things that I have heard from My Father I have made known to you."

John 15:13-15

Names of Christ for Today
Friend of Publicans and Sinners

(Matt. 11:19, KJV)

Prayer to Begin the Lesson
Jesus, thank You for being a friend of sinners. Otherwise, I wouldn't have a chance. Your friendship is the best thing that could ever have happened to me. I want to be Your friend. I pledge to do the things You command me. As I study Your Word, help me to identify the things You desire of me so I can obey. I want fellowship with You. I open my life and invite You to come in and fellowship with me.

Amen.

What does Jesus expect of His friends? ***(v. 14)*** ______________________

What is the difference between a servant and a friend?

____

The ultimate expression of love is to give up one's life for a friend. Jesus did that—not only for His friends who were alive at the time, but also for us! Jesus expected obedience from His friends. When Jesus moved from a master-slave relationship with His disciples to a Friend-friend relationship, He revealed to them the will and heart of His Father.

✳ Based on this passage, how do you rate your Friend-friend relationship with Christ? Check one or write your own.

- **❑ I don't think I'm good enough to be a friend of Christ.**
- **❑ Sometimes I feel a closeness with Christ, and He reveals the Father's will to me. But at other times I seem distanced from the relationship.**
- **❑ Right now I feel a deep closeness to Christ. I would lay down my life for Him if I needed to.**
- **❑ Other** ______________________________

Within the intimate circle of the twelve disciples, Jesus developed an even closer bond with Peter, James, and John. You might consider these three guys as Jesus' close friends. They were the three who witnessed Jesus' transfiguration *(Mark 9:2)*. It was Peter, James, and John who were with Jesus while He prayed in the Garden of Gethsemane *(Mark 14:33)*.

Even in this circle, Jesus had a best friend. The disciple John is referred to as the disciple *whom Jesus loved (John 13:23),* and he was sitting next to Jesus at the Last Supper. Of all the disciples, John was the only one who was present at the foot of the cross. Jesus trusted John to take care of His mother *(John 19:26)*.

Today we've seen Jesus' friendships. Even Jesus needed a group of close, trusted friends. He needed a best friend who stuck by Him to the very end. If Jesus needed that in His life, how much more do we need it in ours?

✳ Refer to the diagram "Jesus' Circle of Friends" and complete the diagram "My Circle of Friends" on pages 221-222. Spend some time today meditating on your friendships. Who in your life would you put in each level of friendship? Do your friendships honor God and draw you closer to Christ? End today's lesson by spending time with Jesus—the Best Friend of all. Express thanks to Him for His friendship. Share with Him your joys and concerns. Respond to His love. Ask Jesus to guide you in cultivating godly friendships.

Jesus' Speech

✱ **Begin today's lesson by reading the Bible verse and the name of Christ for today. Work on your memory verse. Then use the suggested prayer to begin your study.**

✱ **Read Today's Bible Meditation again, and underline three things these verses tell you about Jesus' speech.**

The conversation on the church basketball court began innocently enough. Several of the players were "cracking" on each other—putting each other down, light-heartedly making fun of each other. They were all good friends, active in the youth group, and none of them meant anything by it. But then, one of the "good-natured" put-downs hit a little too close to home, and the "cracking" took on a different flavor. Tempers started to rise, and soon, good friends and solid Christians were on the verge of a fist fight.

Can you relate to this scene? It happens all the time. Today humor is often at the expense of someone else. TV sitcoms are full of biting, cruel sarcasm, and even Christians can get sucked into putting each other down instead of building each other up. We can learn a lot from the example of Jesus.

Peter says there was, *no deceit found in His mouth (v.22).* When Jesus was verbally abused, Jesus didn't retaliate by abusing back. When Jesus suffered, He didn't lash back with threats. When Jesus became frustrated with His disciples' slowness to catch on, He didn't "crack" on them or put them down. While He did rebuke them for their lack of understanding, He never launched personal verbal attacks. Jesus demonstrated perfect self-control in His speech.

There are several biblical passages that relate to control over the tongue. I would encourage you to study *James 3* if you are struggling with this. Today, we're going to look at the example of Jesus' life. How did Jesus use speech?

Much of Jesus' speech was in teaching and preaching. Matthew says He went about *all the cities and the villages, teaching in their synagogues (Matt. 9:35). Matthew 5-7* is the greatest single body of His teaching, the Sermon on the Mount. Jesus also taught in parables—short stories with a profound spiritual truth (see *Mark 4:2).* The crowds were amazed at His teaching, because it was so different from the legalistic teaching of the day (see *Mark 6:2).*

✱ **What is one way Jesus used His speech? He** ______________________

What is one way you could apply this way of using speech to your life?

____

Jesus' commission to ministry was to preach (see *Luke 4:18).* He went about *preaching the gospel of the kingdom (Matt. 9:35,* KJV). Teaching instructs; preaching convinces. Jesus placed a high value on preaching. Later, Jesus said that His gospel would be preached in the whole world (see *Matt. 24:14).* You may or may not be called to preach sermons. But remember: teaching instructs; preaching convinces. Anytime you are trying to convince someone else of the truth of the gospel, you are acting as a preacher.

Today's Bible Meditation
Who committed no sin, nor was any deceit found in His mouth; and while being reviled, He did not revile in return; while suffering, He uttered no threats, but kept entrusting Himself to Him who judges righteously; and He Himself bore our sins in His body on the cross, that we might die to sin and live to righteousness; for by His wounds you were healed.
1 Peter 2:22-24

Names of Christ for Today
Faithful and True Witness
(Rev. 3:14)

Prayer to Begin the Lesson
Faithful and True Witness, You perfectly reflected the Father through Your life. Everything about You is genuine, faithful, and true. I confess to You that I have trouble controlling my speech. I say things I regret. I ask You to continue Your work of developing my self-control regarding my tongue. Help me to listen more than I speak, and to speak only that which is true and wholesome. Enable me to reflect You in the way I speak.
Amen.

✱ What is a second way Jesus used His speech? He ______________________ .

What is one way you could apply this way of using speech to your life?

____

✱ Here are some other ways Jesus used His speech. Underline any you identify with. If you could imagine yourself in a similar situation, underline it.

- Jesus showed incredible skill in using questions as a teaching device.
- Sometimes Jesus warned people about coming difficulties or temptations.
- Jesus usually answered the questions that were asked of Him. He did not, however, answer the Pharisees demand for a sign.
- Jesus effectively used logical arguments, for example, when He was accused of casting out demons using the power of Satan *(Matt. 12:24-29).*
- At times, Jesus severely reproached unresponsive people and cities.
- Jesus even reproached His disciples for their lack of faith.
- Jesus denounced the hypocrisy of the Pharisees.
- Jesus complimented a few individuals for their faith or faithfulness.
- Jesus frequently reassured people, telling them not to be afraid.

Jesus' use of words was economical. He never "ran off at the mouth." He never backed down from what needed to be said, however. His words were always appropriate and timed perfectly. If encouragement was necessary, Jesus spoke as the occasion demanded. Jesus took every opportunity to speak very seriously. When He said, *"Every careless word that men shall speak, they shall render account for it in the day of judgment" (Matt. 12:36),* He applied that standard to Himself as well.

✱ How important is it for you to be careful about the way you speak? Check one.

❑ Not very important. After all, I'm forgiven. What I say now doesn't really matter.

❑ Very important. God is keeping track of every careless word, and I will have to give Him an explanation on the day of judgment.

❑ Other: ____

Having the mind of Christ means being careful and appropriate in our use of words. *Ephesians 4:29* says, *Do not let any unwholesome talk come out of your mouths, but only what is helpful for building others up according to their needs, that it may benefit those who listen* (NIV). We've all seen how "unwholesome talk" can really hurt an individual relationship or a youth group. Even when put-downs are meant in fun, they do nothing to build up one another. There are too many other things for Christians to focus their attention on to waste time on "cracking" on each other.

✱ Turn to page 202 and review the Lifelong Help on Self-Control.

✱ Close today's session by talking to the Lord. If you don't normally pray aloud, consider praying out loud, just to hear your own speech to God. Confess any careless or inappropriate words you recently used that come to mind. Ask God to strengthen you with a Christ-controlled tongue that never dishonors Him.

Living in the Spirit

Hymn Part 4—Christ's Humanity
[Jesus] was made in the likeness of men... And... found in appearance as a man (Phil. 2:7-8)

What Is in This Unit for Me?

Last week, we talked about the material world. This week, you'll understand how Christ lived in the material world, but still lived in the Spirit. From the example of Christ, you will learn ways to give greater control to the spiritual dimensions of your life. You will be able to identify with Christ and follow His example in your relationship to the Father and Holy Spirit.

Lifelong Objective

In Christ, you will seek to live in a proper relationship to the Father and the Holy Spirit. You will continue to emphasize the spiritual over the material.

How God Will Be Working in You

Christ's spirituality within you begins with a mind-set that concentrates spiritually first and materially second. The greater your spiritual perception, the more God is able to guide you. Measure yourself against the standard of Christ's life. Your growth in Christ can only be measured by your dependence on the Holy Spirit. God will direct your outer life through His inner spirit.

Unit Learning Goals

- You will understand that the spiritual is more important than the material.
- You will demonstrate a desire to emphasize the spiritual over the material.
- You will understand the source and nature of Jesus' purposes for His life and ministry.
- You will show a desire to know and do the will of the Heavenly Father.
- You will understand the ways Jesus related to the Father and how you can relate to the Heavenly Father.
- You will understand the ways Jesus related to the Holy Spirit and how you can relate to the Holy Spirit.
- You will understand the ways Jesus used Scripture and practiced prayer.

What You Will Do to Begin Living in the Spirit

- You will study and seek to imitate the examples of Jesus.
- You will examine the Scriptures that speak clearly about your relationship to the Father and Holy Spirit.
- You will spend time meditating on the Scriptures and praying so God can conform your mind to reflect the image of His Son Jesus.

Lifelong Helps Related to This Unit

Your Relationship to the Father and the Holy Spirit (pp. 212-213)

The Mind of Christ Card Related to This Unit

5A. Unit 10: Scripture Memory—*John 6:63*

UNIT 10

Scripture Memory Verse
"It is the Spirit who gives life; the flesh profits nothing; the words that I have spoken to you are spirit and are life."
John 6:63

DAY 1

Today's Bible Meditation
So also it is written, "The first man, Adam, became a living soul." The last Adam became a life-giving spirit. However, the spiritual is not first, but the natural; then the spiritual. The first man is from the earth, earthy; the second man is from heaven. As is the earthy, so also are those who are earthy; and as is the heavenly, so also are those who are heavenly. And just as we have borne the image of the earthy, we shall also bear the image of the heavenly.
1 Corinthians 15:45-49

Names of Christ for Today
A Lamb Unblemished and Spotless
(1 Pet. 1:19)

Prayer to Begin the Lesson
Lord Jesus,
I long to bear Your image more clearly. The material world has such a hold on my life. Teach me today to give priority to the spiritual, as You did in Your earthly life. Cleanse me from the contamination of the world, and make me without blemish and spot.
Amen.

The Spiritual Controls the Material

✳ Begin today's lesson by reading the Bible verse and the name of Christ for today. Work on your memory verse. Then use the suggested prayer to begin your study.

All of us are challenged with trying to be spiritual in the midst of a material world. We are torn between two opposing forces. On one side, there is the Spiritual world—the promise of increased fellowship and relationship with God. On the other side is the pull of the material—a thousand and one things that compete with God for attention. Within that realm are material goods, success, wealth, and prestige. On one side are your wants and purposes. On the other side are Christ's desires and purposes. Right now, take an inventory of how you are doing in the battle.

✳ If God were to evaluate your life right now, how do you think He would rank your life on the following scales? Circle the number on the scale between the two extremes.

Focused on the Material World	1	2	3	4	5	6	7	8	9	10	**Focused on the Spiritual World**
Focused on My Purposes	1	2	3	4	5	6	7	8	9	10	**Focused on Christ's Purposes**

You have to focus on the material world some. You need to make a living. The basic necessities cost money. If your youth group has a lot of activities, those activities cost money. Life in high school places pressures on how to dress, how to make a good impression, and whom to associate with. And money for school activities is a big issue also. So when does that become sin? Jesus denounced the scribes and Pharisees for being too concerned with the things of the world: *"You are of this world, I am not of this world" (John 8:23).* The more you give your attention to the things of the world, the more you allow Satan to control and manipulate you. We can't help living in the material world. It becomes sin when you focus on your purposes rather than Christ's purposes. That's when we become of the world, and not just in the world.

We've seen that one of God's purposes in coming to the world was to show us how to live life as God intended it. That's why God became flesh, and that's why you are seeking to imitate the perfect humanity of Jesus' earthly life. Jesus' example shows how to live a spiritual life in a material world.

Jesus Emphasized the Spiritual Over the Material

Jesus had nothing to do with the world's system. He told the Jews, *"I am not of this world" (John 8:23).* His told His disciples, *"The ruler of the world is coming, and he has nothing in Me" (John 14:30).* He told Pilate, *"My kingdom is not of this world" (John 18:36).* Jesus trained His disciples so well that He said of them, *"They are not of the world, even as I am not of the world" (John 17:16).*

✱ As Christ's disciple, which of the following should you be? Check one:

❑ I am to live like the world with a focus on the material.

❑ I am to live like Christ, with a focus on the spiritual.

Jesus knew how to live His life in the spiritual realm. One of the secrets to His success was that He knew which controlled which. Sometimes we think that the material controls the spiritual. The opposite is true. We've all seen what happens to an athlete when "his head isn't into the game." He may be in top physical condition and have the best equipment. But if he isn't focused, and concentrating on the game, the physical won't matter at all. Jesus worked knowing that the spiritual controlled the physical. Consider these examples:

- In the physical world, there was a bad storm on the Sea of Galilee. But because the spiritual controlled the physical, Jesus was able to calm the storm (see *Mark 4:36-41).*
- In the physical world, there wasn't enough food to feed five thousand men, not to mention the women and children in the crowd. But because the spiritual controlled the physical, twelve baskets of bread and fish were left over after the multitude ate their fill (see *Luke 9:12-17).*

We could go on and on, noting the healings, the casting out of demons, the control over nature, that characterized Jesus' ministry. But the point is clear. The spiritual is always more important and more powerful than the material. There's nothing wrong with the material. Jesus never said it was evil. But it must always be subjected to the spiritual.

All Right, So What Do I Do About It?

We've seen how Jesus emphasized the spiritual over the material in His ministry. We who desire the mind of Christ must be willing to express in tangible ways our conviction that the spiritual is greater than the material.

- Giving demonstrates the value you place on the spiritual over the material. Providing financially or materially for spiritual concerns can help you gain victory over a materialistic spirit. A youth determined how much he would give to his church's annual Christmas offering by matching the amount he had spent on the most expensive Christmas present he bought .
- Jesus would often stay up and pray all night. Going without sleep for the purpose of a spiritual activity can help you accomplish spiritual aims. One youth group I've heard of participated in a "cardboard campout." In order to become more spiritually sensitive to the homeless, they spent the night in their church's parking lot, sleeping in shelters they had made out of cardboard boxes and masking tape.
- Fasting[1] (denying food to your body for a set period of time) can be a way of saying "My body is subject to my spirit." I have heard of some people who will skip a meal or two and give the money they would spend on those meals to a hunger offering.

✱ Ask God to help you identify areas where the material may have too much importance or influence in your life. Are any of the following areas too important? Which ones? Check all that apply. If you know of others write them on the line.

❑ school	❑ car	❑ clothes	❑ music
❑ collections	❑ eating	❑ hobbies	❑ TV
❑ exercise	❑ money	❑ sports	❑ movies
❑ part-time job	❑ other: ______________________		

✷ **Ask the Lord to guide you to victory over the areas you checked above. Do the following:**

- **Set your mind on things above—the spiritual.**
- **Allow God to renew your mind with a Christlike mindset.**
- **Deny yourself and the importance of the material.**
- **Follow Christ in giving priority and emphasis to the spiritual.**
- **Ask God to help you emphasize the spiritual in practical ways.**
- **Write notes to yourself about the things you sense God is guiding you to do.**

✷ **Conclude today's lesson with this prayer:**

Father, I want to see life as You see it, and as Jesus sees it. Give me spiritual perception. Then, through Your Spirit, give me the spiritual energy to follow and do all You want me to do. I ask this in the name and the power of Jesus. Amen.

DAY 2

Today's Bible Meditations
"I have come down from heaven, not to do My own will, but the will of Him who sent Me."
John 6:38

"As the Father has sent Me, I also send you."
John 20:21

Names of Christ for Today
The Power of God
(1 Cor. 1:24)

Christ's Statements of Purpose

✷ **Begin today's lesson by reading the Bible verse and the name of Christ for today. Work on your memory verse. Then use the suggested prayer to begin your study.**

Our church finished what we called our visioning process. We came up with a document saying what we hoped to accomplish as a church during the next five years. This document begins with a "Purpose Statement"—it explains who we are as a church and what we see as our purpose.

Every organization has a purpose statement, whether it's written or unwritten. A football team's purpose statement ought to be "to win football games" (otherwise, they will have a pretty lousy season!). A fast-food restaurant chain's mission statement might be, "To deliver the best possible food with the best possible service to the most possible people at the lowest possible price." Nearly all purpose statements will follow the formula of "infinitive + verb." "To Win…" "To Deliver…" "To Provide…"

During Jesus' ministry, He made several statements that indicated His purpose. They all indicate that Jesus was focused and concentrated on one goal: to establish God's Kingdom on earth.

✷ **Read the following purpose statements of Jesus and underline words or phrases that indicate what Jesus saw as His purposes for life and ministry. Remember the "infinitive + verb" formula, although not all of them will follow it exactly.**

Prayer to Begin the Lesson
Heavenly Father,
You have placed Your Son in me. You have also given me the calling to follow in His steps with a purpose that reflects His purposes for life and ministry. Please help me to know Your purposes for my life and ministry, and then work through me to accomplish them in Your power.
Amen.

Purpose Statements of Jesus

- *The Spirit of the Lord God is upon me, because the Lord has anointed me to bring good news to the afflicted; He has sent me to bind up the brokenhearted, to proclaim liberty to captives, and freedom to prisoners; to proclaim the favorable year of the Lord, and the day of vengeance of our God; to comfort all who mourn (Isa. 61:1-2).*
- *"My food is to do the will of Him who sent Me, and to accomplish his work" (John 4:34).*
- *"I have come down from heaven, not to do My own will, but the will of Him that sent Me" (John 6:38).*
- *"I must preach the kingdom of God to other cities also, for I was sent for this purpose" (Luke 4:43).*
- *"The Son of Man has come to seek and to save that which was lost" (Luke 19:10).*
- *"For this I have been born, and for this I have come into the world, to bear witness to the truth" (John 18:37).*

✳ Jesus used statements like "The Spirit of the Lord… anointed Me," "Him that sent me," and "I came down from heaven" to describe the source of His purposes. What was the source of Jesus' purposes?
- ❑ the world and worldly concerns
- ❑ God and spiritual concerns

Jesus described His purposes as coming from heaven and from the One who sent Him. His purposes did not come from the world system. They begin with God Himself.

✳ Read Today's Bible Meditations again. The first deals with Christ being sent. But the second, *John 20:21,* says, *"As the Father has sent Me, I also send you."* We've looked at the purpose of Jesus' ministry, why He was sent from God. Jesus was sent by God to help accomplish God's purposes. You have been sent by Jesus to help accomplish Jesus' purposes. Consider your own Purpose Statement.

Jesus was sent to the poor, needy, and oppressed. I help accomplish His purpose by ______________________________

Jesus was sent to do the will of the Father. I help accomplish His purpose by

____

____

Jesus was sent to carry the good news to people in other geographic areas. I help accomplish His purpose by______________________________

____

Jesus was sent to seek and save lost people. I help accomplish His purpose by

____

____

In the movie *Forrest Gump*, Forrest has just enlisted in the Army. While he is standing at attention, his drill sergeant rushes up to him and screams in his face, "Gump! What's your sole purpose in this army?" Forrest replies by shouting back, "To do whatever you tell me to do, Drill Sergeant, sir!" Forrest had the right idea. He succeeded in the army because he had a clear statement of purpose.

Jesus' earthly ministry changed the world. It succeeded because His purpose statement was not much different than Forrest Gump's:

Jesus therefore answered and was saying to them, "Truly, truly, I say to you, the Son can do nothing of Himself, unless it is something He sees the Father doing; for whatever the Father does, these things the Son also does in like manner" (John 5:19).

✳ Write a personal Purpose Statement. Imagine that someone has come to you and said, "What is your sole purpose in life?" What do you say? Using the formula of infinitive + verb, began formulating a Purpose Statement. You may want to expand on it a little in your journal.

"My sole purpose in life is to ______________________."

✳ End today's lesson by talking to your Commanding Officer—your Heavenly Father. Ask Him how His purpose for you might be fulfilled in your family, neighborhood, church, and at work.

Christ and the Father

DAY 3

✷ **Begin today's lesson by reading the Bible verse and the name of Christ for today. Work on your memory verse. Then use the suggested prayer to begin your study.**

In the science of fingerprinting, fingerprint analysts look for certain points of similarity between the prints found at a crime scene and the prints on file. When there are a sufficient number of ridges, curves, and whorls that match up, the analysts are able to come up with a positive identification. So that's what we're going to do today. We're going to analyze the points of identification between the Son and the Father, and see if we can make a positive ID. It is important for us to see Jesus' particular points of identification with the Father so that we can find our points of identification with the Son.

Today's Bible Meditation
See how great a love the Father has bestowed upon us, that we should be called children of God.
1 John 3:1

Names of Christ for Today
Son of the Most High God
(Mark 5:7)

Prayer to Begin the Lesson
Heavenly Father,
You have lavished incredible love on me by adopting me into Your family. There is no other love like this. Thank you for sending Your Son Jesus as the sacrifice for my sins. Father, I want to move into a deeper and more personal love relationship with You. Teach me today how I can respond to You in a proper relationship. I ask this in Jesus' name.
Amen.

Point of Identification #1—His Work

Jesus' work identified Himself with His Father. We looked at *John 5:19* at the close of yesterday's lesson. Let's look at it again. *"Truly, truly, I say to you, the Son can do nothing of Himself, unless it is something He sees the Father doing; for whatever the Father does, these things the Son also does in like manner."* Jesus told the Jews, *"I do nothing on my own initiative, but I speak these things as the Father taught Me... I always do the things that are pleasing to Him" (John 8:28-29).* Jesus placed His work in opposition to that of the Jews: *"I speak the things which I have seen with My Father; therefore you also do the things which you heard from your father* [the devil]*" (John 8:38).* The Father's work was Jesus' work.

✷ **Name one point of identification between Jesus and the Father:**

____

✷ **Which of the following best describes one way you should relate to the Heavenly Father? Check one:**

❑ **I should watch to see what the Father is doing. When He chooses to show me what He's doing, I should get involved with it. The Father's work should be my work.**

❑ **I should plan on what I want to do for God, and then ask Him to bless it. He will adjust His work to the great things I'm going to do for Him.**

We don't have God's permission to set our own agendas. God doesn't adjust to us. He invites us to get involved in His work.

Point of Identification #2—His Words

Jesus claimed, *"I did not speak on My own initiative, but the Father Himself who sent Me has given Me commandment, what to say, and what to speak... therefore the things I speak, I speak just as the Father has told Me" (John 12:49-50).* He also said, *"The words that I say to you I do not speak on My own initiative, but the Father abiding in Me does His works" (John 14:10).*

Point of Identification #3—His Possessions

Jesus claimed that the Father's possessions were also His own. When the 70 returned from their preaching mission, Jesus told them, *"All things have been handed over to Me by My Father" (Luke 10:22).* Jesus prayed, *"All I have is yours, and all you have is mine. And glory has come to me through them" (John 17:10,* NIV*).* The Father could not have something that was not Christ's at the same time.

✻ What are the three points of identification we have so far?

Point #1: His ______________________________

Point #2: His ______________________________

Point #3: His ______________________________

Point of Identification #4—Substance

Christ is One with the Father in substance. That means that physically, Jesus and God are composed of the same stuff. Although God is spirit *(John 4:24),* and Jesus was flesh and blood *(John 1:14),* they are still one in nature and substance. Jesus claimed, *"I and the Father are one" (John 10:30).* Once, the disciple Philip asked Him to show the disciples the Father. Jesus replied, *"He who has seen Me has seen the Father; how do you say, 'Show us the Father'? Do you not believe that I am in the Father, and the Father is in Me?" (John 14:9-10).*

Jesus is one with the Father in unity. In *John 17:22,* He said, *"I have given them the glory that you gave me, that they may be one as we are one"* (NIV). While we can't identify with Christ in His divine substance, we can be one with Him in unity. Jesus was able to totally identify with both God and humanity.

When you check Jesus' "thumbprint" against God's, as we have today, you can see how Christ was identified with God. The good news is, as we develop the mind of Christ, our "thumbprint" can be matched with Christ's!

- We can identify with Him in His **works**—always teaching to the poor, the hurting, the needy.
- We can identify with Him in His **words**—we should do our best to imitate Christ in His speech (review Day 5 of last week's lesson). Our words should be simple and direct (see *Matt. 5:37),* gracious (see *Col. 4:6),* purposeful (see *Matt. 12:36),* and exemplary (see *1 Tim. 4:12).*
- We can identify with Him in His **possessions.** Christ was heir to the entire kingdom of God, but according to *Romans 8:17,* we are joint-heirs with Him!
- We can identify with Him in **unity** (see *John 17:21-23).*

✻ Turn to pages 212-213 in the Lifelong Helps and complete the activity related to "Your Relationship with Your Heavenly Father." Close your study today with this activity and a time of prayer with the Heavenly Father.

Christ and the Holy Spirit

DAY 4

✱ **Begin today's lesson by reading the Bible verse and the name of Christ for today. Work on your memory verse. Then use the suggested prayer to begin your study.**

It's a He, Not a What!

Today's lesson will talk about Jesus' relationship with the Holy Spirit. Right away, I'd like to clear up a misconception a lot of Christians have. Sometimes, we speak of the Holy Spirit as an impersonal "it"—as in, "The holy spirit? Sure, it's in my life." The Holy Spirit is a distinct personality of the Trinity, along with the Father and the Son. In the verse we looked at a couple of days ago, Jesus quoted *Isaiah 61:1-2*. Look closely at what He says: *"The Spirit of the Lord is upon me, because **he** anointed me to preach the gospel" (Luke 4:18* emphasis mine). Jesus told the disciples in the Upper Room, *"But the Helper, the Holy Spirit, whom the Father will send in My name, He will teach you all things, and bring to your remembrance all that I said to you" (John 14:26)*. As we talk about Jesus' relationship to the Holy Spirit, keep in mind that you can't have a relationship with an impersonal energy. The Holy Spirit is a He, not an It!

Throughout His earthly ministry, Jesus had a close relationship with the Holy Spirit. Before His birth, Jesus' mother was *found to be with child by the Holy Spirit (Matt. 1:18)*. The work of the Holy Spirit is indicated by Jesus' advanced insight and understanding at the temple when He was 12. Mark describes this scene at His baptism: *Coming up out of the water, He saw the heavens opening, and the Spirit like a dove descending upon* [Jesus] *(Mark 1:10)*.

Jesus was *led up by the spirit (Matt. 4:1)* and *full of the Holy Spirit (Luke 4:1)* as He was tempted by Satan. His response to the temptation is a clear sign that the Holy Spirit was active in Jesus' life. Afterwards, Jesus *returned to Galilee in the power of the Spirit (Luke 4:14)*.

Jesus began His ministry by announcing: *"The spirit of the Lord is upon me" (Luke 4:18)*. This led to the greatest spiritual work in the history of the planet. Jesus' work was done through the Holy Spirit. He specifically said, *"I cast out devils by the Spirit of God" (Matt. 12:28*, KJV). Jesus' life fulfilled the prophecy, *The Spirit of the Lord will rest on Him, the spirit of wisdom and understanding, the spirit of counsel and strength, the spirit of knowledge and fear of the Lord (Isa. 11:2)*.

Jesus strictly forbade blaspheming the Holy Spirit (see *Matt. 12:31-32)*. He highly regarded the Holy Spirit, depended on the Holy Spirit, and followed the Holy Spirit closely throughout His life. This is the mind of Christ.

✱ **In the list below are ways Jesus related to the Holy Spirit during His earthly life and ministry. Check all that apply.**

- ❑ Anointed by the Spirit
- ❑ Blasphemed the Spirit
- ❑ Controlled by the Spirit
- ❑ Ignored the Spirit
- ❑ Jealous for the Spirit
- ❑ Led by the Spirit

Today's Bible Meditation
"Be not drunk with wine, wherein is excess; but be filled with the Spirit."
Ephesians 5:18, KJV

Names of Christ for Today
Mediator of a New Covenant
(Heb. 9:15)

Prayer to Begin the Lesson
Jesus, my Lord,
I am thankful that You did not leave us without another Comforter—the Holy Spirit. I realize, however, that I have probably never experienced the fullness of Your Spirit the way You have intended. I want to be filled with the Spirit and walk in the Spirit.
Amen.

- ❑ Depended on the Spirit
- ❑ Filled with the Spirit
- ❑ Followed the Spirit
- ❑ Grieved the Spirit
- ❑ Quenched the Spirit
- ❑ Experienced the power of the Spirit
- ❑ Resisted the leadership of the Spirit

✳ Turn to pages 212-213 in the Lifelong Helps and complete the activity related to "Your Relationship with the Holy Spirit." Close your study today with this activity and a time of prayer seeking to rightly relate to the Holy Spirit. If time permits, review the Scriptures you read yesterday about your relationship to the Heavenly Father.

DAY 5

Today's Bible Meditation
They said to one another, "Were not our hearts burning within us while He was speaking to us on the road, while He was explaining the Scriptures to us?"
Luke 24:32

Names of Christ for Today
The Word of God
(Rev. 19:13)

Prayer to Begin the Lesson
Word of God,
I want my heart to burn inside me the way the hearts burned of those two

Christ, the Scriptures, and Prayer

✳ Begin today's lesson by reading the Bible verse and the name of Christ for today. Work on your memory verse. Then use the suggested prayer to begin your study.

Jesus showed an incredible familiarity with the Old Testament. Now, you might be saying, "Well of course He did. Jesus was God—He wrote the Old Testament!" But you need to keep in mind our passage for this study, *Philippians 2:5-11*. When Jesus emptied Himself to take on the form of a human being, that means that He had no special knowledge of Scripture. I believe He had to learn Scripture the way everyone else does. During Jesus' ministry, He quoted directly from 16 different Old Testament Books, and referred to many others. The Scriptures were a vital part of Jesus' ministry. Look at some of the different ways He used Scripture:

- He used Scripture to combat temptation. When He was in the wilderness being tempted by the devil, He answered each of the temptations with Scripture from Deuteronomy (see *Matt. 4:4*, and compare it to *Deut. 8:3; Matt 4:7* and *Deut. 6:16;* and *Matt. 4:10,* from *Deut. 6:13).* It is also important to realize that Jesus knew Scripture well enough to be ready when Satan tried to twist it. Satan took a passage from *Psalm 91* completely out of context in the second temptation. Jesus was ready for him.
- He used Scripture to answer criticism. On one occasion, the Pharisees were criticizing Jesus' disciples for breaking off heads of grain and eating the grain on the Sabbath—which the Pharisees considered harvesting. Jesus reminded them of David's eating the *consecrated bread* (compare *Matt. 12:3-4* to *1 Sam. 21:3-6).* Another time, when the Pharisees asked Jesus' disciples why He ate with sinners, Jesus quoted *Hosea 6:6, "I desire compassion, and not sacrifice" (Matt. 9:13).*

- He based His actions on Scripture. When Jesus cleansed the Temple in *Mark 11:17,* He used the term *house of prayer* from *Isaiah 56:7,* and accused the people of making it a *den of robbers,* as Jeremiah had stated (see *Jer. 7:11).*
- He used Scripture to teach. In His parables, Jesus drew freely from phrases used in the Old Testament. The parable of the vine-growers tending the vineyard derives from *Isaiah 5:2.*
- He used the Scriptures as *a witness to Himself.* When John the Baptist's disciples came asking about Him, He sent them back to John with words from *Isaiah 35:5-6* (see *Luke 7:22).* After His resurrection, He started with *Moses and all the prophets* explained to the two disciples on the road to Emmaus *what was said in all the Scriptures concerning Himself (Luke 24:27,* NIV).
- He used Scripture *to point to end times.* In His explanation of the parable of the weeds, Jesus drew from *Daniel 12:3* about the righteous who will shine in the kingdom of their Father (see *Matt. 13:43).*

disciples on the way to Emmaus. I want You to be so real to me as we journey through the Scriptures together that it is as though You are right beside me, explaining them to me as we go along. Open up my mind and give me new understanding. Teach me how to relate Your Word to my everyday life. Help me to pray in ways that will please You.

Amen.

✳ **Without looking back, see if you can describe in your own words at least three ways Jesus used the Scriptures.**

1. ______________________________

2. ______________________________

3. ______________________________

Many times we Christians tend to ignore the Old Testament and do most of our devotional reading and study from the New. It is crucial for us to spend time in the Old Testament as well as the New. Obviously, Jesus and Paul didn't have a New Testament because it had not yet been written. But they found tremendous value in this part of the Scriptures. It would be a mistake for you to bypass it!

Jesus demonstrated that the spiritual mind finds great insight in the Scripture. He emphasized that *"the Scripture cannot be broken" (John 10:35).* You won't find a stronger statement of this than the Sermon on the Mount: *"Truly I say to you, until heaven and earth pass away, not the smallest letter or stroke shall pass away from the Law, until all is accomplished" (Matt. 5:18).* Jesus revered the Scripture, based His actions on it, and even used it to point to the end times.

Earlier I mentioned that when I began these studies, the Lord led me to read nothing but the Bible for four years. During that time, I discovered a technique that proved helpful in understanding the Bible. I memorized a passage, and then would spend months meditating on it. Most of what I learned came from meditating on memorized Scriptures. If you desire the Mind of Christ, you must follow His example in relation to Scripture.

✳ **Pause for a few minutes and think back on one or two of the verses you have memorized in the past 10 weeks. Meditate on the Scripture. Ask God to help you see an insight into it that you didn't have before. Ask God to help you see how that Scripture applies to your life today, right now, where you are. Have your journal with you, and record any new insights you have from your meditation time. You may want to stop the study for today at this point, and come back to the second half tomorrow.**

Jesus' Practice of Prayer

We learned on Day One of this week that the spiritual controls the material. Naturally, then, prayer can be considered the most powerful force on earth, since prayer is our means of connecting to the spiritual world. In the Bible, there are more recorded prayers of David and Paul. However, the Bible says more about the prayers of Jesus than any other character. Jesus also taught more about prayer than any other person in the Bible. If we are to have the mind of Christ, we must imitate His prayer life.

• Jesus preferred to be alone and in a private place when He prayed. Even after a long day of public ministry, He would routinely get up in the early morning, while it was still dark, and get away by Himself to pray (see *Mark 1:35)*. There's no possibility to be phony when you're praying by yourself. You've got no one looking on, no one to put on a show for. It's just you and God.

• Jesus did pray publicly, however. He prayed on all sorts of occasions, and in groups of varying size. On one occasion, Jesus prayed aloud to encourage those around Him. At the raising of Lazarus, Jesus prayed, So they took away the stone. Then Jesus looked up and said, *"Father, I thank you that you have heard me. I knew that you always hear me, but I said this for the benefit of the people standing here, that they may believe that you sent me" (John 11:41-42).* Youth are often self-conscious about praying aloud. But praying aloud for someone else, especially if that someone is in the room with you, can help both you and the other person grow spiritually.

• Jesus prayed before making important decisions. The night before He selected the twelve disciples was spent entirely in prayer.

• Jesus prayed at important events in His own life, such as His baptism and His transfiguration.

Are you familiar with the ACTS-PI acronym? It is a useful way to remember the different types of prayer. There is Adoration, or praise, Confession, Thanksgiving, and Supplication. Supplication means asking for things. There are two types of supplication: Petition, in which you are praying for your own needs, and Intercession, in which you are praying for the needs of others. Jesus prayed all kinds of prayers, except for confession of sin. We find Jesus praying Adoration *(Matt. 11:25),* Thanksgiving *(Matt. 14:19),* Petition *(John 17:1-5),* and Intercession *(John 7:6-26).*

✻ Put your hand over the above section, and try to remember at least three situations or ways in which Jesus prayed.

1. ______________________________

2. ______________________________

3. ______________________________

✻ In your own words, describe the importance of prayer in the life and ministry of Jesus.

____

____

✱ If prayer was that important for the Son of God, how important is it in your life?

____

✱ Conclude today's study and this unit by practicing prayer. Find a place where you can be alone and talk to God. Use the ACTS-PI formula:

- ***A*doration. Praise God for who He is. Acknowledge His greatness. Approach Him as you would a king. Use one or more of your favorite names of Christ.**
- ***C*onfession. Seek God's cleansing before you go any further in your prayer.**
- ***T*hanksgiving. Thank God for forgiving you of your sin, and specifically thank God for His material blessings on your life.**
- ***S*upplication**
- ***P*etition. Let God guide your asking, so you can become more like Him.**
- ***I*ntercession. Join God in His work by praying for others according to His will.**

[1]In thinking about fasting for spiritual purposes, one word of warning must be said. Many teenagers suffer from serious eating disorders. You *must not* confuse the two. Fasting is a controlled discipline of not eating *for a brief period* in order to concentrate on spiritual things. Eating disorders, such as anorexia, are compulsive (uncontrolled) behaviors. If you have struggled in the past with eating disorders, or are dealing with them now, this spiritual discipline *is not for you!* A helpful resource for you and your youth leader to look at together is Robert McGee's *The Search* study course. Talk to your youth leader about it

UNIT 11

Day 1
Getting Holiness and Love Back Together Again

Day 2
How Holiness Looks and How It Acts

Day 3
Love Is a Verb, Part 1

Day 4
Love Is a Verb, Part 2

Day 5
Love Is Also a Noun!

Scripture Memory Verse
Like the Holy One who called you, be holy yourselves also in all your behavior; because it is written, "You shall be holy, for I am holy."
1 Peter 1:15-16

Holiness and Love

Hymn Part 5—Christ's Love and Holiness
[Jesus] humbled Himself by becoming obedient to the point of death, even death on a cross (Phil. 2:8).

What Is in This Unit for Me?

You will understand how Christ brings together holiness and love. Christ desires that we, His disciples, be like Him in these qualities. This unit will help you know how to cooperate with the Holy Spirit to be made holy and to practice love out of your inner being.

Lifelong Objective

In Christ you will be set apart from the world as holy. You will demonstrate Christlike love in your relationship to God and to others.

How God Will be Working In You

Christ's holiness within you allows you to be separated from the world. God's goal is your maturity. Your growth in holiness can only be measured against the sacrifice of Christ—the supreme example of holiness. Holiness and love complement and strengthen one another. Christ's example is our goal in holiness and love. Christ is perfecting these qualities in you.

Unit Learning Goals

- You will understand the way holiness and love work together.
- You will understand the characteristics and behaviors of holiness.
- You will demonstrate your dedication to the Lord.
- You will learn and begin to practice 15 behaviors of Christlike love.

What You Will Do to Develop Holiness and Love

- You will examine your separation from the world, and take necessary steps to display holiness in relation to your world.
- You will dedicate your body to the Lord to be used for His purpose.
- You will look for ways to act out the characteristics of love found in *1 Corinthians 13.*
- You will review ways you can practice the principles of longing for and identifying with Christ.

Lifelong Helps Related to This Unit

Christlike Virtues—Love (pp. 197-198)

The Mind of Christ Cards Related to This Unit

5B. Unit 11: Scripture Memory—*1 Peter 1:15-16*
13. Love Is—*1 Corinthians 13*

Getting Holiness and Love Back Together Again

DAY 1

Today's Bible Meditation
And there is no creature hidden from His sight, but all things are open and laid bare to the eyes of Him with whom we have to do. Since we have a great high priest who has passed through the heavens, Jesus the Son of God, let us hold fast our confession. For we do not have a high priest who cannot sympathize with our weaknesses, but one who has been tempted in all things as we are, yet without sin.
Hebrews 4:13-15

Name of Christ for Today
He That Sanctifies
(Heb. 2:11)

Prayer to Begin the Lesson
Holy God,
because of your holiness,
I am not worthy to stand
in Your presence. But
because of Your love, I am
able to! Once again, I need
Your cleansing, Your mercy,
and Your forgiveness. Wash
me, that I may be clean and
spotless before You. You are
the One who makes me
holy. Teach me to love as
You love.
Amen.

✳ Begin today's lesson by reading the Bible verse and the name of Christ for today. Work on your memory verse. Then use the suggested prayer to begin your study.

After leading a conference in Ohio, a man asked me one of those tough questions: "In the Old Testament, God is so terrifyingly holy that He seems distant. But in the New Testament, God is so warm and loving that He seems to be trying to get close to us. Those seem to be two opposite pictures. Can those two opposites be reconciled?"

Sometimes it seems like the Old Testament God and the New Testament God are two different beings. The core of what we believe as Christians is that God is One. So, how do we reconcile these two pictures? How do we get holiness and love back together again? The truth is, they've never been apart. God is infinite and unchanging. Because our human minds can't comprehend infinity, God reveals to us various aspects of His nature. Sometimes, these aspects appear to be opposites. We can't begin to understand the nature of God without accepting that He can have holiness and love at once.

God's holiness is a wonderful fact. But at the same time, it's scary. When we compare our sinfulness to God's absolute perfection, we can find God's holiness alarming. But on the other hand, God is love, and we have the promise that *"God so loved the world" (John 3:16)*. God went to great lengths to reach out to us with His love. God's love is as great a truth as God's holiness. Holiness causes us to fear, or respect God, while His compassion and love draws us close. These attributes exist in the same magnificent Person. The best example of God's holiness and love coming together is Calvary. Look at the facts:

- Because of God's holiness, sin cannot enter into His presence. If it did, God would no longer be holy.
- Because of God's love, God desires for us to be present with Him.
- Christ, as God, committed no sin. Christ is holy.
- Christ, as God, paid for our sins by dying on the Cross. Christ is love.
- Through Christ, holiness and love come together.

The cross shows us how far God is willing to go to reach us with His infinite love.

✳ What event gives us the clearest picture of God's awesome holiness and His compelling love? Check one:

❑ Destruction of the world with the flood during Noah's time.
❑ The birth of Christ at Bethlehem.
❑ The crucifixion and death of Christ on the cross.
❑ The giving of the Holy Spirit at Pentecost.

We risk irreverence and loss of perspective if we do not acknowledge the holiness of God. We miss God's very nature if we fail to see the immense love revealed through the Person of Jesus Christ. Both God's holiness and His love were demonstrated best in the crucifixion and death of Christ on the cross.

✳ Because Christ's love and holiness are most clearly seen in His crucifixion, we want to give you an assignment to complete in the coming weeks. Your group leader may have announced plans to complete this activity as a large group. If not, consider completing one or more of the following assignments on your own.

- **View *The Mind of Christ Worship Video: The Crucifixion***
- **Listen to *The Mind of Christ Audiocassettes: The Crucifixion***

Hymn Part 5: Christ's Holiness and Love

We've seen how Christ demonstrated His holiness and love on the cross. But did you realize that Christ's death on the cross paves the way for us to be holy as well? "Me? Holy? But you've seen my life! How can I be holy?" The secret is having the mind of Christ. Not only is God holy and loving, but He expects holiness and love from us as well.

> *Just as He chose us in Him before the foundation of the world, that we should be holy and blameless before Him in love (Eph. 1:4).*
>
> *And so, as those who have been chosen of God, holy and beloved, put on a heart of compassion, kindness, humility, gentleness and patience (Col. 3:12).*
>
> *And may the Lord cause you to increase and abound in love for one another, and for all men, just as we also do for you; so that He may establish your hearts unblamable in holiness before our God and Father at the coming of our Lord Jesus with all His saints (1 Thess. 3:12-13).*

Perfecting Holiness in Love

In the life of Jesus, we see a perfect union of two seemingly opposite traits— holiness and love. Jesus was completely holy and separated from the world: *"I am not of this world" (John 8:23).* In all of His actions, behaviors, teachings, or words, you won't find a hint of worldliness. But being separated from the world didn't make Jesus separate or distant. The Bible calls Him a friend of sinners. Even though His inner life was completely holy, in His outer life He demonstrated perfect love.

So how do we bring the two together? Think about another "opposite" such as justice and mercy. Say you're an average student in math. You studied hard all semester, but the final exam comes back and you've missed passing the course by a point. The laws of justice say you get what you deserve if you have to take the course again. But, your teacher saw how hard you studied and could, out of the goodness of her heart, give you that needed point. That's mercy. That's how God works. God's holiness requires justice, yet Christ's forgiveness provides mercy. Justice and mercy, like love and holiness, work together, reinforcing and complementing one another.

In order to understand this, try to imagine one without the other. Without love, holiness would be harsh, legalistic, and unbending. Without holiness, love would be lax, permissive, and spineless. We derive our principles from holiness. Love cultivates holiness and makes it possible. Holiness modifies love and prevents perversion. Only wisdom can make holiness and love work together in perfect balance. Christ brings them together. In Christ, we are holy, and in Christ, we are love.

✳ Fill in the blanks below with holiness or love. Check your answers in the paragraph above.

We derive our principles from ________________________________ .

_______________________ cultivates _______________________ and makes it possible.

_______________________ modifies _______________________ and prevents perversion.

✻ Which of the words below are related to holiness and which are related to love? Write *H* beside the ones related to holiness, and *L* beside the ones related to love.

____ a. In the world
____ b. Separate from the world
____ c. Mercy
____ d. Righteousness
____ e. Sanctification
____ f. Grace
____ g. Justice

✻ End your study time in prayer for God to continue His work of making you holy as He is holy. Ask Him to enable you to love as He loves.

(Answers: Holiness—b, d, e, g; Love—a, c, f.)

DAY 2

How Holiness Looks and How It Acts

✻ Begin today's lesson by reading the Bible verse and the name of Christ for today. Work on your memory verse. Then use the suggested prayer to begin your study.

Today's Bible Meditation
Since all these things are to be destroyed in this way, what sort of people ought you to be in holy conduct and godliness, looking for and hastening the coming of the day of God… Be diligent to be found by Him in peace, spotless and blameless.
2 Peter 3:11-12,14

People in the Bible reacted to God's holiness with terror. For example, Moses hid his face from God (see *Ex. 3:5-6)*. When Isaiah saw God's holiness, he cried out, "*Woe is me, for I am ruined! Because I am a man of unclean lips, and I live among a people of unclean lips" (Isa. 6:5)*. When Peter realized the awesome power of Jesus, he pleaded, *"Depart from me, for I am a sinful man, O Lord!" (Luke 5:8)*. God's holiness is like a spotlight on all of our unworthiness.

How does holiness behave? What is its character? You may be having visions of monks in a monastery right now. Maybe you're thinking of someone who is "holier-than-thou"; someone who thinks Christianity makes them superior to everyone else. Is that "holiness"? Think again. Holiness does not require you to go off and live in a monastery, and it doesn't demand that you stick your nose up in the air and pretend to be better than everyone else.

The Character of Holiness

Purity. Probably the most distinguishing feature of holiness is purity. Jesus was pure.

Name of Christ for Today
Holy One of God
(Luke 4:34)

Prayer to Begin the Lesson
*Holy One of God,
You will come again and judge the world. You already have told us that the evil world will be destroyed by fire. Since this is true, I want to live my life in holiness, godliness, and purity. I'm excited that You will return someday, Lord Jesus, and I long for that day. Help me to live a life of holiness until You come.
Amen.*

Even His enemies acknowledged it when they tried to trap Him with trick questions: *"Teacher, we know that... You are not partial to any" (Luke 20:21).* Jesus' purity came out of loving devotion to the Father. He was so devoted to the Lord that His only desire was to please God. This is what keeps holiness from being "holier-than-thou." When you are focused on God, you're not thinking about how good you are, but how good He is.

✱ **What is one characteristic of holiness?** ______________________________

In your own words define *purity*. ______________________________

____

Godliness. *What sort of people ought you to be in holy conduct and godliness, looking for and hastening the coming of the day of God? (2 Pet. 3:11-12).* Godliness simply means acting like God. Acting like God comes out of a loving reverence for God. Throughout His ministry, Jesus displayed godliness. If there was ever a time for Jesus to not act like God, it was during His trials. He could have cracked, lost His temper, called down fire on His accusers, or simply have broken down from physical exhaustion. Yet Jesus didn't do any of these things. During His trials, and throughout His entire life, He responded with dignity and presence of mind.

✱ **What is a second characteristic of holiness?** ______________________________

In your own words define *godliness*. ______________________________

____

Glory. Holiness is glorious. Moses asked, *"Who is like Thee, majestic in holiness, awesome in praises, working wonders?" (Ex. 15:11).* Jesus lived to bring glory to His Father. At the end of His life, Jesus prayed,*"I glorified Thee on earth, having accomplished the work which Thou hast given Me to do" (John 17:4).* In everything He did, Jesus practiced a loving exaltation of His Father. Once again, in holiness of character we see love behind the scenes, working to produce holiness.

Can you be glorious, or glorified? Only to the extent that you bring glory to God. Remember what John the Baptist said when his disciples expressed worry that Jesus was getting more disciples than he was? *"He must increase, but I must decrease" (John 3:30).* When a person seeks to bring glory to themselves, he or she will ultimately be forgotten. When a person seeks to bring glory to God, he or she will be remembered forever (see *Mark 14:1-9).*

✱ **What is a third characteristic of holiness?** ______________________________

In your own words define *glorious*. ______________________________

____

✱ **Read *Psalm 111:1-9* below and circle the words related to holiness and love.**

Praise the Lord! I will give thanks to the Lord with all my heart, In the

company of the upright and in the assembly. Great are the works of the Lord; They are studied by all who delight in them. Splendid and majestic is His work; And His righteousness endures forever. He has made His wonders to be remembered; The Lord is gracious and compassionate. He has given food to those who fear Him; He will remember His covenant forever. He has made known to His people the power of His works, In giving them the heritage of the nations. The works of His hands are truth and justice; All His precepts are sure. They are upheld forever and ever; They are performed in truth and uprightness. He has sent redemption to His people; He has ordained His covenant forever; Holy and awesome is His name.

The Behavior of Holiness

Separate. Not only does holiness have a certain character, it maintains a certain behavior. Holiness separates itself from the world. The word *holy* means "set apart." Jesus was holy without being distant. Even though He was not of the world, He was in the world. He set the example that you don't have to shut yourself up in a monastery in order to be separate. You can be separate from the world at your school's basketball game. Remember our discussion yesterday of how Jesus was a friend of sinners? Jesus ate with tax-gatherers, He talked with sinful women, and He kept company with common, everyday, sinful people. Separation is not physically distancing yourself from people and things. It is a spiritual exercise of not allowing physical things to have power over you. Review Week Ten, Day One—"The Spiritual Controls the Material," for more help with this concept.

✳ **What is one behavior of holiness?** ______________________

In your own words define *separate*. ______________________

____

Dedicate. Closely related to holiness is dedication. The word *dedicate* means "to set something aside for one use only." For example, when Solomon dedicated the Temple, he said, *"Behold, I am about to build a house for the name of the Lord my God, dedicating it to Him" (2 Chron. 2:4).* In this verse, Solomon states that he is dedicating the Temple for burning incense, setting out the consecrated bread, and for offering sacrifices. Later, Isaiah summarized the temple's purpose as a *"house of prayer" (Isa. 56:7).* The temple was dedicated for one thing only: to connect humans to God through prayer. This was why Jesus had to drive the money changers out of the temple. A place dedicated to prayer had been made into a den of robbers (see *Mark 11:17).*

Our dedication must be to God and to God alone. Remember last week, when you wrote a personal purpose statement. It began, "My sole purpose in life is to..." That is a statement of dedication.

✳ **What is a second behavior of holiness?** ______________________

In your own words define *dedicate*. ______________________

____

In *Leviticus 8:22-24,* an interesting ceremony is recorded for the dedication of the temple priests. God instructed Moses to put ram's blood on the lobe of the priests' right ears, the thumbs of their right hands, and the big toes of their right feet. The symbolism of this act was that the priest's were being dedicated "head to toe" to God's service. Several years ago, when I realized what Jesus had done for me, I dedicated myself "Head to toe" to Him. In prayer, I dedicated my body parts to Him, one by one. I told God, "I dedicate my mouth to you. It will only speak that which is wholesome and of which you would approve. My tongue will serve You." In this way, I dedicated to the Lord my mind, my hands, my feet, my ears, my eyes (your music/movie choices may be affected if you dedicate your ears and eyes to the Lord!), and even my stomach. I've guarded what I put into my stomach since then!

I want to urge you to do the same thing, dedicate your body parts to God. Your body must serve no purpose other than what God wants for it. For the rest of your life, you will remember that the parts of your body have been given to God.

✱ **Below, there are two pledges. One is a pledge of dedication. One is a pledge of willingness. If you are willing to dedicate your body part by part to the Lord Jesus, start now. In your journal, name each body part and how you desire to let the Lord use it. If you are not willing, ask the Lord to make you willing. Spend time in prayer.**

____

(date)

On the above date, I dedicated my body to the Lord for His purposes alone.

____

(signed)

____

(date)

Lord, I am not willing to make this decision. Please make me willing. Identify to me what is standing in the way of my willingness, and prepare me to make this decision soon. Amen.

____

(signed)

Love Is a Verb, Part 1

DAY 3

✻ **Begin today's lesson by reading the Bible verse and the name of Christ for today. Work on your memory verse. Then use the suggested prayer to begin your study.**

✻ **As you study Christlike love, several study aids have been prepared for you.**
- **Cut out the Mind of Christ Cards 12 and 13 for review.**
- **Turn to and mark for future use the Lifelong Help on Love under the Christlike Virtues on pages 197-198.**

The Word *Love*

A dictionary describes *love* in several different ways. One description is a "deep, tender feeling of affection toward a person" such as one's parents and friends. Other descriptions include an "intense emotional attachment to an object" such as a house or car; to "embrace, caress, or have sexual intercourse with"; to "like enthusiastically" such as to love swimming; and to "thrive on or need" such as a cactus loves hot, dry air.

The word *love* is used for everything from describing the way a cactus feels about air to describing the act of sex. One thing is clear: *love* is a verb.

First Corinthians 13 is referred to as the Bible's love chapter. It's used in many weddings. Unlike the English language, Greek, the New Testament language, uses different words for love. *Eros,* for example, describes romantic or sexual love. *Phileo* describes brotherly love. But the word used in *1 Corinthians 13* is *agape*. It describes "godly, holy, unconditional love." Agape love is not based on feelings or circumstances; it sometimes acts contrary to feelings. Where human love sometimes says, "I love you if," or "I love you because," agape says "I love you anyway." It is an act of the will.

First Corinthians 13:4-7 describes 15 characteristics of agape. In Greek, all 15 characteristics are verbs. There is a specific dimension of holiness that each of these characteristics of love produce. Check out the chart:

✻ **Read the Lifelong Help on Love (pp. 197-198), "Showing Love." The practice of the behaviors of love will be long-term. Ask the Lord to help you love with unconditional, agape love. Watch for opportunities, and record in your journal your actions. Ask God to keep you from pride or self-righteousness and to help you to love like He loves.**

We'll look at specific examples of Jesus demonstrating characteristics of *agape* love. As you study these examples, think of ways you can demonstrate the same characteristics. So, right now, stop for a minute. Imagine your school and the people in your classes. Imagine your youth group. Imagine your parents. Imagine your brother or sister. These are your test subjects for agape love!

Today's Bible Meditation
Love is patient, love is kind, and is not jealous; love does not brag and is not arrogant, does not act unbecomingly; it does not seek its own, is not provoked, does not take into account a wrong suffered, does not rejoice in unrighteousness, but rejoices with the truth; bears all things, believes all things, hopes all things, endures all things.
1 Corinthians 13:4-7

Name of Christ for Today
Him That Loved Us and Washed Us From Our Sins in His Own Blood
(Rev. 1:5-6)

Prayer to Begin the Lesson
Loving Lord Jesus, You have loved me with a perfect love. You have washed and forgiven me of my sins by Your own sacrifice on the cross. I love You for first loving me. Teach me to love like You loved.
Amen.

CHARACTERISTICS OF CHRISTLIKE LOVE

Love	Holiness
Is patient	Holy Relationships
Is kind	Holy Purposes
Is not jealous	Holy Heart
Does not brag	Holy Speech
Is not arrogant	Holy Service
Does not act unbecomingly	Holy Behavior
Does not seek its own	Holy Desires
Is not provoked	Holy Self-Control
Does not take into account a wrong	Holy Forgiveness
Does not rejoice in unrighteousness	Holy Conscience
Rejoices in the truth	Holy Mind
Bears all things	Holy Stability
Believes all things	Holy Values
Hopes all things	Holy Expectations
Endures all things	Holy Sacrifice

Love Is Patient (Holy Relationships)

I can show that love is patient by:

____

Jesus was incredibly patient with His disciples, who were pretty slow to catch on. Look how He related to James and John: *When His disciples James and John saw this, they said, "Lord, do You want us to command fire to come down from heaven and consume them?" But He turned and rebuked them, and said, "You do not know what kind of spirit you are of; for the Son of Man did not come to destroy men's lives, but to save them." And they went on to another village (Luke 9:54-56).*

James and John were slow to develop Christ's mindset. Jesus was forevermore waiting on the disciples to play catch-up with trying to understand His character and intentions. The real root to Jesus' patience was that He maintained holy relationships.

Love Is Kind (Holy Purposes)

I can show that love is kind by:

____

After Jesus fed the five thousand (which, by the way, is in itself a huge act of kindness), Jesus sent the disciples across the lake while He went up onto a mountain to pray. While He was praying, He could see them on the lake:

And seeing them straining at the oars, for the wind was against them, at about the fourth watch of the night, He came to them, walking on the sea; and He intended to pass by them. But when they saw Him walking on the sea, they supposed that it was a ghost, and cried out; for they all saw Him and were frightened. But immediately He spoke with them and said to them, "Take courage; it is I, do not be afraid" (Mark 6:48-50).

Jesus' kindness is a demonstration of holiness of purpose. All of His intentions were holy and loving.

Love Does Not Envy (Holy Heart)

I can show that love does not envy by:

___

Envy comes from desiring what somebody else has. Jesus didn't own a thing, and He didn't desire anything anyone else had, either. He didn't seek after material things. For more information, please review "Jesus and Material Things;" Week Nine, Day One. Not envying is a sign of a holy heart. Envy is unholy; self-denial for right purposes can be holy.

Love Does Not Brag (Holy Speech)

I can show that love does not brag by:

___

Bragging is the result of trying to puff yourself up. True, unconditional love is so conscious of others that there is no room for it to be conscious of itself. Jesus said: *"I can do nothing on My own initiative. As I hear, I judge; and My judgment is just, because I do not seek My own will, but the will of Him who sent Me" (John 5:30).* Love can't brag because its speech is holy. Once again, we see holiness and love working together.

Love Is Not Arrogant (Holy Service)

I can show that love is not arrogant by:

___

The opposite of arrogance is humility. There are many examples of Jesus' humble life. *Calling them to Himself, Jesus said to them, "You know that those who are recognized as rulers of the Gentiles lord it over them; and their great men exercise authority over them. But it is not so among you, but whoever wishes to become great among you shall be your servant; and whoever wishes to be first among you shall be slave of all. For even the Son of Man did not come to be served, but to serve, and to give His life a ransom for many" (Mark 10:42-45).* Love actively seeks what it can do for someone else. Arrogance seeks what it can do for self, and it is unholy.

✱ **End today's lesson by asking God to fill you with His love so that you will express that love in your relationships with others. Be specific in the ways you want Him to help you.**

DAY 4

Today's Bible Meditation
The one who does not love does not know God, for God is love. By this the love of God was manifested in us, that God has sent His only begotten Son into the world so that we might live through Him. In this is love, not that we loved God, but that He loved us and sent His Son to be the propitiation for our sins. Beloved, if God so loved us, we also ought to love one another.
1 John 4:8-11

Name of Christ for Today
The Lamb of God
(John 1:29)

Prayer to Begin the Lesson
Lamb of God,
You showed Your love for me by paying the death penalty for my sins. I have been so greatly loved, and therefore I want to love others with Your kind of love. Live in me and love through me so that others can experience Your redeeming love.
Amen.

Love Is a Verb, Part 2

✳ Begin today's lesson by reading the Bible verse and the name of Christ for today. Work on your memory verse. Then use the suggested prayer to begin your study.

Today, we'll finish up our look at love as Paul described it in *1 Corinthians 13.* The following five behaviors were true of Christ and His teachings.

Love Does Not Act Unbecomingly (Holy Behavior)

I can show that love does not act unbecomingly by:

____

When Jesus began His incredible Galileean ministry, He was scheduled to be the teacher of the day in His hometown synagogue in Nazareth. Jesus read to them the prophecy of *Isaiah 61:1-2,* which is a prophecy of His own activity. After reading the scroll, Jesus began His teaching by announcing that He was fulfilling prophecy. To put it mildly, the townspeople were offended:

And all in the synagogue were filled with rage as they heard these things; and they rose up and cast Him out of the city, and led Him to the brow of the hill on which their city had been built, in order to throw Him down the cliff. But passing through their midst, He went His way. (Luke 4:28-30).

What were Jesus' options at this point? He could have called down fire on all of them. He could have disappeared, or even flown away. He was God! But Luke tells us that He simply passed through the crowd and went on His way. He acted totally appropriately. Jesus always displayed a royal dignity that set Him apart from everyone else. We see in Jesus' actions uncommon grace and glory. Love always maintains holy behavior.

Love Does Not Seek Its Own (Holy Desires)

I can show that love does not seek its own by:

____

After the Lord fed the five thousand, the crowd tried to make Him king by force. But the Bible tells us that: *Jesus therefore perceiving that they were intending to come and take Him by force, to make Him king, withdrew again to the mountain by Himself alone (John 6:15).*

Although everything was within Jesus' reach, He never reached for them. Jesus never once performed a miracle for Himself. Love can't seek its own position or pleasure. Love has only holy desires.

Love Is Not Provoked (Holy Temperament)

I can show that love is not easily provoked by:

____

A full year before Judas betrayed Jesus, Jesus spoke an amazing warning to him: Jesus answered him, *"Did I myself not choose you, the twelve, and yet one of you is a devil?" (John 6:70).*

Jesus continued to walk with Judas all that year, knowing full well that Judas would betray Him in the end. He didn't treat Him any differently from any of the other disciples. Even Jesus' last words to Judas were calm: *"What you do, do quickly" (John 13:27).* How could Jesus maintain such calmness in the face of such a painful betrayal by a trusted friend? Love is not easily angered because it has a holy temperament.

Love Does Not Take Into Account a Wrong (Holy Forgiveness)

I can show that love does not take into account a wrong by:

____

Jesus had conflicts with His family, just like everyone else. They thought Jesus was out of His mind: *When his family heard about this, they went to take charge of him, for they said, "He is out of his mind" (Mark 3:21,* NIV).

Jesus' brothers did not believe in Him for His entire ministry (see *John 7:2-5).* Can you imagine how that hurt? Yet, we are told in *1 Corinthians 15:7* that Jesus made a special appearance to His disbelieving brother James to bring him to faith. Jesus did not hold a grudge against His brothers. Instead, He forgave them. By the way, as a result of that forgiveness, both of Jesus' half-brothers, James and Jude, wrote the New Testament books that bear their names.

Love Does Not Rejoice in Unrighteousness (Holy Conscience)

I can show that love does not rejoice in unrighteousness by:

____

When Jesus arrived at the Temple in Jerusalem, there was a great deal of corruption going on. Animals were being sold for outlandish prices to the religious pilgrims, and since foreign currency could not be used for paying tithes, money changers were scamming a lot of money off the top in outrageous exchange rates. When Jesus saw all this going on, the actions He took were taken out of love, because love cannot rejoice in unrighteousness.

He had made a scourge of cords and drove them all out of the temple, with the sheep, and the oxen; and He poured out the coins of the moneychangers, and overturned their tables (John 2:15).

Holy love cannot rejoice when it finds evil in control. Holy love will cast out the moneychangers. This is the kind of love God wants us to have.

✳ End your study in prayer. Think about the people you come into contact with each day. Be specific in asking God to enable you to demonstrate these characteristics of love.

DAY 5

Today's Bible Meditations
No one has beheld God at any time; if we love one another, God abides in us, and His love is perfected in us. By this we know that we abide in Him and He in us, because He has given us of His Spirit. And we have beheld and bear witness that the Father has sent the Son to be the Savior of the world.
1 John 4:12-14

We have come to know and have believed the love which God has for us. God is love, and the one who abides in love abides in God, and God abides in him.
1 John 4:16

Name of Christ for Today
The Propitiation for Our Sins
(1 John 2:2)

Prayer to Begin the Lesson
Lord Jesus,
You made the payment for my sins. You did something for me on the cross that I could never have done for myself. But it cost You

Love Is Also a Noun!

✳ **Begin today's lesson by reading the Bible verses and the name of Christ for today. Work on your memory verse. Then use the suggested prayer to begin your study.**

Today, we'll finish looking at the 15 characteristics of love from *1 Corinthians 13.*

Love Rejoices in the Truth (Holy Mind)

I can show that love bears all things by:

____

Then Jesus' disciples said, "Now you are speaking clearly and without figures of speech. Now we can see that you know all things and that you do not even need to have anyone ask you questions. This makes us believe that you came from God." "You believe at last!" Jesus answered (John 16:29-31, NIV)

We get a hint in these verses of how Jesus must have felt when His disciples finally began to catch on to what He had been trying to teach them. If you have ever had the experience of leading someone to Christ, you know the incredible sense of exhilaration when the person you've been witnessing to and praying for finally sees the truth. That exhilaration comes from holy love.

Love Bears All Things (Holy Stability)

I can show that love bears all things by:

____

One of the clearest examples of holy stability is Jesus' relationship with Simon Peter. There were days when Peter displayed incredible insight (see *Luke 5:8, Matt. 16:16).* But there were other days when his mess-ups were monumental (see *Matt. 16:21-22; 26:69-74).* No other disciple had so many ups and downs. Jesus, knowing that Peter would deny Him, said to Peter: *"...I have prayed for you, that your faith may not fail; and you, when once you have turned again, strengthen your brothers" (Luke 22:32).* Jesus dealt with Peter's struggles and successes often and rewarded him each time he demonstrated insight. Love does not come and go. Love has a holy stability.

Love Believes All Things

I can show that love believes all things by:

____

Jesus had enormous faith in the people He chose. Of all the strange choices He made, perhaps the most questionable was His selection of the despised tax collector, Zaccheus: *And when Jesus came to the place, He looked up and said to him, "Zaccheus, hurry and come down, for today I must stay at your house" (Luke 19:5).*

Jesus had faith in Zaccheus' potential. He believed in him. Because of His belief in him, Zaccheus did a total turn-around. Most of us would have labeled Zaccheus a loser and had nothing to do with him. But Jesus gave him a chance. By the way, if you were Jesus, would you have given someone like you a chance? Jesus believes in you, too!

great suffering and death. I cannot comprehend the depth of Your love. I'm overwhelmed with Your love, and I love You for it. Please work through me to reveal Your love to others, no matter what it costs me. What more could I give after what You've given for me?

Amen.

Love Hopes All Things (Holy Expectations)

I can show that love hopes all things by:

___

Let's go back to Peter again. Jesus chose Simon, knowing he would blow it. Yet, still Jesus gave him a new name: *"And I also say to you that you are Peter, and upon this rock I will build My church; and the gates of Hades shall not overpower it" (Matt. 16:18).*

Love has the ability to see the end from the beginning. Love can look at us, not for what we are now, but for what we will be. Love has holy expectations.

Love Endures All Things (Holy Sacrifice)

I can show that love endures all things by:

___

Jesus could have said no to the cross. According to *Matthew 26:53, "Or do you think that I cannot appeal to My Father, and He will at once put at My disposal more than twelve legions of angels?"*

Jesus finished what He started. *Hebrews 12:2* tells us that Jesus, *For the joy set before Him endured the cross, despising the shame.* Perfect love perseveres. Only perfect love can make the kind of holy sacrifice that Jesus made.

You may have noticed that all these characteristics complement one another. A love which believes all things will also hope all things. The various characteristics of perfect love enhance one another. The deeper we get into the mind of Christ, the more we see wholeness and unity.

But Love Is a Noun, Too!

For the last three days we've talked about the outward actions of love. But the most profound statement about love in the entire Bible doesn't deal with outward, observable actions of love, but with the nature of God Himself. *First John 4:16* says, *God is love.* So, not only is *love* a verb, it is also a noun. And not only is God love, we need to become love. Love will be the essential characteristic of our inner being, if we are to have the mind of Christ.

Love as a verb is an act of the will, and requires doing. *Love* as a noun is a fruit of the indwelling spirit, and requires being. Any Christian is capable of performing the actions of love by an exercising of the will. When we obey the commands of Scripture, we're basically performing the actions of love.

But we are to do more than act like Christ. We are to become like Christ. When we understand more about the nature of love as a noun, we can realize that love is a product of the indwelling Holy Spirit. We depend entirely on the Spirit to produce love in us. But this process of becoming love will not progress without prayer.

✱ Conclude by spending time in prayer: Consider praying a prayer like this one:

Heavenly Father, I'm beginning to understand more about the relationship of holiness and love. Help me to be obedient to the actions of love. Help me to be sensitive to the workings of Your Spirit within me so that I can be love. I want to be love to my friends at school. I want to be love to my family. I want to be love to those who don't know You. Help me to act out love to them so that I can be love for them. This was the example of Jesus, and it is in His name I pray. Amen.

Exalting Christ

UNIT 12

Day 1
Prophet, Priest, and King

Day 2
Names of Christ, Part 1

Day 3
Names of Christ, Part 2

Day 4
Victory in Christ

Day 5
Pressing On!

Scripture Memory Verse
He is also head of the body, the church; and He is the beginning, the first-born from the dead; so that He Himself might come to have first place in everything.
Colossians 1:18

Hymn Part 6—Christ's Name
Therefore also God highly exalted Him, and bestowed on Him the name which is above every name, that at the name of Jesus every knee should bow, of those who are in heaven, and on earth, and under the earth, and that every tongue should confess that Jesus Christ is Lord, to the glory of God the Father (Phil. 2:9-11).

What Is in This Unit for Me?

The names and roles of Christ will inspire you to worship and exalt Him. You will realize how Jesus relates to you in many different ways. As your love for Christ increases, you will surrender to His absolute lordship in your life. Finally, you will review what God has been doing in your life and you will set your mind pressing on toward the mark of the high calling of God in Christ.

Lifelong Objective

You will surrender to Christ's lordship and worship Him in Spirit and truth.

How God Will be Working In You

When you keep the names of Christ in mind at all times, it will help you think His thoughts and show His character. Just knowing His position, His authority, and His work causes you to desire to worship Him. God's goal is the lordship of Christ.

Unit Learning Goals

- You will understand the roles, or offices of Christ as prophet, priest, and king, and the ways by which His names can be grouped.
- You will demonstrate your surrender to His lordship over your life.
- You will demonstrate your worship, reverence, awe, and gratitude to Him in prayer.
- You will understand the nature and source of your victory in Christ.
- You will demonstrate your lifelong commitment to daily Bible study and prayer.

What You Will Do to Exalt Christ

- You will study the names and offices of Christ.
- You will pray exalting Christ through worship, praise, and thanksgiving.
- You will respond to an invitation to allow Christ's absolute lordship over your life.
- You will review your study of *The Mind of Christ* and identify some of the areas God has been working on in your life.
- You will begin praying for your youth group and for your church to be a pure and beautiful bride of Christ.

Lifelong Helps Related to This Unit

Names, Titles, and Descriptions of Jesus Christ (pp. 214-215)

The Mind of Christ Cards Related to This Unit

5B. Unit 12: Scripture Memory—*Colossians 1:18*

DAY 1

Today's Bible Meditations
Therefore also God highly exalted Him,and bestowed on Him the name which is above every name, that at the name of Jesus every knee should bow, of those who are in heaven, and on earth, and under the earth, and that every tongue should confess that Jesus Christ is Lord, to the glory of God the Father.
Philippians 2:9-11

An hour is coming, and now is, when the true worshipers shall worship the Father in spirit and truth; for such people the Father seeks to be His worshipers. God is spirit, and those who worship Him must worship in spirit and truth.
John 4:23-24

Name of Christ for Today
The Prophet
(John 7:40)

Prayer to Begin the Lesson
Lord Jesus Christ,
You are Prophet, Priest, and King. You do more for me than I can ever hope to understand. Yet, I'm related

Prophet, Priest, and King

✳ Begin today's lesson by reading the Bible verse and the name of Christ for today. Work on your memory verse. Then use the suggested prayer to begin your study.

Hymn Part 6: Christ's Name

Our journey through the hymn of *Philippians 2* is almost complete. We have looked at Christ's Freedom, Christ's Lifestyle, Christ's Servanthood, Christ's Humanity, and Christ's Holiness and Love. This week, we'll look at Christ's Name. It's a name which is above every other name. *Verses 9-11* promise that Christ's name will cause every person to bow to Him, and every tongue to proclaim that He is Lord. What a powerful name! During this final week, let's look at the names of Jesus and the Person those names represent. Our purpose is to worship Jesus Christ as Lord, and thus bring glory to God the Father.

✳ Why did God exalt His Son Jesus?________________________________

____

The sixth characteristic of a Christlike mind is peace. Christ's death bought us peace with God. His victory at the cross made peace with God a real possibility. Through His death, resurrection, and exaltation, we can experience genuine peace.

✳ What did Jesus purchase for you through His death on Calvary?

____

✳ Stop right here, and connect with God for a few minutes:

- **Pray and thank God for providing peace for you through the sacrifice of His Son.**
- **Praise God for the victory Christ won over sin and death through His resurrection.**
- **Tell Christ how much you love Him for the supreme sacrifice He made for you.**

Three Offices of Christ

At our church, whenever anyone is baptized, the pastor asks them, "What is your testimony of faith?" The person being baptized says, "Jesus Christ is Lord." This testimony of faith goes back as far as the beginning of the Christian church itself. You see it in *Philippians 2:11*. It is also in *Romans 10:9*, where Paul says, *"Jesus is Lord"* (NIV). Paul wrote the Corinthian church, *No one can say, "Jesus is Lord," except by the Holy Spirit (1 Cor. 12:3)*. There are many times in the New Testament that these three titles, *Jesus, Christ,* and *Lord* occur together. Each name refers to a special role, or office, that Christ holds. Let's look at them one at a time.

Jesus is Prophet. Jesus was the human name of God in the flesh. In this human nature, Jesus functioned as Prophet (see *Acts 3:22*), the first of His three offices. Now, we usually think of a prophet as one who makes a prediction about the future, but that's a pretty limited definition of what a prophet is. A *prophet* is simply "one through whom God speaks." This was the primary function of Jesus while He was on earth. God spoke through Him in mighty ways.

to You! I was chosen by You to be in Your family! Wow! Draw me closer to Yourself in worship today. Teach me what You mean by worshiping in spirit and truth. Be exalted in my life for Your Father's glory.
Amen.

✳ What is the first of Jesus' offices? ______________________________

Read *Acts 3:22* and *26*. What was the purpose of Jesus coming as prophet?

____

Christ as Priest. As prophet, Jesus came to bless us and turn us away from sin. The name Christ helps us understand Him as Priest. *Hebrews 9:11-12* says *Christ appeared as a high priest of the good things to come… through His own blood, He entered the holy place once for all, having obtained eternal redemption* [for us]. Christ functions as our priest in two ways. First, He is an Intercessor (see *Heb. 7:25).* An *intercessor* is "one who prays on behalf of someone else." Jesus prays to the Father on your behalf! Second, Christ is our Mediator *(1 Tim. 2:5). Mediate* is a legal term, meaning, "To resolve or settle differences by working with all the conflicting parties." So a mediator is one who helps resolve differences between two conflicting parties. Christ is the Mediator between us and God, because our sin has made us enemies with God (see *Rom. 5:10).*

✳ What are two ways Christ functions as our Priest?

I ________________ **and M** ________________

The Lord is King. Jesus' third great office is that of King (see *Rev. 19:16).* His name as King is Lord *(Phil 2:11).* If Jesus is the name that relates to the human nature of God, Lord relates to the divine nature. In medieval times, a lord was the ruler over a region. Jesus is Lord over all the earth, and, to the extent that you let Him, over all your life.

All three offices come together in the formula *Jesus Christ is Lord (Phil. 2:11).* As a human, Jesus was a Prophet. That refers to His past work. As Christ, He is Priest, which deals with His present work. In the future, when He returns, every person on earth will acknowledge Him as Lord. Prophet, Priest, and King. Past, Present, and Future. Jesus, Christ, Lord. That's where it all comes together!

✳ Write the corresponding office next to the name.

Jesus ______________________________

Christ ______________________________

Lord ______________________________

✳ What is the creed of a New Testament Church?

J ____________ **C** ____________ **is L** ____________

- **Because Jesus is a Prophet, I listen to His Word.**
- **Because Jesus is a Priest, I have security in my relationship with God.**
- **Because Jesus is King, I obey Him. I acknowledge Jesus' total lordship over every area of my life.**

✻ Jesus loved us so much that He gave His own life to redeem us. Out of love for Him, bow and confess to Him, "Jesus Christ, You are Lord." Whether or not you normally pray on your knees, I would like you to literally pray on your knees today. Take time as you wrap up this lesson to worship Jesus as Prophet, Priest, and King.

DAY 2

Today's Bible Meditation
"Because of the tender mercy of our God, with which the Sunrise from on high shall visit us, to shine upon those who sit in darkness and the shadow of death, to guide our feet into the way of peace."
Luke 1:78-79

Name of Christ for Today
Immanuel [God with us]
(Matt. 1:23)

Prayer to Begin the Lesson
Immanuel,
You are right where I am. I praise You for coming to

Names of Christ, Part 1

✻ Begin today's lesson by reading the Bible verse and the name of Christ for today. Work on your memory verse. Then use the suggested prayer to begin your study.

Ever since we started *The Mind of Christ,* you have been given names of Christ from Scripture on which to focus your attention. The names of Christ are ways to worship, submit, and exalt Christ. They help us love Him more fully and appropriately. They help us understand the many dimensions of who He is.

✻ Every week, your small group leader has asked you to mark the Name of Christ which stood out to you that week. Take some time now to scan back through the lessons. Is there one name of Christ which stands out above all the others? Which one, and why?

____

____

In a Mind of Christ small group that I led, one young lady was consistently drawn to names of Christ which compared Him to nourishment. She described herself as hungry to know more about God, so names like "Bread of Life," "Living Water," and "The Vine" really appealed to her. Another guy in our group was on the football team at school, and he was used to having coaches direct the plays that he made. So the names of Christ that really stood out to him were names like "Shepherd and Bishop of Our Souls," "Master," and "Wonderful Counselor."

We often think of Jesus as our Personal Savior. Part of what that means is that Jesus meets us where we are, according to our need. I think one of the reasons Jesus has so many names in Scripture is because different people relate to Him in different ways, according to their need. You yourself will relate to Him in different ways at different times. When you need boldness to witness to others, you can relate to Jesus as the Light of the World. When you need comforting for personal sadness, Jesus comes to you as the Good Shepherd. As we look at the names of Christ, it's incredible to realize that Jesus is all of these at the same time!

✱ **Why does Jesus have so many names in the Scripture?**

____

Do you see a pattern in the names you relate to the most? What is the pattern? What do you think that says about you?

____

____

I'd like to share with you some principles for organizing the names of Christ. These principles are not mutually exclusive—that is, a name can be in more than one category. This will help us get a handle on the names of Christ.

Deity Names

Christ's deity or divine names refer to Him as God. Because of the deity names, we worship Christ as well as the Father and the Holy Spirit. God has revealed Himself through the Incarnation, for Jesus is God. Listed below are some of His deity names.

- Creator *(Col. 1:16)*
- Truth *(John 14:6)*
- Mighty God *(Isa. 9:6)*
- Son of God *(John 1:49)*
- Holy One of God *(Luke 4:34)*
- Lord from Heaven *(1 Cor. 15:47)*
- Image of the Invisible God *(Col. 1:15)*
- Immanuel [God With Us] *(Matt. 1:23)*

Perhaps the most important of the divine names is Jesus' own claim to be the *"I Am" (John 8:58)*. This was an incredibly important name to the Jews because this was the name God revealed to Moses at the burning bush (see *Ex. 3:14)*. By calling Himself I Am, Jesus was identifying Himself with the eternal God of Moses.

✱ **Take a prayer break to worship Christ as God.**

Functioning Names

These names describe Christ in terms of what He does. They are action names. Since they describe what Jesus did specifically to redeem us, some of them could be called Redemption Names. Jesus is:

- Deliverer *(Rom. 11:26)*
- He that Sanctifies *(Heb. 2:11)*
- Shepherd and Bishop [Guardian] of Our Souls *(1 Pet. 2:25)*
- Savior of the world *(John 4:42)*
- Wonderful Counselor *(Isa. 9:6)*

✱ **Take another prayer break. Acknowledge Christ for who He is, and thank Him for the things He does for you.**

Light Names

No, these are not names with just one calorie! Jesus is often described as the True Light. When you think about all the sun does for the earth, it's an appropriate com-

dwell among humanity. You are Immanuel when I go to school. You are Immanuel when I am at home. You are Immanuel when I am frustrated or depressed. Everywhere I go, You are God With Me. I can't understand why You have chosen to live with me, but I praise You for it. Shine in me, and shine through me to reveal Your light to those who live in darkness. Guide my feet in the ways of peace.

Amen.

parison when you think about all the Son does for us! Here are some of Jesus' light names:

- Dayspring [Sunrise] *(Luke 1:78)*
- Light of Life *(John 8:12)*
- Light of Men *(John 1:4)*
- Day Star *(2 Pet. 1:19)*
- Light of the World *(John 8:12)*
- Light of Revelation to the Gentiles *(Luke 2:32)*

In Jesus' last words in the New Testament, He called Himself *"the bright morning star" (Rev. 22:16)*. There is a lot of hope in this name. The morning star is the one that comes out just before the dawn, when night is darkest. In the New Jerusalem, the city of Heaven, Revelation promises us that *"the city has no need of the sun or of the moon to shine upon it, for the glory of God has illumined it, and its lamp is the Lamb" (Rev. 21:23)*.

✳ Close your time with the Lord today by praising Him for His glory.

DAY 3

Today's Bible Meditation
"I am the Alpha and the Omega, the first and the last, the beginning and the end."
Revelation 22:13

Name of Christ for Today
Alpha and Omega, the Beginning and the End
(Rev. 21:6)

Prayer to Begin the Lesson
Alpha and Omega,
You are the beginner and

Names of Christ, Part 2

✳ Begin today's lesson by reading the Bible verse and the name of Christ for today. Work on your memory verse. Then use the suggested prayer to begin your study.

Complement Principle

Bread and Butter. Car and Driver. Lamp and Lampshade. Player and Coach. There are some concepts that go together. We call these complementary concepts. Many of the names of Christ have a complementary role for us. The name describes what He does, our role describes what we are supposed to do or be in response to it.

CHRIST'S NAME	OUR ROLE
Shepherd *(John 10:11)*	Sheep
Father *(Isa. 9:6)*	Child
Brother *(Heb. 2:11)*	Brother or Sister
Teacher *(John 3:2)*	Student (Disciple)
Master *(2 Tim. 2:21)*	Servant
Vine *(John 15:1)*	Branch
Bridegroom *(Mark 2:19)*	Bride of Christ (the church)

Identity Principle

When we apply the Identity Principle, we identify with Christ in terms of His names. For example, in *John 8:12,* Jesus called Himself the Light of the World. But in *Matthew 5:14,* He calls us the light of the world. This is the identity principle at work.

We are to grow in His likeness, and become like Christ.

- God's Beloved *(Matt. 12:18)*. We are beloved by God *(Rom. 1:7)*.
- Chosen One *(Isa. 42:1)*. We are chosen by God *(2 Tim. 2:10)*.
- Heir of All Things *(Heb. 1:2)*. We are joint-heirs with Christ *(Rom. 8:17)*.
- Rock *(1 Cor. 10:4)*. We are to be solid and steady.
- Jesus Christ the Righteous *(1 John 2:1)*. In Him we are righteous *(Jer. 23:6)*.
- Last Adam *(1 Cor. 15:45)*. We become fully human when we live like Christ lived.

Some of these names tell us where we need to be. But some of them tell us what we already are. We are beloved. We are joint-heirs. We are chosen. We are righteous.

the finisher of everything! You started Creation; You will bring it to completion. You began a good work in me, and You are able to finish it. Holy Spirit, as I study more about Christ's names today, please continue to enlarge my knowledge and understanding of Him. Exalt Him in my life. Then, enable me to lift Him up in the eyes of others as I declare His greatness to those around me.

Amen.

✳ **Review the list and ask God if there is one particular area He would like to work on to bring you closer to Christ's likeness. Thank God that you are beloved, chosen, and a joint-heir with Christ.**

The Life Principle

Many of Jesus' names indicate that He is the Source of Life. Whenever a name is repeated in its various forms, that's a clue that God really wants us to get the idea. Above all else, Christ is our source of nourishment and sustenance. Christ is:

- The Bread of Life *(John 6:35)*
- The Life *(John 14:6)*
- Light of Life *(John 8:12)*
- The Word of Life *(1 John 1:1)*
- Eternal Life *(1 John 5:20)*
- Our Life *(Col. 3:4)*
- Prince of Life *(Acts 3:15)*
- The Resurrection and the Life *(John 11:25)*

✳ **Take a prayer break. Pause to agree with Christ that He is your life, and ask Him to do whatever it takes for His life to be clearly reflected in you.**

The Sovereign Principle

Sovereign is a big word we don't use very often anymore. An easy way to remember its meaning is to look at the word within the word: *Sov-e-reign. Sovereign* means that "Jesus reigns." Jesus is in control over everything that happens. These names indicate the sovereignty and royalty of Christ.

- Governor *(Matt. 2:6)*
- King of Saints *(Rev. 15:3)*
- Thy King *(Matt. 21:5)*
- Good Master *(Mark 10:17)*
- Prince of Life *(Acts 3:15)*
- Prince of the Kings of the Earth *(Rev. 1:5)*
- King that Comes in the Name of the Lord *(Luke 19:38)*
- King of Kings *(1 Tim. 6:15)*
- King of the Jews *(Matt. 27:11)*
- Lord of Lords *(1 Tim. 6:15)*
- Messiah the Prince *(Dan. 9:25)*
- Prince of Peace *(Isa. 9:6)*
- King Eternal, Immortal, Invisible *(1 Tim. 1:17)*
- Leader and Commander to the People *(Isa. 55:4)*

The Preeminence Principle

Another big word, *preeminence* simply means "first" or "foremost." Not only is Christ absolute ruler, but He is to be first or foremost in all things.

- God of the Whole Earth *(Isa. 54:5)*
- Firstborn of Every Creature *(Col. 1:15)*
- Head of Every Man *(1 Cor. 11:3)*
- Firstborn Among Many Brethren *(Rom. 8:29)*
- Head of the Body, the Church *(Col. 1:18)*

- Head of all Principality and Power *(Col. 2:10)*
- Lord Over All *(Rom. 10:12)*

These are important names, because Jesus wants to have preeminence in our lives. He wants to be first and foremost. Is Jesus Lord over all in your life?

✳ Take another prayer break, focus on Christ as your ruler. On your knees submit to His Lordship in your life, your family, your work, your school, and your church. Review the lists of the names of Christ. End by expressing your worship, praise, and thanksgiving to Christ. God wants Christ to be exalted in your mind and in your life.

DAY 4

Today's Bible Meditations
For whatever is born of God overcomes the world; and this is the victory that has overcome the world—our faith. And who is the one who overcomes the world, but he who believes that Jesus is the Son of God?

1 John 5:4-5

I urge you therefore, brethren, by the mercies of God, to present your bodies a living and holy sacrifice, acceptable to God, which is your spiritual service of worship. And do not be conformed to this world, but be transformed by the

Victory in Christ

✳ Begin today's lesson by reading the Bible verse and the name of Christ for today. Work on your memory verse. Then use the suggested prayer to begin your study.

You're Drafted!

Every day of your Christian life, you are involved in a battle. Not a physical one, but a spiritual one. The battles you fight are just a part of a war that has been going on since the beginning of time. The good news is, we know that God's already won the war. We read in the Book of Revelation that ultimately, victory is guaranteed for our side. The challenging news is, no one is exempt from the fight. Once you become a Christian, you basically get a draft card.

Like we said, it's not a physical battle. Paul says that *our struggle is not against flesh and blood, but against the rulers, against the powers, against the world forces of this darkness, against the spiritual forces of wickedness in the heavenly places (Eph. 6:12).* When Paul talks about "rulers" and "world forces," he is not talking about earthly political rulers or governments. He is talking about spiritual warfare—where the battle is not fought on a field, in a desert, or in a jungle, but in your mind. Satan and his forces are determined to get a foothold in your mind, and God is just as determined to keep your mind pure. So, if you're going to have the mind of Christ, you're going to struggle. Every day.

✳ What is one way you have experienced spiritual battles in your mind?

____

____

Our Battle Gear

Okay, so you know there's a battle. And you know that we can win it. Paul expresses great confidence in our ability to defeat Satan:

The weapons we fight with are not the weapons of the world. On the contrary, they have divine power to demolish strongholds. We demolish arguments and every pretension that sets itself up against the knowledge of God, and we take captive every thought to make it obedient to Christ (2 Cor. 10:4-5, NIV).

Okay, so what are the weapons, and how do we use them? For all the times you've felt like your thought life is out of control, isn't it good news to know that we've got weapons at our disposal that can *take every thought captive to the obedience of Christ? Ephesians 6:13-18* list the weapons we have to *fight the good fight of faith (1 Tim. 6:12).*

✻ **Read *Ephesians 6:10-18* below. Circle all the defensive pieces of spiritual armor we have. Then, underline the one offensive weapon we have.**

Finally, be strong in the Lord, and in the strength of His might. Put on the full armor of God, that you may be able to stand firm against the schemes of the devil. For our struggle is not against flesh and blood, but against the rulers, against the powers, against the world forces of this darkness, against the spiritual forces of wickedness in the heavenly places. Therefore, take up the full armor of God, that you may be able to resist in the evil day, and having done everything, to stand firm. Stand firm therefore, having girded your loins with truth, and having put on the breastplate of righteousness, and having shod your feet with the preparation of the gospel of peace; in addition to all, taking up the shield of faith with which you will be able to extinguish all the flaming missiles of the evil one. And take the helmet of salvation, and the sword of the Spirit, which is the word of God. With all prayer and petition pray at all times in the Spirit, and with this in view, be on the alert with all perseverance and petition for all the saints.

✻ **What is the one thing we are to do *at all times*?** ______________________

What is our offensive weapon? ______________________________

According to Ephesians, the only offensive weapon is the *sword of the Spirit,* which is the Word of God. The Bible is powerful because it contains what we need to fight the enemy.

The Battle and the Victory are the Lord's

Maybe the reason God didn't give us more offensive weapons is so that we will always remember who the battle really belongs to. *Second Chronicles 20:15* reminds us that *"the battle is not yours but God's."* Paul said, *But thanks be to God, who always leads us **in His triumph** in Christ, and manifests through us the sweet aroma of the knowledge of Him in every place (2 Cor. 2:14)* [bold is mine]. Victory is not an outcome to be achieved (because it already has been), but a process to follow, as God leads us in His triumph. When we walk in Christ, and He is shown and exalted in our life, we walk in victory. If you are a Christian seeking after the mind of Christ, victory is not an event. Victory is when the Victor abides in us.

For whatever is born of God overcomes the world; and this is the victory that has overcome the world—our faith. And who is the one who overcomes the world, but he

renewing of your mind, that you may prove what the will of God is, that which is good and acceptable and perfect.

Romans 12:1-2

Name of Christ for Today
Our Savior Jesus Christ
(2 Pet. 1:1)

Prayer to Begin the Lesson
Jesus,
You are my Savior.
In You I have victory over the world. How can I begin to say thanks? Nothing I do would be adequate. I can only place my life on the altar as a living sacrifice to You in an act of worship. Continue to renew my mind that I may be pleasing to You. Please accept my humble thanks for the victory You give.
Amen.

who believes that Jesus is the Son of God? (1 John 5:4-5). How is our faith proven? It's not by success, not by number of friends won to Christ, not even by answered prayer. The proof of our faith is in our endurance.

✳ Which of the following best describes spiritual victory in Christ?

- ❑ **Spiritual victory in Christ is a future hope. I hope He wins.**
- ❑ **Spiritual victory in Christ is a present reality. He has won already.**

Christ has won already. Not even death can defeat Him. He Himself conquered death when He rose from the grave, and because of that, death is defeated for believers as well:

> *When this perishable will have put on the imperishable, and this mortal will have put on immortality, then will come about the saying that is written, "Death is swallowed up in victory. O death, where is your victory? O death, where is your sting?" The sting of death is sin, and the power of sin is the law; but thanks be to God, who gives us the victory through our Lord Jesus Christ (1 Cor. 15:54-57).*

For believers, death is nothing. It's just a brief passage into the presence of Christ. On the other side of death is the reward we were seeking as we struggled with the forces of the world.

But for now, don't be surprised if the devil tries to mess up what you've learned in this course. Since he knows he won't win in the end, he will do everything he can to win in the short term. Jesus never promised that living this life would be easy. Even though we get the mind of Christ at our spiritual birth, that baby mind's gotta grow. The growth of that mind can be stunted by the habits of a sinful lifestyle, the obstruction of Satan, and the lure of the world. But victory is yours! Your triumph was accomplished two thousand years ago when Christ conquered death on the cross and ascended to intercede for us until the final battle is over. Here's a great thought: Jesus has been praying for you all the way through this course!

- ❑ **Conclude in prayer. Claim your victory in Christ. Ask God to teach you to use your spiritual weapons to make every though obedient to Christ.**
- ❑ **As a follow-up to the previous assignment on page 162 to view or listen to the tapes on *The Crucifixion*, this is an appropriate time in your study to complete the following assignments, either individually or as a group (check with your small group leader).**
- ❑ **View *The Mind of Christ Worship Video: The Resurrection***
- ❑ **Listen to *The Mind of Christ Audiocassettes: The Resurrection***

Pressing On!

Today's Bible Meditation
"Hallelujah! For the Lord our God, the Almighty, reigns. Let us rejoice and be glad and give the glory to Him, for the marriage of the Lamb has come and his bride has made herself ready." And it was given to her to clothe herself in fine linen, bright and clean; for the fine linen is the righteous acts of the saints.
Revelation 19:6-8

Name of Christ for Today
Author and Perfecter of Faith
(Heb. 12:2)

Prayer to Begin the Lesson
Jesus,
Author and Finisher of my faith, twelve weeks ago You began a good work in my life when we began The Mind of Christ. Even before that, You began a good work when You saved me. I pray now that You will continue to accomplish Your purposes in my life to mold and shape my life into Your image. I exalt You! I worship You! I adore You! I bow before You and proclaim that You are my Lord Jesus Christ.
Amen.

✻ **Begin today's lesson by reading the Bible verse and the name of Christ for today. Work on your memory verse. Then use the suggested prayer to begin your study.**

Conforming to Christ's Image

As I look back over this course, I believe the Lord had several purposes in leading me to write it. He led me to write it, and I believe He led you to study it. The first group of purposes relate to you as an individual.

Purpose #1: God wants to conform you to the image of His Son.

You have studied so many names and offices of Christ these past few months. He is your Creator (see *Col. 1:16),* your Redeemer, and your Sustainer (see *Col. 1:14,17*). He is Head over every Rule and Authority (see *Col. 2:10*). But as great as Christ is, He is your Brother if you are a Christian (see *Heb. 2:11).* You are to look like your Big Brother. You are to resemble Him, and live a life that parallels His. Even though you live in the material world, you are a spiritual creature. God is molding you into that image: *Just as we have borne the image of the earthy, we shall also bear the image of the heavenly (1 Cor. 15:49).*

You can take part in that process of being conformed to Christ's image. It's a matter of realizing in thought and deed all that was born in you when you became a Christian. Reviewing what you have studied in *The Mind of Christ* gives you some specifics in the mind of Christ to which you can conform:

- The virtues of godly wisdom in *James 3:17.*
- The fruit of the Spirit in *Galatians 5:22-23.*
- The characteristics of the servant mind.
- The qualities described in the Beatitudes of *Matthew 5:3-10.*
- The model of Christ in expressing emotions.
- The model of Christ in relationship to things and people.
- The model of Christ in relationship to the Father and the Holy Spirit.
- The model of Christ's use of the Scriptures and prayer.
- The character and behavior of holiness.
- The actions of Christlike love.

✻ **Which area(s) found in this list did God emphasize in your life over the course of *The Mind of Christ?* Underline those areas.**

✻ **Think back to where you were in your spiritual life when you started this course. Are you more like Christ now, or less like Christ?**

____

Why? ____

____

Conforming to the image of Christ is accomplished through a process (see *Mark 4:26-29)*. We participate in that process. This is why your will is so important. You must *be transformed by the renewing of your mind (Rom. 12:2).*

Purpose #2: God wants you to gain knowledge of Christ.

This book has given you basic information about the mind and Person of Christ. If we are to be conformed, we must have specific information about what we are being conformed to. Over the years, I have filled 21 notebooks (not to mention the many books in my library) with information on the Person of Christ. This course barely scratches the surface! I've still got a lot to learn, and so do you. Jesus invites us, *"Take My yoke upon you, and learn from Me" (Matt. 11:29).*

✳ **Think back on all the things you have learned about Christ during *The Mind of Christ.* What one thing seems to stand out as most interesting, meaningful, inspiring, or challenging?**

____

We've said it over and over again—this course is only a beginning. There is so much knowledge to be gained every single time you open your Bible. The Old Testament is full of God's actions through history, prophecies about Christ's coming, poetry about who Christ is, and His names. The New Testament tells of Jesus' earthly ministry and His heavenly work in energizing the church. I've known people who have memorized major sections of the Bible, yet still find something new every time they open it up to study from it. There is nothing better that you can do for yourself than to develop the discipline of a daily quiet time. Make a commitment to spending time with God, in His word, and in prayer. Make Jesus and His plan the basis for everything you do. As you go through your daily routine, embrace Jesus as you plan, as you study, as you hang out with friends, as you go to wrestling practice, as you shop at the mall, even as you sit down to dinner with your parents. Embrace Jesus.

Think about what it takes to get to know a boyfriend or girlfriend. You've got to spend time talking with them. You've got to listen to them. You write notes back and forth to each other during third period! Getting to know Jesus Christ and becoming like Him isn't that much different. You've got to:

- Take time to talk with Him in prayer.
- Take time to listen to His instruction and guidance.
- Take time reading His Word to know Him, His purposes, and His ways more clearly.
- Take time to meditate on the person and work of Christ as a model for your life.

✳ **All right. We've got one more long-term assignment for you. First, read the following verses:**

> ***When you make a vow to God, do not be late in paying it, for He takes no delight in fools. Pay what you vow! It is better that you should not vow than than that you should vow and not pay (Eccl. 5:4-5).***

Now, with that verse in mind, realizing how serious a vow before God is, consider this request carefully and prayerfully. Will you commit yourself to spend time with

the Lord in prayer, Scripture study, and meditation daily?

❑ Yes ❑ I'm not ready to do that yet. ❑ No

If you are willing, how much time are you willing to pledge to Jesus with the intention of keeping your vow to Him for the rest of your life? Check your response.

❑ 15 minutes daily
❑ 30 minutes daily
❑ 45 minutes daily
❑ 60 minutes daily
❑ Other: ________________ daily

A long time ago, I made a commitment to spend at least 30 minutes a day with the Lord. God has enabled me to keep that commitment to Him, and He has rewarded me with His presence and guidance. If you have just made a vow to the Lord, check out this model prayer from the Psalms:

> *Thou hast heard my vows, O God; Thou hast given me the inheritance of those who fear Thy name… So I will sing praise unto Thy name forever, that I may pay my vows day by day (Ps. 61:5,8).*
>
> *"Offer to God a sacrifice of thanksgiving, and pay your vows to the Most High; and call upon Me in the day of trouble; I shall rescue you, and you will honor Me" (Ps. 50:14-15).*

Purpose #3: Preparing the Bride of Christ

There are many times in Scripture when the church is called the Bride of Christ. As I wrote *The Mind of Christ,* my constant desire was to see the church purified and cleansed. For you, that may start with your youth group. How often do you pray that your youth group and your church can be a pure Bride for Christ? Here are some things to pray for:

- Pray that your youth group will be pure. Pray that people will be involved in your group for more than just the fun trips and activities. Pray that your youth group will consistently seek God's purposes for it. Ask God to cleanse it from sin.
- Pray that your youth group and your church will come under the unconditional lordship of Jesus. Keep this in mind: *Christ can never be head of your youth group if He isn't Head over your life. Christ can never be head of your church if He isn't Head over your youth group.* You see, you're a part of your youth group, your youth group is part of your church, your church may be part of a larger association of churches which is part of the larger kingdom of God. If you are going to pray for your youth group to be ready for Christ, you have to start by praying for yourself to be ready.
- Pray that your youth group will truly love Christ—the Bridegroom. There are lots of people in youth groups around the country that come because of the personality of the youth workers, or because of the church's facilities, or because their boyfriend or girlfriend goes to that church. Pray that your youth group will totally fall in love with Christ.

✳ **Take a few moments to pray these prayers for yourself, your youth group, and your church.**

If you don't mind, I'd like to pray for you and your group.

Heavenly Father,

I ask that my friends finishing this course today never forget the glory and accomplishments of Jesus. I pray that they will always glorify Christ in their lives above all else. I ask that You remind my friends of those things to be praying for in their own lives and in the lives of their friends in the youth group. Help them to be aware of the larger church family that their youth group is a part of.

Lord Jesus, I pray that we will lift up You in our groups. When people visit our group, let them see You, not our accomplishments or activities. Great God, exalt the name of Christ like it has never been exalted before. Let it be high and holy in our youth group.

Dear Father, fulfill the purpose You originally had in the writing of this course. In Jesus' name.

Amen.

Continuing the Process

You have concluded your study of this introduction to the lifelong process of letting the mind of Christ be developed in you. This is just the beginning. Continue to grow in the grace and knowledge of your Lord and Savior Jesus Christ.

✳ **Consider praying this prayer. Respond to God in whatever way you sense would be appropriate.**

Lord,

I understand more clearly now that Jesus was how You chose to reveal Yourself to me. As I get to know Jesus, I get to know You and Your nature. With all my heart, I thank You for revealing Yourself to us so clearly. I understand that all revelation is summarized in the Person of Christ.

I want to live His life today. Through Him, You are bringing many children to glory. I know that I've just started this process. I ask You to carry that process through to its final conclusion that You have in mind for me. I want to do all I can to help You accomplish Your purpose for my life.

I make Jesus Christ the absolute Lord of my life. I won't question your plan for me, for Jesus is my Master.

I love You very much. With all the adoration possible to me at this stage of my growth, I love You with my whole being. I commit myself to let You perfect fully all that You intend to finish in me. In Jesus' name, I am Yours.

Amen.

Lifelong Helps for Developing the Mind of Christ

Bondage to Freedom Lists

Jesus wants you to be free from every bondage to sin, self, and the world's mind-set. The first step in developing the mind of Christ is to experience the freedom Christ provides. When I made these lists for myself, I evaluated my thinking and true mind-set. Under the leadership of the Holy Spirit, God helped me identify things that are not like the mind of Christ. Then He guided me to be more in line with the mind of Christ.

These lists are connected with Weeks 2 and 3, but working on these lists is a lifelong process. God continually renews your mind, so you will continually be reviewing, updating, changing, crossing out, and adding in items on this list. If you have a journal, that is a great place for these lists. A loose-leaf notebook also works fine, especially as you add and remove pages. Here are some hints:

1. Title and date your lists and updates. See how God works to remove and add items from and to your lists.
2. Be totally honest with God as you make your lists. It's pretty useless to lie to God.
3. Don't go to the suggested categories until you've run out of things for your own list.
4. These may not be the only areas of bondage in your life. If the Holy Spirit leads you, list new categories.
5. Evaluate your lists using Scripture and the life of Jesus. Study your Bible closely. Use a topical index as well as a concordance, to look up Scripture. Ask your youth minister for help.
6. Review the lists periodically to check your progress and to identify new areas of bondage.

LIST 1—Lusts/Wants/Desires

If you are having difficulty in making your list or want to be more thorough, consider wants or desires related to the following categories:

- opposite sex relationships
- athletic excellence
- material things
- academic recognition
- money
- morality
- spiritual character
- attitudes/behaviors

Evaluating Your Desires—Ask God to help you identify the self-seeking items and the ones that are Kingdom seeking. God's goal is to move your desires from selfish desires to Kingdom desires.

LIST 2—Habits

If you are having difficulty in making your list or want to be more thorough, consider habits related to the following categories:

- Bible study, prayer
- keeping promises
- reading
- speech/language
- exercise
- punctuality
- recreation
- use of free time

Evaluating Your Habits—Evaluate your habits and ask God to help you identify the careless habits and the Spirit-controlled habits. God's desire is to move your habits from being careless to being Spirit-controlled.

LIST 3—Loyalties

If you are having difficulty in making your list or want to be more thorough, consider loyalties related to the following categories:

- family
- friends
- social club
- athletic team
- youth group
- part-time job
- school
- future college

Evaluating Your Loyalties—Evaluate your loyalties asking God to help you identify the scattered loyalties and the prayerful loyalties. God's goal is to move your loyalties from scattered to prayerful.

LIST 4— Relationships

If you are having difficulty in making your list or want to be more thorough, consider relationships related to the following categories:

- teachers
- church members
- friends
- family members
- Sunday School teacher
- classmates
- co-workers
- neighbors
- girlfriend/boyfriend
- youth leader/pastor

Evaluating Your Relationships—Evaluate your relationships asking God to help you identify the self-serving ones and the ones serving Him. God's goal is to move your relationships from serving self to serving God.

LIST 5—Prejudices

If you are having difficulty in making your list or want to be more thorough, consider prejudices related to the following categories:

- other ethnic backgrounds
- well-educated/poorly educated
- homosexuals
- other religions
- other schools
- rich or poor
- homeless persons
- the opposite sex

Evaluating Your Prejudices—Evaluate your prejudices, ask God to help you identify the ones contrary to Scripture and which, if any, are scriptural. If you don't know what the Bible has to say about an area, study the Bible for your response. God's goal is to move your prejudices from being contrary to Scripture to being scriptural.

LIST 6—Ambitions

If you are having difficulty in making your list or want to be more thorough, consider ambitions (goals, purposes, objectives, hopes, dreams) related to the following categories:

- beauty/good looks
- college
- athletic achievement
- good grades
- popularity
- wealth
- career
- marriage
- things
- fame

Evaluating Your Ambitions—Evaluate your ambitions asking God to help you identify the ones honoring self and those honoring God. God's goal is to move your ambitions from honoring self to honoring God.

LIST 7—Duties

If you are having difficulty in making your list or want to be more thorough, consider duties related to the following categories:

- school
- social clubs
- God
- self
- church
- part-time job
- family members
- friends

Evaluating Your Duties—Evaluate your duties asking God to help you identify insignificant duties and eternally significant duties. God's goal is to move your duties from insignificant to eternal significance.

LIST 8—Debts

If you are having difficulty in making your list or want to be more thorough, consider debts (including favors owed) related to the following categories:

- money you owe parents
- money you owe friends
- showing hospitality
- church
- giving gifts
- thank you notes

Evaluating Your Debts—Ask God to help you identify obligation debts and gratitude debts. God's goal is to move your debts from obligation to gratitude.

LIST 9—Possessions

If you are having difficulty in making your list, consider possessions related to the following :

- recreation equipment
- stereo equipment
- computers/computer games
- collections (comics, sports cards)
- money
- jewelry
- CDs
- car

Evaluating Your Possessions—Ask God to help you identify the possessions you relate to as owner, and those you relate to as steward. God desires to move your relationship to possessions from ownership to stewardship.

Are your possessions idols to you? Do they take God's place in your life? God may ask you to get rid of them because you love them more than you love God. Giving them away or sharing them may move you from being an owner to being a steward. God requires us to tithe to remind us that He provides everything we have. Be sensitive.

LIST 10—Fears

If you are having difficulty in making your list or want to be more thorough, consider fears or worries related to the following categories:

- college choice
- violence
- finding a spouse
- health
- death
- parents fighting
- safety, security
- having money
- natural disaster
- grades
- family trouble

Evaluating Your Fears—Ask God to help you move from being self-protective to being secure in Christ. God's goal is to change you from being one who is self-protective to one whose only security is in Christ.

LIST 11—Weaknesses

If you are having difficulty in making your list or want to be more thorough, consider weaknesses related to the following categories:

- family background
- mental disability
- physical disability
- character flaws (short-tempered, etc.)
- age
- uneducated
- unskilled

Evaluation of Your Weaknesses—Ask God to help you identify the weaknesses being used by Satan and the ones being used by God. God's goal is to change your weaknesses from being Satan's tools to God's tools.

LIST 12—Hurts

If you are having difficulty in making your list or want to be more thorough, consider hurts, grudges, or resentments related to the following categories:

- misunderstanding arguments
- failure
- crimes committed against you
- abuse
- childhood experiences with family or relatives
- childhood experiences with friends or neighbors
- friends letting you down or turning on you

Evaluation of Your Hurts—Ask God to help you identify the hurts you respond to with resentment, and the ones you respond to with love. God's goal is to move your hurts from producing resentment to producing love.

Note: If you are dealing with abuse in your life, either going on now or in your past, you need to get help. Please talk to your group leader, your minister, or a counselor.

Lifelong Helps for Developing the Mind of Christ

Christlike Virtues

Pure:
blameless, clean,
chaste, spotless, unblemished,
innocent, stainless, uncontaminated, above reproach

Opposites of *Pure:*
lustful, carnal,
fleshly, lewd, impure, dirty,
tainted, stained, corrupt,
immoral, depraved

Perversions of *Pure:*
puritanical,
rigid, overly strict,
self-righteous, holier-than-thou, prudish, pharisaical

PURE

For additional help on becoming pure see pages 64-67.

Possible Points of Temptation

As a Christian teen, you're going to battle impurity in two main areas: (1) Lust for what you're not supposed to have; and (2) Lust for power. Lust for what you're not supposed to have is expressed by preoccupation with anything unlawful, immoral, or wrong. This might include sexual impurity, relying on horoscopes or psychic phone networks, watching X-rated movies, downloading computer pornography, and other such activities. Temptation also comes through attitudes expressed in TV, movies, magazines, newspapers, music, jokes, and gossip. Lust for power is expressed either in lust for wealth or lust for position. You can spot lust for power in how it affects your motives for doing things. For example, if you are running for student council because you have some ideas for positive changes at school, that's one thing. But if you're running so you can be perceived as being in "the popular crowd," then student council is a point of temptation to impurity.

Becoming Pure

We become pure by constantly practicing the presence of God.

- Recognize that God is present with you.
- Screen your thoughts, what you look at, and what you listen to.
- Evaluate the purity of your thoughts, sights, and sounds according to the purity of Christ.
- When possible, avoid impure communication (turn off the TV or radio, close the book or magazine, leave the room, log off the computer, etc.).
- Identify regular problem areas (activities you do, places you go, things you watch or read that frequently cause you to have impure thoughts).
- Get rid of temptations that are always present.
- Find pure alternatives. Look for Christian music to replace your non-Christian music. Make a list with your girlfriend or boyfriend of every possible thing you might do on a date besides making out.

Scriptures for Meditation

As you read the following Scriptures, ask God to speak to you about the purity or impurity of your life. Watch for specific ways God may guide you to avoid impurities or to develop purity.

> *Finally, brethren, whatever is true, whatever is honorable, whatever is right, whatever is pure, whatever is lovely, whatever is of good repute, if there*

is any excellence and if anything worthy of praise, let your mind dwell on these things (Phil. 4:8).

Beloved, now we are children of God, and it has not appeared as yet what we shall be. We know that, when He appears, we shall be like Him, because we shall see Him just as He is. And everyone who has this hope fixed on Him purifies himself, just as He is pure (1 John 3:2-3).

PEACEABLE

For additional help on becoming peaceable see pages 68-69.

Possible Points of Temptation

When you are hungry, tired, fatigued, or stressed-out, your peaceable spirit may be tested. Peaceableness can also be tested when you're trying to impress someone, show someone else up or put them down, or when you're around people who love to argue and debate meaningless issues.

Becoming Peaceable

You can become peaceable by bringing into harmony the perfections of Christ in you with those of others.

- Learn to recognize times when peace is needed.
- When you recognize times when peace is needed, pray to the Prince of Peace for godly wisdom in responding to the circumstances.
- Ask God to help you display a servant heart.
- Will a humble spirit or forgiveness help ease the tensions? If so, do what you can to show such a spirit.
- Suggest a cooling-off time, or call the people involved to prayer.
- Seek to maintain a spirit of unity in the bond of peace.
- See if there is any way you can help meet the needs of the people in conflict.
- Watch for ways you can help bring about agreement, but don't compromise on convictions or truth.

Scriptures for Meditation

As you read the following Scriptures, ask God to speak to you about peaceable behavior. Watch for specific ways God may guide you to choose peace and harmony over strife.

Live in peace with one another. And we urge you, brethren, admonish the unruly, encourage the fainthearted, help the weak, be patient with all men. See that no one repays another with evil for evil, but always seek after that which is good for one another and for all men (1 Thess. 5:13-15).

Pursue peace with all men, and the sanctification without which no one will see the Lord (Heb. 12:14).

GENTLE

For additional help on becoming gentle, see pages 70-71.

Becoming Gentle

You can become gentle by applying the perfect skill of Christ to the removal of the imperfections in the body of Christ.

Peaceable:
peaceful, friendly, harmonious, orderly, quiet, content, reconciling, calm, agreeable, compatible

Opposites of *Peaceable:*
fussy, nit-picking, picky, contentious, argumentative, ornery, controversial, disagreeable, mean, obstinate, bad-tempered

Perversions of *Peaceable:*
compromising, wishy-washy, people-pleaser

Gentle:
fair, moderate, considerate, approachable, pleasant, nurturing, tender, tactful, delicate, gracious, considerate, kind-hearted

Opposites of *Gentle:*
harsh, caustic, rough, abusive, hard, stiff, bitter, cruel, fierce, violent, blunt, brash, rude, snappy, short, snippy, grating

Perversions of *Gentle:*
unkind restraint, negligent, spoiling, careless, neglectful, inattentive, reckless

- Examine yourself *(Matt. 7:3-5).*
- Act only out of love, desiring what is best for the body of Christ.
- Pray carefully about when and how to respond.
- Treat others as brothers and sisters, or as gently as children.

Scriptures for Meditation

As you read the following Scriptures, ask God to speak to you about gentleness or harshness in your life. Watch for specific ways God may guide you to respond to others with a gentle spirit.

> *The Lord's bond-servant must not be quarrelsome, but be kind to all, able to teach, patient when wronged (2 Tim. 2:24).*

> *Remind them to be subject to rulers, to authorities, to be obedient, to be ready for every good deed, to malign no one, to be uncontentious, gentle, showing every consideration for all men. For we also once were foolish ourselves, disobedient, deceived, enslaved to various lusts and pleasures, spending our life in malice and envy, hateful, hating one another (Titus 3:1-3).*

Reasonable:
approachable, cordial, helpful, accessible, available, open, reachable, cooperative, willing, inclined, accommodating, responsive

Opposites of *Reasonable:*
unapproachable, cold, cool, distant, uncooperative, inaccessible, closed, frigid, introverted

Perversions of *Reasonable:*
yes-person, brown-noser, pushover, sucker

REASONABLE

For additional help on becoming reasonable see pages 71-72.

Becoming Reasonable

You can become reasonable by making yourself available, knowing that God only allows circumstances in your life that build the body of Christ.

- Look at every circumstance as an event that God has permitted, or sometimes even planned!
- Develop an intimacy with God so that you are always in a spirit of prayer—"pray without ceasing."
- When someone asks you for something, look for God's perspective on how to respond.

Scriptures for Meditation

Read the following Scriptures to prepare your mind to respond to requests in God's way.

> *"And whoever shall force you to go one mile, go with him two. Give to him who asks of you, and do not turn away from him who wants to borrow from you" (Matt. 5:41-42).*

> *If your enemy is hungry, give him food to eat; And if he is thirsty, give him water to drink (Prov. 25:21).*

Merciful:
caring, forgiving, gracious, decent, noble, sympathetic, tolerant, compassionate, charitable, benevolent

Opposites of *Merciful:*
merciless, unmerciful, unsympathetic, compassionless, hardened, pitiless, spiteful, sadistic

Perversions of *Merciful:*
indulgent, lenient, permissive

MERCIFUL

For additional help on becoming merciful see pages 72-73.

Possible Points of Temptation

The world that tells us to get even, to stand up for our rights, to look out for number one, and to give other people what they've got coming to them. God's way is different. To be merciful is to remember how much mercy God has shown us. *Matthew 18:21-35* is a great story about an unmerciful servant.

Becoming Merciful
You can become merciful by desiring to express the mercy of God.

Scriptures for Meditation
As you read the following Scriptures, ask God to speak to you about being merciful. Watch for specific ways God can guide you to forgive someone or show mercy.

> *"Be merciful, just as your Father is merciful" (Luke 6:36).*

> *"If you forgive men for their transgressions, your heavenly Father will also forgive you. But if you do not forgive men, then your Father will not forgive your transgressions" (Matt. 6:14-15).*

FRUITFUL
For additional help on becoming fruitful see page 74.

Fruitful:
productive, fertile, prolific, constructive, high yield

Opposites of *Fruitful:*
fruitless, unproductive, non-productive, ineffective, worthless, waste of time, empty, hollow, profitless

Perversions of *Fruitful:*
fruit-obsessed, success-driven, workaholic, obsessed with numbers, vain, showy

Possible Points of Temptation
When you try to explain away your fruitfulness by pointing to your circumstances, you indicate a lack of trust in God. Nothing is impossible with God. Jesus said, *"I will build My church; and the gates of Hades shall not overpower it" (Matt. 16:18).* Nothing Satan tries to do can stop what God intends to do through you!

Another danger is going for success in the world's eyes. Let's say that your youth group is trying to grow. So, you decide you'll do a free pizza-feed lock-in every weekend. Sounds great, and chances are your group will grow. But if you never share the gospel, and if you never work on discipleship with the folks that are showing up for pizza, then all you'll have are a bunch of people showing up for pizza (and no money left in your youth ministry budget). The Great Commission says to make disciples, and teach them to obey everything that Christ commands. Is it possible that God will grant you the success you desire without the blessing of His presence? Of course! Like I said, your youth group will grow if you totally focus on fun activities. So it is possible. But think about this story: In Exodus, God told Moses to go in and take the promised land. God said He would send an angel to drive out the inhabitants; but He would not be with them Himself, or He might destroy the people for their rebellion. Moses could have had success, but it would have been at the cost of God's presence. So Moses, a wise spiritual leader, prayed:

> *"If Thy presence does not go with us, do not lead us up from here. For how then can it be known that I have found favor in Thy sight, I and Thy people? Is it not by Thy going with us, so that we, I and Thy people, may be distinguished from all the other people who are upon the face of the earth?" (Ex. 33:15-16).*

Becoming Fruitful
You can become fruitful by cultivating processes and methods which produce godly results.

- Study the Scriptures with a ready heart to know God's ways. Watch for contrasts between God's ways and the world's ways.
- When God gives you an assignment, continue praying until He guides you in the way or method.
- Ask other believers, such as your Mind of Christ small group or your youth minister, to help you evaluate the fruit of your life.

Scriptures for Meditation

Read the following Scriptures asking God to speak to you about your fruitfulness. What is the quality and quantity of fruit in your life? Watch for specific things in your life that God may want to prune away so that you will become more fruitful.

"Abide in Me, and I in you. As the branch cannot bear fruit of itself, unless it abides in the vine, so neither can you, unless you abide in Me. I am the vine, you are the branches; he who abides in Me, and I in him, he bears much fruit; for apart from Me you can do nothing" (John 15:4-5).

"You did not choose Me, but I chose you, and appointed you, that you should go and bear fruit, and that your fruit should remain, that whatever you ask of the Father in My name, He may give to you" (John 15:16).

Steadfast:
firm, unshakable, sure, never-failing, enduring, long-lasting, resolute, constant, devoted, steady, immovable, resolved, uncompromising

Opposites of *Steadfast:*
wavering, waffling, unsure, weak, unstable, wobbly, fickle, flimsy, shaky, faltering, halting, hesitant, indecisive, reluctant, wayward

Perversions of *Steadfast:*
inflexible, rigid, narrow-minded, obstinate, stubborn, unbendable, bullheaded, hardheaded, authoritarian, tyrannical, severe

STEADFAST

For additional help on becoming steadfast, see page 75.

Possible Points of Temptation

Paul gave Timothy this advice: *Guard what has been entrusted to you, avoiding worldly and empty chatter and the opposing arguments of what is falsely called "knowledge"—which some have professed and thus gone astray from the faith (1 Tim. 6:20-21).* In other words, avoid getting caught up in debates about truth which could lead you astray rather than keep you on track.

Becoming Steadfast

You can become steadfast by believing that God has a strong preference about your behavior for every circumstance He allows in your life.

- Give God the right to dictate how you will live your life.
- Develop an intimate relationship with God in prayer.
- When you are faced with a situation that would cause you to waver, turn to Christ—your sure foundation.

Scriptures for Meditation

Read these Scriptures and ask God about your steadfastness or wavering. Watch for ways He guides you to avoid wavering or to develop steadfastness.

Therefore, my beloved brethren, be steadfast, immovable, always abounding in the work of the Lord, knowing that your toil is not in vain in the Lord (1 Cor. 15:58).

Be of sober spirit, be on the alert. Your adversary, the devil, prowls about like a roaring lion, seeking someone to devour. But resist him, firm in your faith, knowing that the same experiences of suffering are being accomplished by your brethren who are in the world. And after you have suffered for a little while, the God of all grace, who called you to His eternal glory in Christ, will Himself perfect, confirm, strengthen and establish you (1 Pet. 5:8-10).

HONEST

For additional help on becoming honest, see pages 75-77.

Possible Points of Temptation
Learn to say no at the slightest hint of dishonesty or falsehood. Temptation lures you further and further from the truth, until you find great difficulty in being honest. Don't let yourself stray even the slightest bit from the truth.

Becoming Honest
You can become honest by representing God appropriately to every person God allows in your life.
- Keep your life clean, pure, and holy so others will see Christ is in you.
- Allow God's love to flow through you in relationships with others.
- Let every word be truthful so that people will not question your honesty/integrity.
- Let love guide your speech if you are in a situation where you need to correct or confront somebody.

Scriptures for Meditation
As you read the following Scriptures, ask God to speak to you about your honesty and sincerity. Watch for specific ways God may guide you to avoid hypocrisy or to develop honesty.

> *This I pray, that your love may abound still more and more in real knowledge and all discernment, so that you may approve the things that are excellent, in order to be sincere and blameless until the day of Christ (Phil. 1:9-10).*

> *Keep your behavior excellent among the Gentiles, so that in the thing in which they slander you as evildoers, they may on account of your good deeds, as they observe them, glorify God in the day of visitation (1 Pet. 2:12).*

Honest:
sincere, true, genuine, ethical, sound, trustworthy, upright, straightforward, factual, candid, real

Opposites of *Honest:*
lying, dishonest, hypocritical, fake, phony, fraudulent, crooked, deceitful, scheming, shady, corrupt

Perversions of *Honest:*
brutal, cruel, callous, pitiless, ruthless, spiteful, unrelenting, vicious, unkind, indifferent

LOVE
For additional help on showing love, see pages 80-81.

Possible Points of Temptation
Our greatest temptation is to base love on feelings or circumstances. The challenge is to base your love on a decision, or an act of the will. Love is not just an emotion. It involves action. Love must be demonstrated.

Showing Love
You can show love by perfect giving of yourself to others. Try to apply the following list of 15 behaviors of love to your relationships with others. Watch for opportunities God may send your way in order for you to learn love more perfectly. Review this list (*The Mind of Christ Card 13*) periodically and ask God to help you evaluate your love life based on the perfect standard of Christ. Check the behaviors that you have the opportunity to act upon. You may want to make space in your journal to describe the experiences in which you demonstrate such behavior.

Love:
- ❑ Is patient (holy relationships).
- ❑ Is kind (holy purposes).
- ❑ Is not jealous (holy heart).
- ❑ Does not brag (holy speech).

Love:
affection, compassion, benevolence, adoration, fondness, commitment

Opposites of *Love:*
hate, animosity, dislike, enmity, hostility, ill-will, malice, vindictiveness

Perversions of *Love:*
possessive, overly protective, permissive, smothering love, manipulative

❑ Is not arrogant (holy service).
❑ Does not act unbecomingly (holy behavior).
❑ Does not seek its own (holy desires).
❑ Is not provoked (holy self-control).
❑ Does not take into account a wrong (holy forgiveness).
❑ Does not rejoice in unrighteousness (holy conscience).
❑ Rejoices in the truth (holy mind).
❑ Bears all things (holy stability).
❑ Believes all things (holy values).
❑ Hopes all things (holy expectations).
❑ Endures all things (holy sacrifice).

Scriptures for Meditation

As you read the following Scriptures, ask God to speak to you about love. Watch for specific ways God may guide you to show your love to others.

> *"'Love the Lord your God with all your heart, and with all your soul, and with all your mind, and with all your strength.' The second is this: 'You shall love your neighbor as yourself.' There is no other commandment greater than these" (Mark 12:30-31).*

> *"A new command I give you, that you love one another, even as I have loved you, that you also love one another. By this all men will know that you are My disciples, if you have love for one another" (John 13:34-35).*

JOY

For additional help on showing joy, see pages 81-82.

Joy:
delight, gladness, calm, cheerfulness, bliss, enjoyment, contentment, radiance

Opposites of *Joy:*
pain, hurt, agony, anguish, distress, misery, torment, woe

Perversions of *Joy:*
frenzy, maniacal, crazed excitement, hysteria

Showing Joy

You can show joy by choosing to focus on God's glory in every circumstance.

- Memorize Scriptures that remind you of God's truth.
- Ask God to give you understanding from His perspective about your circumstance. Continue to trust that God is in control, and that He deeply loves you, even if He doesn't give you an answer.
- Think about your circumstances in an eternal perspective, not just for the present time.
- Remember that God's grace is enough for you, even in times of weakness.
- Seek to bring glory to God in the way you respond to every circumstance.

Scriptures for Meditation

As you read the following Scriptures, ask God to speak to you about joy. Watch for specific ways God may guide you to show your joy in difficult circumstances. Select Scriptures for memorization that may be helpful to you in tough times.

> *Restore to me the joy of Thy salvation, and sustain me with a willing spirit. Then I will teach transgressors Thy ways, and sinners will be converted to Thee (Ps. 51:12-13).*

> *Now may the God of hope fill you with all joy and peace in believing, that you may abound in hope by the power of the Holy Spirit (Rom. 15:13).*

PEACE

For additional help on showing peace, see pages 82-84.

Peace:
rest, quietness, tranquillity, harmony, serenity

Opposites of *Peace:*
war, rage, havoc, discord, conflict, strife, rivalry, clash, feud, brawl, rift, worry

Perversions of *Peace:*
neutrality, lukewarmness, indifference, detached, uncommitted, uninvolved

Possible Points of Temptation

Peace comes from within, not from outward circumstances. Unconfessed sin in your life is a destroyer of peace. When lusts and desires wage war against each other within you, peace is sacrificed.

Showing Peace

You show peace by resting on the achievements and the character of Christ. When peace is not present, ask God to help you identify the sin or conflicting desires that are robbing you of the peace He wants to manifest in you.

Scriptures for Meditation

As you read the following Scriptures, ask God to speak to you about peace. Watch for specific ways God may allow you to manifest His perfect peace in you—a peace that is beyond understanding.

> *"The steadfast of mind Thou wilt keep in perfect peace, Because he trusts in Thee. Trust in the Lord forever, For in God the Lord, we have an everlasting Rock" (Isa. 26:3-4).*
>
> *Therefore having been justified by faith, we have peace with God through our Lord Jesus Christ (Rom. 5:1).*

PATIENCE

For additional help on showing patience, see pages 85-86.

Patient:
endurance, constancy, hanging in there, steadfastness, perseverance

Opposites of *Patient:*
impatient, edgy, chafing, crabby, touchy, hotheaded, rash, impulsive

Perversions of *Patient:*
lenient, indulgent, permissive

Possible Points of Temptation

In order to allow God to develop patience in your life, you must not place limits on your willingness to endure. When you limit your willingness, the enemy knows and will test those limits.

Showing Patience

You can show patience by cooperating with God in the process of bringing others toward becoming more Christlike.

Scriptures for Meditation

As you read the following Scriptures, ask God to speak to you about patience. Watch for specific ways God may guide you to show patience in your relationships with others. Look for Scriptures that tell you how God will be working to develop your patience. Submit to those circumstances instead of fighting them. Thank God for them.

> *We urge you, brethren, admonish the unruly, encourage the fainthearted, help the weak, be patient with all men (1 Thess. 5:14).*
>
> *Consider it all joy, my brethren, when you encounter various trials, knowing that the testing of your faith produces endurance. And let endurance have its perfect result, that you may be perfect and complete, lacking in nothing (Jas. 1:2-4).*

Kindness:
goodness of heart, integrity, goodness in deeds or actions

Opposites of *Kindness:*
hard, severity, harsh, rough, abusive, bitter, cruel, violent, fierce, blunt, brash, rude, short, unkind

Perversions of *Kindness:*
mushy, sappy, negligence, inattentive, careless, unchecked, coddling, indulgent

KINDNESS

For additional help on showing kindness, see pages 86-87.

Possible Points of Temptation

What is inside your mind and heart will show in your actions. If you have a hard heart, or are prejudiced toward other people, you will not act with kindness. If your actions are hard and reflect the opposites or perversions of kindness, something is wrong on the inside. Ask God to examine your heart and mind and reveal the problem area.

Showing Kindness

You can show kindness by seeing others the way God sees them.

Scriptures for Meditation

As you read the following Scriptures, ask God to speak to you about kindness. Watch for specific ways God may guide you to show kindness to others.

> *For His lovingkindness is great toward us, And the truth of the Lord is everlasting. Praise the Lord! (Ps. 117:2)*

> *Now for this very reason also, applying all diligence, in your faith supply moral excellence, and in your moral excellence, knowledge; and in your knowledge, self-control, and in your self-control, perseverance, and in your perseverance, godliness; and in your godliness, brotherly kindness, and in your brotherly kindness, love (2 Pet. 1:5-7).*

Goodness:
uprightness of heart and life, moral, wholesome, productive, functioning, working order

Opposites of *Goodness:*
badness, unwholesome, evil, corruption, depravity, immorality, spoiled, wickedness, non-functioning, non-productive

Perversions of *Goodness:*
goody-two-shoes, self-righteous

GOODNESS

For additional help on showing goodness, see pages 88-89.

Possible Points of Temptation

The greatest temptation is to think that goodness comes from ourselves and not from God. Because of sin, there is none who does good, no, not one (see *Rom. 3:12).* Claiming a good life in your own self-righteousness is foolishness (see *Prov. 20:6).* Badness, unwholesomeness, or fruitlessness are indications of a more serious problem. Good trees produce good fruit, and vice-versa. Your spiritual nature can be determined by the fruit you bear.

Showing Goodness

You can show goodness by working with God in His way.

Scriptures for Meditation

As you read the following Scriptures, ask God to speak to you about goodness. Watch for specific ways God may guide you to show goodness in your work with Him. Notice God's goodness as you read these Scriptures.

> *Surely goodness and lovingkindness will follow me all the days of my life, And I will dwell in the house of the Lord forever (Ps. 23:6).*

> *Concerning you, my brethren, I myself also am convinced that you yourselves are full of goodness, filled with all knowledge, and able also to admonish one another (Rom. 15:14).*

FAITH/FAITHFULNESS

For additional help on showing faith or faithfulness, see pages 89-90.

Possible Points of Temptation

When you are faithful for a long time, and then are confronted with persecution, frustration, or weariness, you might be tempted to let up or give in, rather than persevere. The perversion of faithfulness is also common. Sometimes, people think that the amount or difficulty of their "work for God" somehow earns His love or pleasure. But God's love is not for sale; it is unconditional. Wrong motivations can move a person from being faithful to being legalistic. Some Christians take every job that comes along, trying to do enough. The result is a religious workaholic—very busy, but not very fruitful. God would rather you be faithful just to the assignments He gives, instead of being faithful to a bunch of stuff that He hasn't given you. Avoid getting distracted by busywork that people come up with rather than the assignments God gives you. Trust God to help you know the difference.

Showing Faith/Faithfulness

You can show faithfulness by obeying God's commands and completing work He assigns to you.

- Begin by obeying what you already know God has commanded you to do.
- Be a faithful steward of the time and resources God gives you.
- When God gives you an assignment, keep doing it until the job is complete, or until God moves you to the next assignment.

Scriptures for Meditation

As you read the following Scriptures, ask God to speak to you about faithfulness. Watch for specific ways God may guide you to show or express faithfulness.

> *A faithful man will abound with blessings, but he who makes haste to be rich will not go unpunished (Prov. 28:20).*

> *"His master said to him, 'Well done, good and faithful slave; you were faithful with a few things, I will put you in charge of many things, enter into the joy of your master'" (Matt. 25:21).*

Faithfulness:
trustworthiness, integrity, reliability, loyalty, dependability, consistency

Opposites of ***Faithfulness:***
faithlessness, fickleness, untrustworthiness, inconsistency, unreliability, uncertainty

Perversions of ***Faithfulness:***
legalism, workaholism, over-committed, fanatical, overly zealous, extremism

GENTLENESS (MEEKNESS)

For additional help on showing gentleness, see pages 91-92.

Possible Points of Temptation

The greatest temptation against this virtue is to let pride cause you to assert yourself because of your own self-interest.

Showing Gentleness

You can show gentleness by not getting caught up in the trappings of worldly power.

Scriptures for Meditation

As you read the following Scriptures, ask God to speak to you about gentleness. Watch for specific ways God may guide you to show gentleness.

Gentleness:
meekness, humility, accepting God's dealings with us as good without resisting Him, a fruit of power, lowly before God and humble before people

Opposite of ***Gentleness:***
arrogance, haughtiness, pride, cockiness, egotism, vanity, conceit

Perversions of ***Gentleness:***
weakness, wimpy, cowardly, spinelessness, timidity

"Take My yoke upon you, and learn from Me, for I am gentle and humble in heart; and you shall find rest for your souls" (Matt. 11:29).

Brethren, even if a man is caught in any trespass, you who are spiritual, restore such a one in a spirit of gentleness; each one looking to yourself, lest you too be tempted (Gal. 6:1).

Self-Control:
strength, discipline, restraint, willpower under the direction and operation of the Holy Spirit, mastery over sinful desires

Opposites of *Self-Control:*
undisciplined, self-indulgent, slothful, lazy, compulsive, sluggish

Perversions of *Self-Control:*
Stoic, fleshly effort, self-effort, obsessive

SELF-CONTROL

For additional help on showing self-control, see pages 92-93.

Possible Points of Temptation

Watch out for areas in which you may lose self-control. Here are some areas in which addiction is common: eating, gossip, alcohol, drugs, gambling, pornography, television, exercise. Basically any activity that you can overdo can be a point of temptation for you.

Showing Self-Control

You can show self-control by accepting and applying the Holy Spirit's guidance as you master your desires and sensual appetites.

Scriptures for Meditation

As you read the following Scriptures, ask God to speak to you about self-control. Watch for specific ways God may guide you to develop or show self-control. As God leads, confess, repent, and turn to Him for help.

Everyone who competes in the games exercises self-control in all things. They then do it to receive a perishable wreath, but we an imperishable. Therefore I run in such a way, as not without aim; I box in such a way, as not beating the air; but I buffet my body and make it my slave, lest possibly, after I have preached to others, I myself should be disqualified (1 Cor. 9:25-27).

Therefore do not let sin reign in your mortal body that you should obey its lusts (Rom. 6:12).

Lifelong Helps for Developing the Mind of Christ

Servanthood Instrument

✳ The following instrument is provided for you to measure your growth as a servant of Christ. Read each of the statements. Evaluate the attitudes of your servant mind. Use the following scale and place the appropriate number in each blank. The higher your total score, the closer you believe you are to attaining servanthood.

1—No, that's not me.
2—That's me sometimes.
3—That's me often.
4—Yes, that's definitely me.

Humble—Proper attitude toward the Master's work in others.
________ I see my work as a part of God's plan.

Obedient—Understanding the authority of the Master over my time and life.
________ I am obeying all known commands of Scripture.

Willing—Identity with the Master's attitudes.
________ My great desire is to be about the Father's business.

Loyal—Unswerving devotion to the Master.
________ I get my joy from the company of the Master, rather than what will enrich me.

Faithful—Confidence that anticipates the Master continuing His plan.
________ God has enriched His kingdom through my work.

Watchful—Attentiveness to the Master's voice.
________ I have learned recently something new about God.

Courageous—Conviction about the Master's priorities.
________ My conviction is so strong that I cannot deny Christ any request He makes of me.

Not Quarrelsome—Peace that awakes the Master's work in others.
________ I have no quarrel with any brother or sister in God's family.

Gentle—Respect that enhances the work of others for the Master.
________ My desire is to enhance the work of my brothers and sisters, not that they make me look good.

Able to Teach—Understanding the Master's work.
________ My concern is the authority of Christ. I desire His Word and will, not my opinion.

Patient—Forbearance that values the Master's purposes for others.
________ I am willing to wait on the growth process in others.

Meek—Disciplined sensitivity to the Master.
________ I am sensitive to the Master.

Good—Applied trust in the Master's excellence.
________ All the fruit you can see in my life was produced by the Holy Spirit.

Wise—Dependence on the Master's method.
________ I use God's method in doing my work rather than my method.

________ **Total Score (range: 14-56)**

Lifelong Helps for Developing the Mind of Christ

The Beatitudes
Matthew 5:3-12

A—First Four Beatitudes

1. Blessed are the poor in spirit: for theirs is the kingdom of heaven.
2. Blessed are those who mourn: for they shall be comforted.
3. Blessed are the gentle, for they shall inherit the earth.
4. Blessed are those who hunger and thirst for righteousness, for they shall be satisfied.

A-1: Poor in Spirit	Principle of Need
A-2: Mourn	Principle of Brokenness
A-3: Gentle	Principle of Submission
A-4: Hungry	Principle of Yearning

- *Basis for Happiness*—Your need
- *Keys* to God's Heart
- *Focus*—Turn your mind toward God. You learn about God. You learn that God is God.
- *Command*—Love God—"*You shall love the Lord your God with all your heart, and with all your soul, and with all your mind, and with all your strength" (Mark 12:30).*
- *Object*—God gives according to your need to mold and shape you into the image of Christ. He equips you with the character of Christ.
- *Door* to Greatness
- *Worship*—Lower Levels of Worship–Praise to God comes out of your need and His sufficiency to meet your need.

B—Second Four Beatitudes

5. Blessed are the merciful, for they shall receive mercy.
6. Blessed are the pure in heart, for they shall see God.
7. Blessed are the peacemakers, for they shall be called sons of God.
8. Blessed are those who have been persecuted for the sake of righteousness, for theirs is the kingdom of heaven. Blessed are you when men cast insults at you, and persecute you, and say all kinds of evil against you falsely, on account of Me. Rejoice, and be glad, for your reward in heaven is great, for so they persecuted the prophets who were before you.

B-1: Merciful	Principle of Reciprocity
B-2: Pure in Heart	Principle of Perfect Heart
B-3: Peacemakers	Principle of Reconciliation
B-4: Persecuted	Principle of Identification

- *Basis for Happiness*—Your giving
- *Keys* to Christ's Character
- *Focus*—Turn your mind toward others. You serve in Christ's spirit. You reflect Christ to a watching world.
- *Command*—Love Others–"*You shall love your neighbor as yourself" (Mark 12:31).*
- *Object*—God works through you to reveal Himself to a watching world. You become identified with Christ as you reveal His character to others.
- *Practice* of Greatness
- *Worship*—Higher Levels of Worship–Praise to God comes from the exercise of your character as you reveal the character of Christ to others.

God's Training for Royalty and Nobility

Circumstances in life become opportunities for God to work in and through you. God uses circumstances in life to develop these qualities (Beatitudes) in your life. Every circumstance in life can become an adventure as you turn to God to see what He may want to do to develop your character or to work through you to reveal His character to others. God is working to train you for a noble future. You are a child of the King. God will take you through this cycle over and over again in order to train you for your royal and noble future reign with Christ.

✱ **Pause and pray. Ask God to take you through circumstances in order to train you fully for your royal and noble future reign with Christ.**

Using This Lifelong Helps

The following pages describe each of the eight Beatitudes in detail. Following the same format for each Beatitude, you can study each one to understand what it would look like in your life.

- You will see what the Beatitude is and what it is not.
- You will look at an example from the life of Jesus as He manifested this quality in His life.
- You will look at one or more examples from the Bible of other people who demonstrated this quality.
- God is going to be taking you through circumstances to mold this quality into your life. "What God Is Doing in Me" will help you see the goal God has in mind for you.
- "Circumstances Through Which God May Work" will give you an idea of the kinds of circumstances God may use to develop this trait in your life. If these circumstances come to you, consider them as God's invitation for spiritual growth. They may not all be pleasant. However, happy is the one who submits to God's process. Even when "bad" things happen, *"God causes all things to work together for good to those who love God, to those who are called according to His purpose" (Rom. 8:28).*
- "How I Express This Attitude" will give you some ideas of practical ways this attitude might show in your life. You may intentionally choose some of these as an "action plan" to work on developing the quality in your daily living.
- "Prayers" will give you an idea of ways you can express this attitude before God (First Four Beatitudes). Or how you may seek God's assistance as you express these attitudes toward others (Second Four Beatitudes).
- "Response in Worship" describes the way this attitude would be reflected in your worship. This section includes such things as a definition, biblical commands, promised blessings, biblical prayers, and biblical applications.

The Mind of Christ Cards

The Mind of Christ Cards summarize the following helps. Carry these cards with you for meditation, review, or application of the attitudes in your life. Cards related to the Beatitudes are:

6. Scripture Memory—*Matthew 5:3-10*
20. Poor in Spirit
21. Mourn
22. Meek
23. Hungry
24. Merciful
25. Pure in Heart
26. Peacemakers
27. Persecuted

For more information on the Beatitudes see unit 7—The Beatitudes (pp. 113-123).

A-1

Poor in Spirit

"Blessed are the poor in spirit: for theirs is the kingdom of heaven" (Matt. 5:3).

Examples

JESUS: *Jesus said, "Let the children alone, and do not hinder them from coming to Me; for the kingdom of heaven belongs to such as these" (Matt. 19:14).*

THE PHARISEE AND THE PUBLICAN: *"Two men went up into the temple to pray, one a Pharisee, and the other a tax-gatherer. The Pharisee stood and was praying thus to himself, 'God, I thank Thee, that I am not like other people: swindlers, unjust, adulterers, or even like this tax-gatherer. I fast twice a week; I pay tithes of all that I get.' But the tax-gatherer, standing some distance away, was even unwilling to lift up his eyes to heaven, but was beating his breast, saying, 'God, be merciful to me, the sinner!' I tell you, this man went down to his house justified rather than the other; for everyone who exalts himself shall be humbled, but he who humbles himself shall be exalted" (Luke 18:10-14).*

What God Is Doing in Me

God prepares me to be merciful to others (see B-1, pp. 208-209).

Prayers

- I am needy, Lord.
- I am nothing and can do nothing without You.
- I need You to ...
- I need You because...
- What do I need You to do in me?
- What do You have that I need?

Response in Worship: Fear God

DEFINITION: Respect God, reverence God, display piety toward God; not a fear of God's power or His righteous retribution, instead of obedience to God because He is God. *"The fear of the Lord is to hate evil; pride and arrogance and the evil way, and the perverted mouth, I hate" (Prov. 8:13).*

COMMAND: *"You shall follow the Lord your God and fear Him; and you shall keep His commandments, listen to His voice, serve Him, and cling to him" (Deut. 13:4).*

BLESSINGS: *Let all the earth fear the Lord; let all the inhabitants of the world stand in awe of Him... Behold, the eye of the Lord is on those who fear Him, on those who hope for His lovingkindness (Ps. 33:8,18).*

The fear of the Lord is the beginning of wisdom; a good understanding have all those who do His commandments (Ps. 111:10).

The fear of the Lord leads to life, so that one may sleep satisfied, untouched by evil (Prov. 19:23).

The fear of the Lord is a fountain of life (Prov. 14:27).

PRAYER: *Teach me Thy way, O Lord; I will walk in Thy truth; unite my heart to fear Thy name (Ps. 86:11).*

APPLIED: *Be subject to one another in the fear of Christ (Eph. 5:21).*

Therefore, since we receive a kingdom which cannot be shaken, let us show gratitude, by which we may offer to God an acceptable service with reverence and awe (Heb. 12:28).

A-2

Mourn

"Blessed are they that mourn: for they shall be comforted" (Matt. 5:4).

Examples

JESUS: *He was despised and forsaken of men, a man of sorrows, and acquainted with grief; and like one from whom men hide their face, He was despised, and we did not esteem Him (Isa. 53:3).*

MARY, MARTHA, AND JESUS: *When Mary came where Jesus was, she saw Him, and fell at His feet, saying to Him, "Lord, if You had been here, my brother would not have died." When Jesus therefore saw her weeping, and the Jews who came with her, also weeping, He was deeply moved in spirit, and was troubled, and said "Where have you laid him?" They said to Him, "Lord, come and see." Jesus wept (John 11:32-35).*

What God Is Doing in Me

God uses difficult circumstances to purify me. Like a Refiner's Fire, God works in me to develop a pure heart (see B-2, pp. 209-210).

Prayers

- I need Your comfort, Lord. Would You just hold me for a little while?
- How can I bring glory to You through this experience?
- What impurities in me do You want to burn out through this experience?
- What do You want to do in me to cause this experience to work together for good?
- What needs to be broken in me or broken away from me?

Response in Worship: Ascribe Credit to God

DEFINITION: To give credit to God; to bestow, report, mention, or utter.

COMMEND: *Ascribe to the Lord, O sons of the mighty, ascribe to the Lord glory and strength. Ascribe to the Lord the glory due to His name; worship the Lord in holy array (Ps. 29:1-2).*

Ascribe strength to God; His majesty is over Israel, and His strength is in the skies (Ps. 68:34).

PRAYER: *The Lord is my rock and my fortress and my deliverer, my God, my rock, in whom I take refuge; my shield and the horn of my salvation, my stronghold (Ps. 18:2).*

APPLIED: *"I proclaim the name of the Lord; ascribe greatness to our God! The Rock! His work is perfect, for all His ways are just; a God of faithfulness and without injustice, righteous and upright is He" (Deut. 32:3-4).*

A-3

"Blessed are the meek: for they shall inherit the earth" (MATT. 5:5).

Examples

JESUS: *"Take My yoke upon you, and learn from Me; for I am gentle and humble in heart; and you shall find rest for your souls" (Matt. 11:29).*

MARY: *Mary said: "My soul exalts the Lord, and my spirit has rejoiced in God my Savior. For He has had regard for the humble state of His bondslave; for behold, from this time on all generations will count me blessed. For the Mighty One has done great things for me; and holy is His name. And His mercy is upon generation after generation toward those who fear Him. He has done mighty deeds with His arm; He has scattered those who were proud in the thoughts of their heart. He has brought down rulers from their thrones, and has exalted those who were humble. He has filled the hungry with good things; and sent away the rich empty handed. He has given help to Israel His servant, in remembrance of His mercy, as He spoke to our fathers, to Abraham and his offspring forever" (Luke 1:46-55).*

JOHN THE BAPTIST: *"He must increase, but I must decrease" (John 3:30).*

DAVID: *"From the end of the earth I call to Thee, when my heart is faint; lead me to the rock that is higher than I" (Ps. 61:2).*

What God Is Doing in Me

Through opportunities of submission to God, I learn the value of submission to others. God develops in me the character of a peacemaker (see B-3, p. 210).

Prayers

- Not my will, but Thine be done.
- In what ways can I decrease so You may increase?
- What areas in my life need greater submission to You?
- How can I magnify and exalt You more than I do?
- Show me times when I should stand up for You.

Response in Worship: Magnify, Exalt

DEFINITION: *Magnify:* to make great, to enlarge, to cause to grow. We magnify God when we focus attention on His greatness. *Exalt:* To raise, lift, lift up, set on high.

COMMAND: *I will bless the Lord at all times; His praise shall continually be in my mouth. My soul shall make its boast in the Lord; the humble shall hear it, and rejoice. O magnify the Lord with me, and let us exalt His name together (Ps. 34:1-3).*

Exalt the Lord our God, and worship at His footstool; Holy is He. Exalt the Lord our God, and worship at His holy hill; for holy is the Lord our God (Ps. 99:5,9).

PRAYERS: *"Thine, O Lord, is the greatness and the power and the glory and the victory and the majesty, indeed everything that is in the heavens and the earth; Thine is the dominion, O Lord, and Thou dost rule over all, and in Thy hand is power and might; and it lies in Thy hand to make great, and to strengthen everyone. Now therefore, our God, we thank Thee, and praise Thy glorious name" (1 Chron. 29:11-13).*

Let all who seek Thee rejoice and be glad in Thee; and let those who love Thy salvation say continually, "Let God be magnified" (Ps. 70:4).

O Lord, Thou art my God; I will exalt Thee, I will give thanks to Thy name; for Thou hast worked wonders, Plans formed long ago, with perfect faithfulness (Isa. 25:1).
Be Thou exalted, O Lord, in Thy strength; we will sing and praise Thy power (Ps. 21:13).
APPLIED: *I will praise the name of God with song, and shall magnify Him with thanksgiving (Ps. 69:30).*

A-4

Hungry

"Blessed are those who hunger and thirst for righteousness, for they shall be satisfied" (MATT. 5:6).

Examples
JESUS: *Jesus said to them, "My food is to do the will of Him who sent Me, and to accomplish His work" (John 4:34).*
THE BEREANS: *The brethren immediately sent Paul and Silas away by night to Berea; and when they arrived they went into the synagogue of the Jews. Now these were more noble-minded than those in Thessalonica, for they received the word with great eagerness, examining the Scriptures daily, to see whether these things were so. Many of them therefore believed, along with a number of prominent Greek women and men (Acts 17:10-12).*

What God Is Doing in Me
God is causing me to seek after Him so He can mold and shape me into the image of His Son Jesus.

Prayers
• *My soul pants for Thee, O God. My soul thirsts... for the living God; when shall I come and appear before God? (Ps. 42:1-2).*
• *O God, Thou art my God; I shall seek Thee earnestly; my soul thirsts for Thee, my flesh yearns for Thee, in a dry and weary land where there is no water (Ps. 63:1).*
• *I meditate on all Thy doings; I muse on the work of Thy hands. I stretch out my hands to Thee; my soul longs for Thee, as a parched land. Answer me quickly, O Lord, my spirit fails; do not hide Thy face from me, lest I become like those who go down to the pit. Let me hear Thy lovingkindness in the morning; for I trust in Thee; teach me the way in which I should walk; for to Thee I lift up my soul (Ps. 143:5-8).*

Response in Worship: Thanksgiving
DEFINITION: To give thanks to God for what He has done, expressing gratitude for God's bounty.
COMMAND: *Give thanks to the Lord, for He is good; for His lovingkindness is everlasting (Ps. 118:1).*
Give thanks to the Lord of lords, for His lovingkindness is everlasting. To Him who alone does great wonders, for His lovingkindness is everlasting (Ps. 136:3-4).
PRAYERS: *Lord,... I am Thy servant... the son of Thy handmaid, Thou hast loosed my bonds. To Thee I shall offer a sacrifice of thanksgiving, and call upon the name of the Lord (Ps. 116:16-17).*
Thou hast turned for me my mourning into dancing; Thou hast loosed my sackcloth and girded me with gladness; that my soul may sing praise to Thee, and not be silent. O Lord my God, I will give thanks to Thee forever (Ps. 30:11-12).
APPLIED: *"I will sacrifice to Thee with the voice of thanksgiving. That which I have vowed I will pay. Salvation is from the Lord" (Jonah 2:9).*

B-1

Merciful

"Blessed are the merciful, for they shall receive mercy" (MATT. 5:7).

Examples
JESUS: *Seeing their faith* [Jesus] *said to the paralytic, "Take courage, My son, your sins are forgiven" (Matt. 9:2).*
GOD'S RESPONSE TO OTHERS: *"With the kind Thou dost show Thyself kind, with the blameless Thou dost show Thyself blameless; with the pure Thou dost show Thyself pure, and with the perverted Thou dost show Thyself astute" (2 Sam. 22:26-27).*
PHARAOH'S HARDENED HEART DURING THE PLAGUES IN EGYPT: *Pharaoh's heart was hardened, and he did not listen to them, as the Lord had said. Then Pharaoh turned and went into his house with no concern even for this (Ex. 7:22-23).*
When Pharaoh saw that there was relief, he hardened his heart and did not listen to them, as the Lord had said...Pharaoh hardened his heart this time also, and he did not let the people go (Ex. 8:15,32).

The Lord hardened Pharaoh's heart, and he did not listen to them, just as the Lord had spoken to Moses (Ex. 9:12).

What God Is Doing Through Me

God reveals His mercy, grace, and forgiveness through the way I treat others. God in turn treats me with mercy, grace, and forgiveness in the same way I have treated others.

Prayers

- To whom do I need to show mercy, forgiveness, or grace?
- Lord, increase my faith to be forgiving.
- You have forgiven me so much. I'll forgive likewise.

Response in Worship: Reverence

DEFINITION: A sense of honor, modesty, reverence, regard for others, respect.

COMMAND: *"You shall keep My sabbaths and revere My sanctuary; I am the Lord" (Lev. 19:30).*

Tremble, and do not sin; meditate in your heart upon your bed, and be still (Ps. 4:4).

A God greatly feared in the council of the holy ones, and awesome above all those who are around Him (Ps. 89:7).

Guard your steps as you go to the house of God, and draw near to listen rather than to offer the sacrifice of fools; for they do not know they are doing evil (Eccl. 5:1).

It is the Lord of hosts whom you should regard as holy (Isa. 8:13).

"The Lord is in His holy temple. Let all the earth be silent before Him" (Hab. 2:20).

APPLIED: *He said, "Do not come near here; remove your sandals ... for the place...is holy ground" (Ex. 3:5).*

Since we receive a kingdom which cannot be shaken, let us show gratitude, by which we may offer to God an acceptable service with reverence and awe (Heb. 12:28).

B-2

Pure in Heart

"Blessed are the pure in heart, for they shall see God" (Matt. 5:8).

Examples

JESUS: *He was saying to them, "You are from below, I am from above; you are of this world, I am not of this world" (John 8:23).*

DAVID BECOMING KING: *He raised up David to be their king... He also testified and said, "I have found David... a man after My heart, who will do all My will" (Acts 13:22).*

DAVID'S PRAYER AFTER HIS SIN WITH BATHSHEBA: *Purify me ... wash me...Make me to hear joy and gladness... Hide Thy face from my sins, and blot out all my iniquities. Create in me a clean heart, O God, and renew a steadfast spirit within me. Do not cast me away from Thy presence, and do not take Thy Holy Spirit from me. Restore to me the joy of Thy salvation, and sustain me with a willing spirit. Then I will teach transgressors Thy ways, and sinners will be converted to Thee. Deliver me from bloodguiltiness,... then my tongue will joyfully sing of Thy righteousness...open my lips, that my mouth may declare Thy praise. For Thou dost not delight in sacrifice, otherwise I would give it; Thou art not pleased with burnt offering. The sacrifices of God are a broken spirit; a broken and a contrite heart, O God, Thou wilt not despise.... Thou wilt delight in righteous sacrifices, in burnt offering and whole burnt offering; then young bulls will be offered on Thine altar (Ps. 51:7-19).*

What God Is Doing Through Me

God reveals His holiness, righteousness, and purity through my behavior. He allows me to have a greater intimacy with Him. God reveals more of Himself to me.

Prayer

- Lord, cleanse my heart and purify my mind.
- I choose to do Your will, O Lord.
- I love You with all my heart, mind, soul, and strength.
- Lead me not into temptation and deliver me from evil.

Response in Worship: Glorify

DEFINITION: To make honorable, honor, to give glory.

COMMAND: *You who fear the Lord praise Him; all you descendants of Jacob, glorify Him, and stand in awe of Him, all you descendants of Israel (Ps. 22:23).*

"Let your light shine before men in such a way that they may see your good works, and glorify your Father" (Matt. 5:16).

You have been bought with a price: therefore glorify God in your body (1 Cor. 6:20).

BLESSINGS: *"Call upon Me in the day of trouble; I shall rescue you, and you will honor Me" (Ps. 50:15).*

PRAYER: *All nations whom Thou hast made shall come and worship before Thee, O Lord; and they shall glorify Thy*

name. For Thou art great and doest wondrous deeds; Thou alone art God (Ps. 86:9-10).
"Who will not fear, O Lord, and glorify Thy name? For Thou alone art holy; for all the nations will come and worship before Thee, for Thy righteous acts have been revealed"(Rev. 15:4).
APPLIED: *The God who gives perseverance and encouragement grant you to be of the same mind with one another... that with one accord you may with one voice glorify the God and Father of our Lord Jesus Christ.... accept one another, just as Christ also accepted us to the glory of God (Rom. 15:5-7).*
If anyone suffers as a Christian, let him not feel ashamed, but in that name let him glorify God (1 Pet. 4:16).

B-3

Peacemaker

"Blessed are the peacemakers, for they shall be called sons of God" (Matt. 5:9).

Examples

JESUS: *"Salt is good; but if the salt becomes unsalty, with what will you make it salty again? Have salt in yourselves, and be at peace with one another" (Mark 9:50).*
JAMES: *After there had been much debate, Peter stood up and said to them, "Brethren, you know that in the early days God made a choice among you, that by my mouth the Gentiles should hear the word of the gospel and believe. And God, who knows the heart, bore witness to them, giving them the Holy Spirit, just as He also did to us; and He made no distinction between us and them, cleansing their hearts by faith. Now therefore why do you put God to the test by placing upon the neck of the disciples a yoke which neither our fathers nor we have been able to bear? But we believe that we are saved through the grace of the Lord Jesus, in the same way as they also are."*

And all the multitude kept silent, and they were listening to Barnabas and Paul as they were relating what signs and wonders God had done through them among the Gentiles. And after they had stopped speaking, James answered, saying, "Brethren, listen to me. Simeon has related how God first concerned Himself about taking from among the Gentiles a people for His name. And with this the words of the Prophets agree, just as it is written, 'After these things I will return, and I will rebuild the tabernacle of David which has fallen, and I will rebuild its ruins, and I will restore it, in order that the rest of mankind may seek the Lord, and all the Gentiles who are called by My name,' says the Lord, who makes these things known from of old.

Therefore it is my judgment that we do not trouble those who are turning to God from among the Gentiles, but that we write to them that they abstain from things contaminated by idols and from fornication and from what is strangled and from blood. For Moses from ancient generations has in every city those who preach him, since he is read in the synagogues every Sabbath."

Then it seemed good to the apostles and the elders, with the whole church, to choose men from among them to send to Antioch with Paul and Barnabas—Judas called Barsabbas, and Silas, leading men among the brethren, and they sent this letter by them, "The apostles and the brethren who are elders, to the brethren in Antioch and Syria and Cilicia who are from the Gentiles, greetings"(Acts 15:7-23).

What God Is Doing Through Me

God reveals His wholeness to the world and restores wholeness among people. He shows the unity of the Godhead (Father, Son, and Spirit). Jesus is revealed as the Son of God: *"That they may all be one; as Thou, Father, art in Me, and I in Thee, that they also may be in Us: that the world may believe that Thou dist send Me" (John 17:21).*

Prayers

- Help me to know the peace that passes understanding.
- Lord, help me to live in peace with my fellow humans.
- Empower me to carry out the ministry of reconciliation You have assigned to me and the church.
- Bind us together, Lord.

Response in Worship: Extol

DEFINITION: To rise, to lift up, to exalt.
COMMAND: *Sing to God, sing praises to His name; lift up a song for Him who rides through the deserts, whose name is the Lord, and exult before Him (Ps. 68:4).*
PRAYER: *I will extol Thee, O Lord, for Thou hast lifted me up, and hast not let my enemies rejoice over me. O Lord my God, I cried to Thee for help, and Thou didst heal me (Ps. 30:1-2).*
APPLIED: *"Now I Nebuchadnezzar praise, exalt, and honor the King of heaven, for all His works are true and His ways just, and He is able to humble those who walk in pride" (Dan. 4:37).*

B-4

Persecuted

"Blessed are those who have been persecuted for the sake of righteousness, for theirs is the kingdom of heaven. Blessed are you when men cast insults at you, and persecute you, and say all kinds of evil against you falsely, on account of Me. Rejoice, and be glad for your reward in heaven is great, for so they persecuted the prophets who were before you" (Matt. 5:10-12).

Examples

JESUS: *Jesus said to him, "No one, after putting his hand to the plow and looking back, is fit for the kingdom of God" (Luke 9:62).*

FIRST CENTURY BELIEVERS: *Be hospitable to one another without complaint. As each one has received a special gift, employ it in serving one another as good stewards of the manifold grace of God. Whoever speaks, let him speak, as it were, the utterances of God; whoever serves, let him do so as by the strength which God supplies; so that in all things God may be glorified through Jesus Christ, to whom belongs the glory and dominion forever and ever. Amen. Beloved, do not be surprised at the fiery ordeal among you, which comes upon you for your testing, as though some strange thing were happening to you; but to the degree that you share the sufferings of Christ, keep on rejoicing; so that also at the revelation of His glory, you may rejoice with exultation. If you are reviled for the name of Christ, you are blessed, because the Spirit of glory and of God rests upon you. By no means let any of you suffer as a murderer, or thief, or evildoer, or a troublesome meddler; but if anyone suffers as a Christian, let him not feel ashamed, but in that name let him glorify God. For it is time for judgment to begin with the household of God; and if it begins with us first, what will be the outcome for those who do not obey the gospel of God? And if it is with difficulty that the righteous is saved, what will become of the godless man and the sinner? Therefore, let those also who suffer according to the will of God entrust their souls to a faithful Creator in doing what is right (1 Pet. 4:9-19).*

PAUL: *That I may know Him, and the power of His resurrection and the fellowship of His sufferings, being conformed to His death (Phil. 3:10).*

What God Is Doing Through Me

God allows me to be identified perfectly with Christ in His suffering as God's servant.

Prayers

- Thank You for allowing me to share in the sufferings of Christ.
- Defend me, O Lord. You are my Righteous Judge.
- If I live, I'll live for You. If I die, let me honor You.
- Into Your hands I entrust my life and reputation.

Response in Worship: Rejoice

DEFINITION: To take pleasure in, to be glad, to exult, to express joy, to delight.

COMMAND: *Rejoice in the Lord always; again I will say, rejoice (Phil. 4:4).*

Let all who take refuge in Thee be glad, let them ever sing for joy; and mayest Thou shelter them, that those who love Thy name may exult in Thee (Ps. 5:11).

Be glad in the Lord and rejoice, you righteous ones, and shout for joy, all you who are upright in heart (Ps. 32:11).

Let the righteous be glad; let them exult before God; yes, let them rejoice with gladness (Ps. 68:3).

BLESSINGS: *Those who sow in tears shall reap with joyful shouting (Ps. 126:5).*

PRAYER: *I have trusted in Thy lovingkindness; my heart shall rejoice in Thy salvation (Ps. 13:5).*

I will rejoice and be glad in Thy lovingkindness, because Thou hast seen my affliction; Thou hast known the troubles of my soul (Ps. 31:7).

My lips will shout for joy when I sing praises to Thee; and my soul, which Thou hast redeemed (Ps. 71:23).

APPLIED: *Now I rejoice in my sufferings for your sake, and in my flesh I do my share on behalf of His body (which is the church) in filling up that which is lacking in Christ's afflictions (Col. 1:24).*

Even if I am being poured out as a drink offering upon the sacrifice and service of your faith, I rejoice and share my joy with you all. And you too, I urge you, rejoice in the same way and share your joy with me (Phil. 2:17-18).

Lifelong Helps for Developing the Mind of Christ

Your Relationship with Your Heavenly Father and the Holy Spirit

✳ Read the following verses that describe ways you should be related to your Heavenly Father and the Holy Spirit. Circle key words that describe the ways. Ask God through the Holy Spirit to help you relate to Him completely. Review these Scriptures periodically.

Heavenly Father

May…Jesus… and God… who has loved us and given us eternal comfort and good hope by grace, comfort and strengthen your hearts in every good work and word (2 Thess. 2:16-17).

See how great a love the Father has bestowed upon us, that we should be called children of God (1 John 3:1).

You have not received a spirit of slavery leading to fear again, but you have received a spirit of adoption as sons by which we cry out, "Abba! Father!" The Spirit Himself bears witness with our spirit that we are children of God… heirs also, heirs of God and fellow heirs with Christ, if indeed we suffer with Him in order that we may also be glorified with Him (Rom. 8:15-17).

"I am in My Father, and you in Me, and I in you. He who has My commandments and keeps them, he it is who loves Me; and he who loves Me shall be loved by My Father, and I will love him, and will disclose Myself to him" (John 14:20-21).

"The Father Himself loves you, because you have loved Me, and have believed that I came forth from the Father" (John 16:27).

"True worshipers shall worship the Father in spirit and in truth… God is spirit, and those who worship Him must worship in spirit and truth" (John 4:23-24).

"In order that all may honor the Son, even as they honor the Father. He who does not honor the Son does not honor the Father who sent Him" (John 5:23).

"I am the true vine, and My Father is the vinedresser. Every branch in Me that does not bear fruit, He takes away; and every branch that bears fruit, He prunes it, that it may bear more fruit" (John 15:1-2).

"If two of you agree on earth about any thing that they may ask, it shall be done for them by My Father" (Matt. 18:19).

"Go into your inner room… shut your door, pray to your Father… [God] *who sees in secret will repay you" (Matt. 6:6).*

"That they may all be one; even as Thou, Father, art in Me, and I in Thee, that they also may be in Us; that the world may believe that Thou didst send Me" (John 17:21).

"Come out from their midst and be separate… do not touch what is unclean; and I will welcome you… you shall be sons and daughters to Me," says the Lord Almighty (2 Cor. 6:17-18).

"You are to be perfect, as your heavenly Father is perfect" (Matt. 5:48).

"If you forgive men… your heavenly Father will also forgive you. But if you do not forgive men, then your Father will not forgive your transgressions" (Matt. 6:14-15).

"Be merciful, just as your Father is merciful" (Luke 6:36).

"If you then, being evil, know how to give good gifts to your children, how much more shall your Father who is in heaven give what is good to those who ask Him" (Matt. 7:11).

Every good thing bestowed and every perfect gift is from above (Jas. 1:17).

Holy Spirit

"Repent, and let each of you be baptized in the name of

Jesus Christ for the forgiveness of your sins; and you shall receive the gift of the Holy Spirit" (Acts 2:38).

You are not in the flesh but in the Spirit, if indeed the Spirit of God dwells in you. But if anyone does not have the Spirit of Christ, he does not belong to Him (Rom. 8:9).

The Spirit Himself bears witness with our spirit that we are children of God (Rom. 8:16).

Do you not know that you are a temple of God, and that the Spirit of God dwells in you (1 Cor. 3:16).

"You shall receive power when the Holy Spirit has come upon you; and you shall be My witnesses… in Jerusalem… Judea and Samaria, and even to the remotest part of the earth" (Acts 1:8).

"The Helper, the Holy Spirit, whom the Father will send in My name, He will teach you all things, and bring to your remembrance all that I said to you" (John 14:26).

"The Spirit… will guide you into all the truth; for He will not speak on His own initiative, but whatever He hears, He will speak; and He will disclose to you what is to come" (John 16:13).

"Any sin and blasphemy shall be forgiven men, but blasphemy against the Spirit shall not be forgiven" (Matt. 12:31).

Do not grieve the Holy Spirit of God, by whom you were sealed for the day of redemption (Eph. 4:30).

Do not quench the Spirit (1 Thess. 5:19).

Walk by the Spirit, and you will not carry out the desire of the flesh (Gal. 5:16).

Do not get drunk with wine… but be filled with the Spirit (Eph. 5:18).

Lifelong Helps for Developing the Mind of Christ

Names, Titles, and Descriptions of Jesus Christ

The following names, titles, and descriptions of Jesus Christ (the second Person of the Trinity) are from the King James Version of the Bible. This is not a complete list, but it may help you relate to Christ in different ways based upon His purposes and upon your needs. Use these names for meditation on the Person of Jesus Christ and in prayer through Him to the Heavenly Father.

From time to time, select one or a few names of Jesus on which to meditate. Read the Scripture listed or use a concordance to read other passages to see if the text gives you more detail about Christ's name and His function. Write the details on a card to carry with you throughout the day. Spend time with Jesus in prayer. Ask yourself questions like:

- What does this name tell me about Jesus Christ? about His nature? His work? (Christ is Faithful and True or He is a Judge.)
- Does this name call me to worship Christ for who He is or to thank Him for what He has done? (I can worship Jesus Christ as the King of Kings and Lord of Lords. I can thank Christ for His great sacrifice as the Lamb of God who took away my sins.)
- Does this name describe a relationship I have or can have with Christ? (Jesus is a Wonderful Counselor and I can seek His counsel. He is Physician and I can be His patient.)
- Is there a reason I need to experience Christ working in my life according to this name? (Jesus is the author of our faith and I need Him to give me faith to follow God in this situation.)
- Do I need to pray to Jesus in this name—to ask Him to function in this role? (Christ is the dayspring from on high, and I want Him to shine His light to my friend who lives in darkness and the shadow of death.)

Jesus Christ is:

- an advocate with the Father *(1 John 2:1)*
- Alpha and Omega *(Rev. 1:8)*
- the Amen *(Rev. 3:14)*
- Ancient of days *(Dan. 7:22)*
- This anointed (Acts 4:27)
- Apostle and High Priest of our profession *(Heb. 3:1)*
- author and finisher of our faith *(Heb. 12:2)*
- the beginning and the end *(Rev. 21:6)*
- the beginning of the creation of God *(Rev. 3:14)*
- the only begotten of the Father *(John 1:14)*
- my beloved *(Matt. 12:18)*
- a righteous Branch *(Jer. 23:5)*
- bread of life *(John 6:35)*
- bridegroom *(Matt. 9:15)*
- the brightness of his [God's] glory *(Heb. 1:3)*
- chosen of God *(Luke 23:35)*
- Christ Jesus my Lord *(Phil. 3:8)*
- the Christ [Anointed One] *(Matt. 16:16)*
- chief cornerstone *(Eph. 2:20)*
- crown of glory *(Isa. 62:3)*
- the dayspring from on high *(Luke 1:78)*
- the Deliverer *(Rom. 11:26)*
- desire of all nations *(Hag. 2:7)*
- door of the sheep *(John 10:7)*
- Emmanuel [God with us] *(Matt. 1:23)*
- Faithful and True *(Rev. 19:11)*
- firstborn from the dead *(Col. 1:18)*
- firstborn of every creature *(Col. 1:15)*
- a sure foundation *(Isa. 28:16)*
- friend of publicans and sinners *(Matt. 11:19)*
- unspeakable gift *(2 Cor. 9:15)*
- God of the whole earth *(Isa. 54:5)*
- the only wise God our Savior *(Jude 1:25)*
- a Governor *(Matt. 2:6)*
- head of the body, the church *(Col. 1:18)*
- head of the church *(Eph. 5:23)*
- head of all principality and power *(Col. 2:10)*
- the head *(Eph. 4:15)*
- heir of all things *(Heb. 1:2)*
- high priest *(Heb. 4:15)*

- a great high priest *(Heb. 4:14)*
- Holy One of God *(Luke 4:34)*
- our hope *(1 Tim. 1:1)*
- horn of salvation *(Luke 1:69)*
- image of God *(2 Cor. 4:4)*
- image of the invisible God *(Col. 1:15)*
- Jesus Christ *(John 1:17)*
- Jesus Christ of Nazareth *(Acts 4:10)*
- Jesus Christ our Savior *(Titus 3:6)*
- Jesus of Nazareth *(John 19:19)*
- righteous judge *(2 Tim. 4:8)*
- King eternal, immortal, invisible *(1 Tim. 1:17)*
- King of kings *(1 Tim. 6:15)*
- King of saints *(Rev. 15:3)*
- King of the Jews *(Matt. 27:11)*
- thy King *(Matt. 21:5)*
- Lamb of God *(John 1:29)*
- the Lamb that was slain *(Rev. 5:12)*
- the last *(Rev. 22:13)*
- lawgiver *(Jas. 4:12)*
- leader and commander to the people *(Isa. 55:4)*
- eternal life *(1 John 5:20)*
- our life *(Col. 3:4)*
- light *(1 John 1:5)*
- light of life *(John 8:12)*
- light of men *(John 1:4)*
- the light of the world *(John 8:12)*
- true Light *(John 1:9)*
- lily of the valleys *(Song of Sol. 2:1)*
- Christ the Lord *(Luke 2:11)*
- Lord and Savior Jesus Christ *(2 Pet. 2:20)*
- the Lord and Savior *(2 Pet. 3:2)*
- the only Lord God *(Jude 1:4)*
- Lord God Almighty *(Rev. 15:3)*
- Lord Jesus Christ *(Gal. 1:3)*
- Lord both of the dead and living *(Rom. 14:9)*
- Lord of lords *(1 Tim. 6:15)*
- Lord of peace *(2 Thess. 3:16)*
- Lord of the harvest *(Matt. 9:38)*
- my Lord and my God *(John 20:28)*
- man of sorrows *(Isa. 53:3)*
- Good Master *(Mark 10:17)*
- your Master *(Matt. 23:8)*
- mediator *(1 Tim. 2:5)*
- the Messiah the Prince *(Dan. 9:25)*
- the most Holy *(Dan. 9:24)*
- a Nazarene *(Matt. 2:23)*
- an offering and a sacrifice to God *(Eph. 5:2)*
- our passover *(1 Cor. 5:7)*
- our peace *(Eph. 2:14)*
- Physician *(Luke 4:23)*
- a Prince and a Savior *(Acts 5:31)*
- Prince of life *(Acts 3:15)*
- Prince of Peace *(Isa. 9:6)*
- the Prophet *(John 7:40)*
- the propitiation for our sins *(1 John 2:2)*
- Rabbi *(John 3:2)*
- Rabboni *(John 20:16)*
- as a refiner and purifier *(Mal. 3:3)*
- the resurrection, and the life *(John 11:25)*
- spiritual Rock *(1 Cor. 10:4)*
- Root of David *(Rev. 5:5)*
- root of Jesse *(Rom. 15:12)*
- thy salvation *(Luke 2:30)*
- our Savior Jesus Christ *(2 Pet. 1:1)*
- Savior of the world *(John 4:42)*
- my [God's] servant *(Matt. 12:18)*
- righteous servant *(Isa. 53:11)*
- Shepherd and Bishop of your souls *(1 Pet. 2:25)*
- great shepherd of the sheep *(Heb. 13:20)*
- chief Shepherd *(1 Pet. 5:4)*
- the good shepherd *(John 10:11)*
- son of Abraham *(Matt. 1:1)*
- son of David *(Matt. 1:1)*
- Son of God *(John 1:49)*
- son of Joseph *(John 6:42)*
- Son of man *(Matt. 12:40)*
- Son of the living God *(Matt. 16:16)*
- Son of God *(John 10:36)*
- the son of Mary *(Mark 6:3)*
- his only begotten Son *(1 John 4:9)*
- a Star *(Num. 24:17)*
- day star *(2 Pet. 1:19)*
- the bright and morning star *(Rev. 22:16)*
- the stone which the builders rejected *(Matt. 21:42)*
- the truth *(John 14:6)*
- the true vine, the vine *(John 15:1,5)*
- the way *(John 14:6)*
- a witness to the people *(Isa. 55:4)*
- faithful and true witness *(Rev. 3:14)*
- The Word of God *(Rev. 19:13)*
- the Word of life *(1 John 1:1)*
- the Word *(John 1:1)*

Lifelong Helps for Developing the Mind of Christ

Readings on the Life, Teaching, and Parables of Christ

Readings on the Life of Christ

The following chart lists events from the life of Jesus. In many cases the references for an event are parallel passages (different accounts of the same event). In some cases a reference may be a related event that may or may not be describing the same event. As you read these passages, ask God to help you identify the mind of Christ at work in how Jesus thought or responded in various situations. The healings have been grouped together. Most of the other events are listed with priority given to the chronology of Matthew's Gospel.

	MATTHEW	MARK	LUKE	JOHN
1. Birth	❑ 1—2		❑ 2:1-40	❑ 1:1-18
2. Age 12 at the Temple			❑ 2:41-52	
3. Baptism	❑ 3:13-17	❑ 1:9-11	❑ 3:21-22	❑ 1:19-34
4. Temptation	❑ 4:1-11	❑ 1:12-13	❑ 4:1-13	
5. Begins Preaching Ministry	❑ 4:12-17	❑ 1:14-15	❑ 3:23	
6. Calling the First Disciples	❑ 4:18-22	❑ 1:16-20	❑ 5:1-11	❑ 1:35-42
7. Calling Philip, Nathaniel				❑ 1:43-51
8. Calling of Levi	❑ 9:9-13	❑ 2:13-17	❑ 5:27-32	
9. Naming the Twelve	❑ 10:2-4	❑ 3:13-19	❑ 6:12-16	
10. Turns Water to Wine				❑ 2:1-11
11. Jesus Heals Many	❑ 4:23-25	❑ 3:7-10	❑ 6:17-19	
	❑ 8:14-17	❑ 1:29-34	❑ 4:38-41	
	❑ 14:34-36	❑ 6:53-56		
12. Leprosy	❑ 8:1-4	❑ 1:40-45	❑ 5:12-15	
13. Evil Spirit		❑ 1:21-28	❑ 4:31-37	
14. Centurion's Servant	❑ 8:5-13		❑ 7:1-10	
15. Official's Son				❑ 4:43-54
16. Invalid at Bethesda Pool				❑ 5:1-15
17. Silences Evil Spirits		❑ 3:11-12		
18. Demon Possessed	❑ 8:28-34	❑ 5:1-20	❑ 8:26-39	
19. Paralytic	❑ 9:1-8	❑ 2:1-12	❑ 5:17-26	
20. Hemorrhaging Woman/ Dead Girl	❑ 9:18-26	❑ 5:21-43	❑ 8:40-56	
21. Two Blind Men	❑ 9:27-31			
22. Demon Possessed Mute	❑ 9:32-34			
23. Man with Withered Hand	❑ 12:9-14	❑ 3:1-6	❑ 6:6-11	
24. Demon Possessed, Blind, Mute	❑ 12:22-23			
25. Raises a Widow's Son			❑ 7:11-17	
26. Daughter of Canaanite Woman	❑ 15:21-28	❑ 7:24-30		

	MATTHEW	MARK	LUKE	JOHN
27. Deaf Mute	❏ 15:29-31	❏ 7:31-37	———	———
28. Blind Man at Bethsaida	———	❏ 8:22-26	———	———
29. Man Born Blind	———	———	———	❏ 9:1-41
30. Boy with Evil Spirit	❏ 17:14-21	❏ 9:14-29	❏ 9:37-43	———
31. Blind Men	❏ 20:29-34	❏ 10:46-52	❏ 18:35-43	———
32. Cripple Woman on Sabbath	———	———	❏ 13:10-17	———
33. Ten with Leprosy	———	———	❏ 17:11-19	———
34. Works Miracles	———	———	———	❏ 2:23-25
35. Must Preach	———	———	❏ 4:42-44	———
36. Prayer in Solitary Place	———	❏ 1:35-38	❏ 5:16	———
37. Calms the Storm	❏ 8:23-27	❏ 4:35-41	❏ 8:22-25	———
38. Questioned about Fasting	❏ 9:14-15	❏ 2:18-20	❏ 5:33-35	———
39. Workers Are Few/ Sends Out 72	❏ 9:35-38	———	❏ 10:1-12,17-20	———
40. Sends Out the Twelve	❏ 10:1—11:1	❏ 6:7-13	❏ 9:1-6	———
41. John's Testimony	———	———	———	❏ 3:22-36
42. Samaritan Woman at Well	———	———	———	❏ 4:1-42
43. John in Prison	❏ 11:1-6	———	❏ 7:18-23	———
44. God's Chosen Servant	❏ 12:15-21	———	———	———
45. Visits Mary and Martha	———	———	❏ 10:38-42	———
46. Accused of Working by Satan	❏ 12:24-37	❏ 3:20-30	❏ 11:14-22	———
47. Refuses to Give a Sign	❏ 12:38-45; 16:1-4	❏ 8:11-13	❏ 11:29-32	❏ 2:18-22
48. Teaches Nicodemus	———	———	———	❏ 3:1-21
49. Rejected at Home/Nazareth	❏ 13:53-58	❏ 6:1-6	❏ 4:14-30	———
50. Family Thinks He's Mad	❏ 12:46-50	❏ 3:20-21,31-34	❏ 8:19-21	———
51. Feeds 5,000	❏ 14:13-21	❏ 6:32-44	❏ 9:10-17	❏ 6:1-15
52. Feeds 4,000	❏ 15:29-39	❏ 8:1-10	———	———
53. Walks on Water	❏ 14:22-33	❏ 6:45-52	———	❏ 6:16-24
54. Many Desert Him	———	———	———	❏ 6:60-71
55. Jesus Anointed	❏ 26:6-13	❏ 14:3-9	❏ 7:36-50	❏ 12:1-8
56. Jesus the Christ	———	———	———	❏ 7:25-44
57. Unbelief of Leaders	———	———	———	❏ 7:45-52
58. Unbelief of Jews	———	———	———	❏ 10:22-42
59. Woman Caught in Adultery	———	———	———	❏ 8:1-11
60. Peter's Confession	❏ 16:13-20	❏ 8:27-30	❏ 9:18-21	———
61. Jesus Predicts His Death (1)	❏ 16:21-28	❏ 8:31—9:1	❏ 9:22-27	———
62. Transfiguration	❏ 17:1-13	❏ 9:2-13	❏ 9:28-36	———
63. Jesus Predicts His Death (2)	❏ 17:22-23	❏ 9:30-32	❏ 9:43-45	———
64. Paying the Temple Tax	❏ 17:24-27	———	———	———
65. Blessing Little Children	❏ 19:13-15	❏ 10:13-16	❏ 18:15-17	———
66. Rich Young Ruler	❏ 19:16-26	❏ 10:17-27	❏ 18:18-27	———
67. Samaritan Opposition	———	———	❏ 9:51-56	———
68. Zacchaeus	———	———	❏ 19:1-10	———
69. Lazarus Dies, Raised	———	———	———	❏ 11:1-44
70. Jesus Predicts His Death (3)	❏ 20:17-19	❏ 10:32-34	❏ 18:31-34	———
71. Triumphal Entry	❏ 21:1-11	❏ 11:1-10	❏ 19:28-40	❏ 12:12-19

	MATTHEW	MARK	LUKE	JOHN
72. Sorrow over Jerusalem	———	———	❑ 13:31-35	———
73. Weeps Over Jerusalem	———	———	❑ 19:41-44	———
74. Cleans the Temple	❑ 21:12-17	❑ 11:12,15-19	❑ 19:45-48	❑ 2:12-17
75. Fig Tree Withers	❑ 21:18-22	❑ 11:12-14,20-26	———	———
76. Jesus' Authority Questioned	❑ 21:23-27	❑ 11:27-33	❑ 20:1-8	———
77. Widow's Offering	———	❑ 12:41-44	❑ 21:1-4	———
78. Predicts Crucifixion	❑ 26:1-2	———	———	❑ 12:20-36
79. Jews Still in Unbelief	———	———	———	❑ 12:37-50
80. Plot by Priests and Elders	❑ 26:3-5	———	———	❑ 11:45-57
81. Lord's Supper	❑ 26:17-30	❑ 14:12-26	❑ 22:7-23	❑ 13:1-30
82. Predicts Peter's Denial	❑ 26:31-35	❑ 14:27-31	❑ 22:31-38	❑ 13:31-38
83. Gethsemane and Arrest	❑ 26:36-56	❑ 14:32-52	❑ 22:39-53	❑ 18:1-11
84. Trial Before Sanhedrin	❑ 26:57-68	❑ 14:53-65	❑ 22:63-71	❑ 18:12-14,19-24
85. Peter's Denial	❑ 26:69-75	❑ 14:66-72	❑ 22:54-62	❑ 18:15-18,25-27
86. Trial Before Pilate	❑ 27:11-31	❑ 15:1-20	❑ 23:1-25	❑ 18:28-19:16
87. Crucifixion	❑ 27:32-56	❑ 15:21-41	❑ 23:26-49	❑ 19:17-37
88. Burial	❑ 27:57-66	❑ 15:42-47	❑ 23:50-56	❑ 19:38-42
89. Resurrection	❑ 28:1-15	❑ 16:1-14	❑ 24:1-12	❑ 20:1-9
90. Resurrection Appearances	———	———	❑ 24:13-49	❑ 20:10-21:14
91. Commissions Peter	———	———	———	❑ 21:15-25
92. Great Commission	❑ 28:16-20	❑ 16:15-16	———	———
93. Ascension	———	❑ 16:19-20	❑ 24:50-53	———

Readings on the Teaching of Christ

The following passages relate to the teaching ministry of Jesus. Of course Jesus taught through what He did, and He taught through the parables which we have in a separate section that follows. Some of the references identify parallel passages while others are passages related to the same or similar topic.

	MATTHEW	MARK	LUKE	JOHN
1. The Beatitudes	❑ 5:3-12	———	❑ 6:20-26	———
2. Salt and Light	❑ 5:13-16	❑ 9:50; 4:21-25	❑ 8:16-18; 11:33-36	———
	———	———	❑ 14:34-35	———
3. Fulfillment of the Law	❑ 5:17-20	———	———	———
4. Murder/Hatred	❑ 5:21-26	———	———	———
5. Adultery	❑ 5:27-30	———	———	———
6. Divorce	❑ 5:31-32; 19:1-9	❑ 10:1-12	❑ 16:18	———
7. Celibacy	❑ 19:10-12	———	———	———
8. Oaths	❑ 5:33-37	———	———	———
9. Eye for Eye	❑ 5:38-42	———	———	———
10. Love Enemies	❑ 5:43-48	———	❑ 6:27-36	———
11. Giving to Needy	❑ 6:1-4	———	———	———
12. Prayer	❑ 6:5-13;7:7-11	———	❑ 11:1-13	———
13. Forgiveness	❑ 6:14	———	❑ 17:3-4	———
14. Fasting	❑ 6:16-18	———	———	———
15. Treasures in Heaven	❑ 6:19-24	———	❑ 18:22	———
16. Don't Worry/Seek the Kingdom	❑ 6:25-34	———	❑ 12:22-34	———

	MATTHEW	MARK	LUKE	JOHN
17. Judging Others	❑ 7:1-6	————	❑ 6:37-42	————
18. Narrow Gate	❑ 7:13-14	————	❑ 13:22-30	————
19. Good and Bad Fruit	❑ 7:15-23	————	❑ 6:43-45	————
20. Cost of Following Jesus	❑ 8:18-22	————	❑ 9:57-62;14:25-33	————
21. Rewards for Following Jesus	❑ 19:27-30	❑ 10:28-31	❑ 18:28-30	————
22. Son Gives Life	————	————	————	❑ 5:16-30
23. Testimonies About Jesus	————	————	————	❑ 5:31-47
24. Jesus' Testimony	————	————	————	❑ 8:12-30,48-59
25. Children of Abraham/Devil	————	————	————	❑ 8:31-47
26. About John the Baptist	❑ 11:7-19	————	❑ 7:24-35	————
27. Woe to Unrepentant Cities	❑ 11:20-24	————	❑ 10:13-16	————
28. Jesus Reveals the Father	❑ 11:25-27	————	❑ 10:21-24	————
29. Rest for the Heavy Laden	❑ 11:28-30	————	————	————
30. Lord of the Sabbath	❑ 12:1-8	❑ 2:23-28	❑ 6:1-5	————
31. Obedience	————	————	❑ 11:27-28	————
32. Bread of Life	————	————	————	❑ 6:25-59
33. Clean and Unclean	❑ 15:1-21	❑ 7:1-23	————	————
34. Yeast of Pharisees/Sadducees	❑ 16:5-12	❑ 8:14-21	❑ 12:1-12	————
35. Greatness in the Kingdom	❑ 18:1-6	❑ 9:33-37	❑ 9:46-48	————
36. James and John	❑ 20:20-28	❑ 10:35-45	❑ 22:24-30	————
37. For or Against Us	————	❑ 9:38-41	❑ 9:49-50	————
38. Things that Cause Sin	❑ 18:7-9	❑ 9:42-48	❑ 17:1-2	————
39. Reconciliation	❑ 18:15-20	————	————	————
40. Faith	————	————	❑ 17:5-6	————
41. Servanthood	————	————	❑ 17:7-10	————
42. Humility	————	————	❑ 14:1-14	————
43. Good News of the Kingdom	————	————	❑ 16:16-17	————
44. Paying Taxes to Caesar	❑ 22:15-22	❑ 12:13-17	❑ 20:20-26	————
45. Marriage at the Resurrection	❑ 22:23-33	❑ 12:18-27	❑ 20:27-40	————
46. Greatest Commandment	❑ 22:34-40	❑ 12:28-34	❑ 10:25-28	————
47. Whose Son Is Christ	❑ 22:41-46	❑ 12:35-37	❑ 20:41-44	————
48. Authority of His Teaching	————	————	————	❑ 7:14-24
49. Good Shepherd	————	————	————	❑ 10:1-21
50. Woes to Teachers and Pharisees	❑ 23:1-39	❑ 12:38-40	❑ 20:45-47	————
51. Six Woes	————	————	❑ 11:37-54	————
52. Division not Peace	❑ 10:34-36	————	❑ 12:49-53	————
53. Interpreting the Times	————	————	❑ 12:54-59	————
54. Repent or Perish	————	————	❑ 13:1-5	————
55. Coming of the Kingdom	————	————	❑ 17:20-37	————
56. Signs of the End of the Age	❑ 24:1-35	❑ 13:1-31	❑ 21:5-38	————
57. Day and Hour Unknown	❑ 24:36-51	❑ 13:32-37	————	————
58. Teaches Disciples at the Supper	————	————	————	❑ 14—17
59. Preparing a place	————	————	————	❑ 14:1-4
60. Way to the Father	————	————	————	❑ 14:5-14
61. Promise of Holy Spirit	————	————	————	❑ 14:15-31
62. The Vine and Branches	————	————	————	❑ 15:1-17

	MATTHEW	MARK	LUKE	JOHN
63. World Will Hate You	———	———	———	❑ 15:18—16:4
64. Work of Holy Spirit	———	———	———	❑ 16:5-16
65. Grief Will Turn to Joy	———	———	———	❑ 16:17-33
66. Prayer for Himself	———	———	———	❑ 17:1-5
67. Prayer for Disciples	———	———	———	❑ 17:6-19
68. Prayer for All Believers	———	———	———	❑ 17:20-26

Readings on the Parables of Christ

The list below includes most of the parables of Jesus. However, some of His teaching includes comparisons or other stories that are considered parables by some. Most scholars believe each parable usually had only one primary theme. As you read and study a parable, ask God to give you understanding about the primary message.

	MATTHEW	MARK	LUKE
1. About teaching with parables	❑ 13:34-35	❑ 4:33-34	———
2. Good Samaritan	———	———	❑ 10:29-37
3. Growing Seed	———	❑ 4:26-29	———
4. Hidden Treasure	❑ 13:44	———	———
5. Lost Coin	———	———	❑ 15:8-10
6. Lost Sheep	❑ 18:10-14	———	❑ 15:1-7
7. Lost Son/Prodigal Son	———	———	❑ 15:11-32
8. Mustard Seed	❑ 13:31-32	❑ 4:30-32	❑ 13:18-19
9. Net	❑ 13:47-51	———	———
10. New and Old Treasures	❑ 13:52	———	———
11. New Wine/Old Wine Skins	❑ 9:17	❑ 2:22	❑ 5:37-39
12. Patched Garment	❑ 9:16	❑ 2:21	❑ 5:36
13. Pearl of Great Price	❑ 13:45-46	———	———
14. Persistent Widow	———	———	❑ 18:1-8
15. Pharisee and Publican	———	———	❑ 18:9-14
16. Rich Fool	———	———	❑ 12:13-21
17. Rich Man and Lazarus	———	———	❑ 16:19-31
18. Sheep and Goats	❑ 25:31-46	———	———
19. Shrewd Manager	———	———	❑ 16:1-15
20. Sower	❑ 13:1-23	❑ 4:1-20	❑ 8:4-15
21. Talents	❑ 25:14-30	———	❑ 19:12-27
22. Ten Virgins	❑ 25:1-13	———	———
23. Thief at Night/Be Watchful	———	———	❑ 12:35-48
24. Two Sons and Obedience	❑ 21:28-32	———	———
25. Unfruitful Fig Tree	———	———	❑ 13:6-9
26. Unmerciful Servant	❑ 18:21-35	———	———
27. Wedding Banquet	❑ 22:1-14	———	❑ 14:15-24
28. Weeds	❑ 13:24-30;36-43	———	———
29. Wicked Tenants	❑ 21:33-46	❑ 12:1-12	❑ 20:9-19
30. Wise Builder/Obedience	❑ 7:24-27	———	❑ 6:46-49
31. Workers in the Vineyard	❑ 20:1-16	———	———
32. Yeast	❑ 13:33	———	❑ 13:20-21

Jesus' Circle of Friends

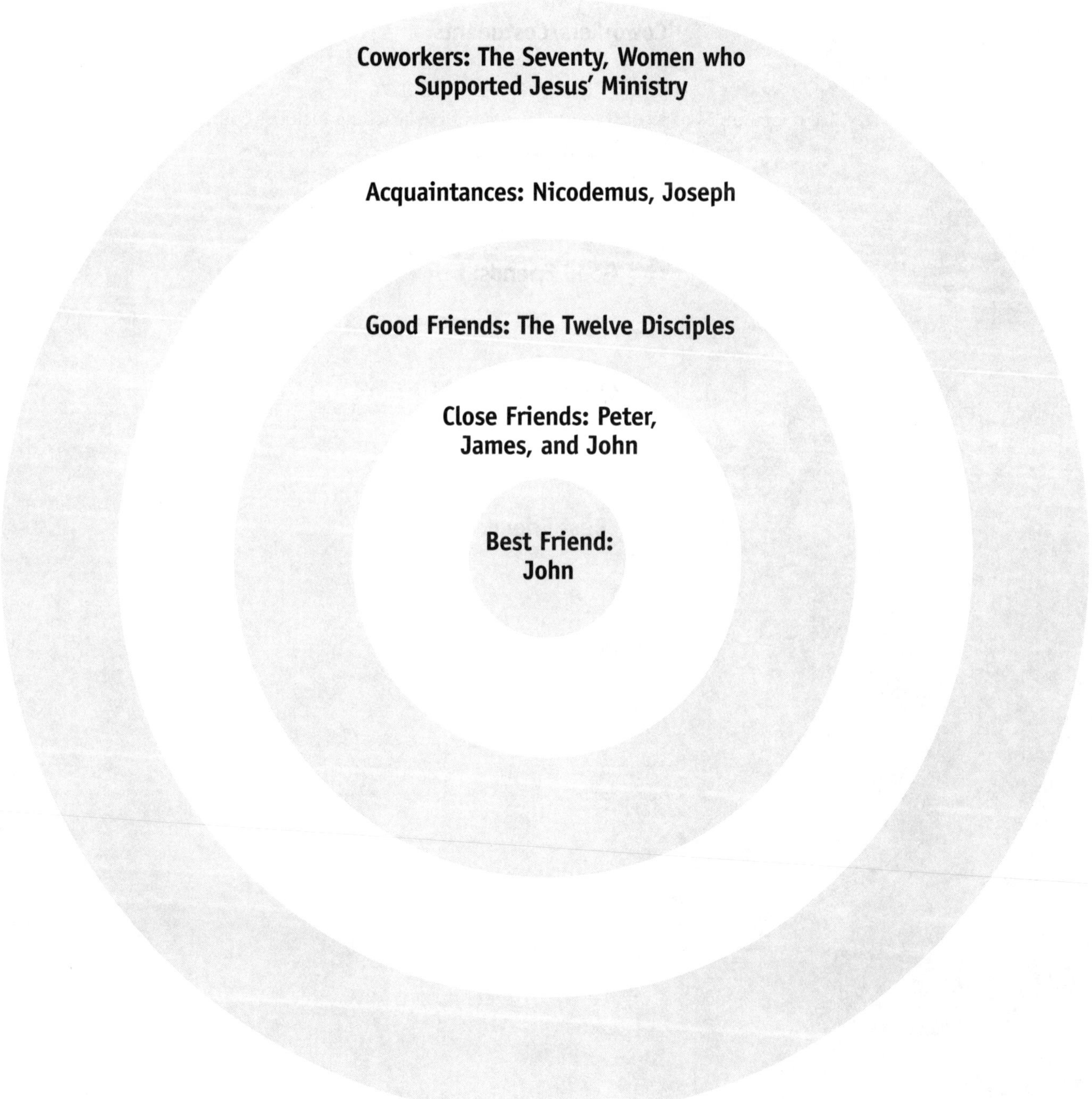

Coworkers: The Seventy, Women who Supported Jesus' Ministry

Acquaintances: Nicodemus, Joseph

Good Friends: The Twelve Disciples

Close Friends: Peter, James, and John

Best Friend: John

My Circle of Friends

Coworkers/Costudents:

Acquaintances:

Good Friends:

Close Friends:

Best Friend:

Notes

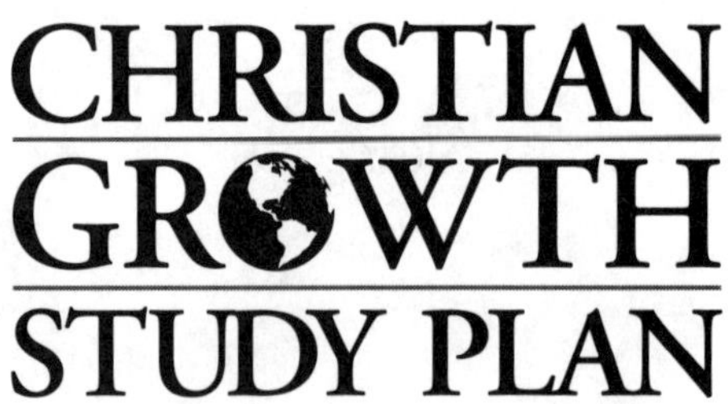

Preparing Christians to Serve

In the **Christian Growth Study Plan (formerly Church Study Course)**, this book *The Mind of Christ, Youth Edition* is a resource for course credit in the subject area "Personal Life" of the Christian Growth category of plans. To receive credit, read the book, complete the learning activities, show your work to your pastor, a staff member or church leader, then complete the following information. This page may be duplicated. Send the completed page to:

Christian Growth Study Plan
One LifeWay Plaza
Nashville, TN 37234-0117
FAX: (615)251-5067
Email: cgspnet@lifeway.com

For information about the Christian Growth Study Plan, refer to the current Christian Growth Study Plan Catalog. It is located online at *www.lifeway.com/cgsp*. If you do not hae access to the Internet, contact the Christian Growth Study Plan office (1.800.968.5519) for the specific plan you need for your ministry.

The Mind of Christ, Youth Edition
COURSE NUMBER: CG- 0253

PARTICIPANT INFORMATION

Social Security Number (USA ONLY-optional)	Personal CGSP Number*	Date of Birth (MONTH, DAY, YEAR)
- -	- -	- -
Name (First, Middle, Last)		Home Phone
		- -
Address (Street, Route, or P.O. Box)	City, State, or Province	Zip/Postal Code

CHURCH INFORMATION

Church Name		
Address (Street, Route, or P.O. Box)	City, State, or Province	Zip/Postal Code

CHANGE REQUEST ONLY

☐ Former Name		
☐ Former Address	City, State, or Province	Zip/Postal Code
☐ Former Church	City, State, or Province	Zip/Postal Code

Signature of Pastor, Conference Leader, or Other Church Leader	Date

*New participants are requested but not required to give SS# and date of birth. Existing participants, please give CGSP# when using SS# for the first time. Thereafter, only one ID# is required. **Mail to:** Christian Growth Study Plan, One LifeWay Plaza, Nashville, TN 37234-0117. Fax: (615)251-5067.

Rev. 5-02